Palgrave's Critical Policing Studies

In a period where police and academics benefit from coproduction in research and education, the need for a critical perspective on key challenges is pressing. Palgrave's Critical Policing Studies is a series of high quality, research-based books which examine a range of cutting-edge challenges and developments to policing and their social and political contexts. They seek to provide evidence-based case studies and high quality research, combined with critique and theory, to address fundamental challenging questions about future directions in policing.

Through a range of formats including monographs, edited collections and short form Pivots, this series provides research at a variety of lengths to suit both academics and practitioners. The series brings together new topics at the forefront of policing scholarship but is also organised around who the contemporary police are, what they do, how they go about it, and the ever-changing external environments which bear upon their work.

The series will cover topics such as: the purpose of policing and public expectations, public health approaches to policing, policing of cyber-crime, environmental policing, digital policing, social media, Artificial Intelligence and big data, accountability of complex networks of actors involved in policing, austerity, public scrutiny, technological and social changes, over-policing and marginalised groups, under-policing and corporate crime, institutional abuses, policing of climate change, ethics, workforce, education, evidence-based policing, and the pluralisation of policing.

Monica Den Boer · Eric Bervoets · Linda Hak
Editors

Plural Policing, Security and the COVID Crisis

Comparative European Perspectives

palgrave
macmillan

Editors
Monica Den Boer
Faculty of Military Sciences
Netherlands Defence Academy
Breda, The Netherlands

Eric Bervoets
Netherlands Defence Academy
Breda, The Netherlands

Linda Hak
National Police of The Netherlands
Noord-Holland, The Netherlands

ISSN 2730-535X ISSN 2730-5368 (electronic)
Palgrave's Critical Policing Studies
ISBN 978-3-031-19176-3 ISBN 978-3-031-19177-0 (eBook)
https://doi.org/10.1007/978-3-031-19177-0

This Palgrave Macmillan imprint is published by the registered company Springer Nature Switzerland AG
The registered company address is: Gewerbestrasse 11, 6330 Cham, Switzerland

Praise for *Plural Policing, Security and the COVID Crisis*

"Monica den Boer, Eric Bervoets and Linda Hak have produced an outstanding book on the dynamics of plural policing, security and the COVID Crisis. By linking empirical insights about our understanding of policing during the COVID pandemic with empirical investigations in highly interesting comparative European case studies, the book makes a substantial contribution to our understanding of both the theoretical and empirical dynamics of the phenomenon. Indeed, this is an excellent book which provides a very interesting and compelling analysis of an important and largely under-researched topic. It is highly recommended for anyone interested in Policing Studies, Political Science, Sociology and Criminology, or International Security more generally."

—Christian Kaunert, *Professor of International Security, Dublin City University, Ireland and Professor of Policing and Security & Director of the International Centre for Policing and Security, University of South Wales, UK*

"Anyone curious about how plural policing unfolds in times of crisis should read this book. Experts empirically describe the dynamics during the fight against COVID-19 in 9 countries and show how existing trends and patterns in plural policing are confirmed or not, making it an attractive read. It reveals an intriguing patchwork and generates insights for academics and practitioners about the (non-)active role of a diversity of actors in the governance of security during crises. This collection contains several insights and lessons learnt for scholars as well as practitioners of policing."

—Marleen Easton, *Professor and head of the research group 'Governing and Policing Security' (GaPS) at the Department of Public Governance and Management at Ghent University, Belgium*

"They say that in crisis management, you should be quick with the facts but slow with the blame. That is precisely what this must-read book does. A number of highly credible observers give a rare insight into how Europe acted upon its worst challenge in our time. By putting light on how a number of different states across Europe acted in these dire times, the authors have been able to catch not only essential learning points for the future - but also add a new understanding of what policing and harm reduction really is. It's not good vs evil. It's more about how to prevent something bad from getting worse."

—Dr. Ivar Fahsing *is a detective chief superintendent and associate professor at the Norwegian Police University College*

Contents

1 **Plural Policing, Security and the COVID-19 Crisis: An Introduction to Comparative European Perspectives** 1
Monica Den Boer, Eric Bervoets, and Linda Hak
1 Introduction 1
2 Leading Questions 4
3 Trends and Patterns 7
4 Comparative Dimension 10
5 Reading Guide to the Chapters 13
6 An Introduction to the Authors 18
References 26

2 **Policing with the Help of Data: The Use of CoroPol in the Pandemic's Early Stages in The Netherlands** 33
Eric Bervoets, Jolijn Broekhuizen, Henk Ferwerda, and Wouter Landman
1 Introduction 33
1.1 Plural Policing 36

2 CoroPol: Collating Information During the Initial Stages of the Pandemic 37
3 Key Observations: Crime Shifts During the Initial Stages of the Pandemic 39
3.1 Opportunities as an Issue 39
3.2 How Vulnerable Persons Turn into Victims 42
3.3 Reflection 45
4 Social Disorder 46
4.1 Actual Tensions and Disorder in The Netherlands During First Pandemic Wave 46
4.2 Background: Decrease in Support (of Measures) and 'Moral Holiday' 47
4.3 Trust in Police 50
5 Key Observations on Plural Policing and Security 52
5.1 Introduction: Observations and Predictions 52
5.2 Circumstances: Little Pluralism, No Protocols, Little Intel, Lack of Proximity 52
5.3 A Classic Police Dilemma in Extraordinary Times 54
5.4 Summary and Reflection: A Quest for Balance 56
6 Conclusions and Critical Assessment 57
References 61

3 Policing and Security in Southern Europe: How the COVID-19 Pandemic Reaffirms Pre-existing Patterns 67
Christian Mouhanna, Anastassia Tsoukala, and Gemma Ubasart-González
1 Introduction 67
2 Spain in the Face of COVID-19: State of Alarm and Decentralised Police Response 71
2.1 State of Alarm 72
2.2 Policing the Lockdown 74
2.3 Restriction on Fundamental Rights and Deprivation of Liberty Management 75

3 France: A Permanent State of Emergency, With or Without COVID-19 78
3.1 A Permanent State of Emergency 79
3.2 Police Practices Towards Hesitant Governmental Strategies 80
3.3 Public Opinion Still Keen to Oppose 83
4 Greece: Authoritarian Modes of Policing 86
4.1 Governmental Communication Strategy on Policing and Security 87
4.2 Maintaining Law and Order During the COVID-19 Crisis 89
5 Discussion 93
5.1 An Emergency Adaptation 95
5.2 Limits to COVID-19 Policing Vary from Country to Country 97
References 100

4 Police and Other Plural Policing Institutions in Central and Eastern Europe Facing COVID-19 Pandemic 107
Branko Lobnikar, László Christián, József Balla, Ádám Kalmár, Irena Cajner Mraović, Krunoslav Borovec, and Andrej Sotlar
1 Introduction 107
2 Policing Pandemic in Central and Eastern European Countries: The Case of Hungary, Croatia and Slovenia 111
2.1 New Legislation and Pandemic Response Organisation 111
2.2 Policing COVID-19 Pandemic in CEE 116
3 Assessment of the Functioning of (Plural) Police Institutions During a Pandemic in CEE Countries 125
4 Discussion and Conclusion 130
References 133

5 Policing the COVID-19 Pandemic in Germany: Challenges and Learnings for Future Crises 139
Hartmut Aden
1 Introduction 139
2 Extended Executive Powers: The German Federal Multilevel Setting During the COVID-19 Pandemic 140
2.1 Rule-Making Under the Pressure of Crises and Uncertainty 141
2.2 Coordination and Conflicts Between Central and De-centralised Levels of Decision-Making in a Multilevel Setting 143
2.3 Lack of Preparedness and Other Shortcomings in the Administration of the COVID-19 Pandemic 145
3 Plural Policing in a Federal Multilevel Setting During the COVID-19 Pandemic 146
3.1 Policing the "Normal" Versus Policing a Pandemic Crisis? 146
3.2 Public Health and Public Order: Distribution of Tasks and Authority Between Police Agencies and Health Administration 147
3.3 Public Policing of Far-Reaching Restrictions to Fundamental rights—Just Another Variation of Police Discretion? 148
3.4 Data Collected for Combating the Pandemic—to Be Used for Policing Purposes? 149
3.5 Problems of Protest Policing During the Pandemic 150
3.6 Plural Policing in a Pandemic: New Tasks for Private Security Forces 151
4 Learning for Future Crises 152
4.1 Uncertainty, Risks and Policing 152
4.2 Towards a Culture of Learning from Errors 154
5 Conclusion and Outlook 154
References 156

6 **Policing by Consent in a Pandemic: Security Governance and Policing of COVID-19 in the United Kingdom** 161
Saskia Hufnagel, Rudi Fortson, Clive Walker, and Megan O'Neill
1 Introduction 161
2 Security Actors Influencing UK COVID-19 Policing 166
3 Implementing COVID-19 Regulations 170
4 COVID-19 Police Surveillance 179
5 Conclusion 181
References 184

Contributors

Hartmut Aden Berlin, Germany

József Balla Ludovika-University of Public Service, Budapest, Hungary

Eric Bervoets Netherlands Defence Academy, Breda, The Netherlands

Krunoslav Borovec Police College, Police Academy Zagreb, Zagreb, Croatia

Jolijn Broekhuizen Bureau Beke, Arnhem, The Netherlands; Bureau Broekhuizen, Amersfoort, The Netherlands

László Christián Ludovika-University of Public Service, Budapest, Hungary

Monica Den Boer Netherlands Defence Academy, Breda, The Netherlands

Henk Ferwerda Bureau Beke, Arnhem, The Netherlands

Rudi Fortson Leeds, UK

Linda Hak National Police of The Netherlands, Noord-Holland, The Netherlands

Saskia Hufnagel Leeds, UK

Ádám Kalmár Baranya County Police Headquarters, Pécs, Hungary

Wouter Landman Bureau Beke, Arnhem, The Netherlands; Bureau Landman, Hengelo, The Netherlands

Branko Lobnikar Faculty of Criminal Justice and Security, University of Maribor, Ljubljana, Slovenia

Christian Mouhanna Paris, France

Irena Cajner Mraović Faculty of Croatian Studies, University of Zagreb, Zagreb, Croatia

Megan O'Neill Leeds, UK

Andrej Sotlar Faculty of Criminal Justice and Security, University of Maribor, Ljubljana, Slovenia

Anastassia Tsoukala Paris, France

Gemma Ubasart-González Political Science Research Group, University of Girona, Girona, Spain

Clive Walker Leeds, UK

List of Figures

Chapter 1

Fig. 1 Plural policing during COVID-19 12
Fig. 2 Comparative spheres of policing 13

1

Plural Policing, Security and the COVID-19 Crisis: An Introduction to Comparative European Perspectives

Monica Den Boer, Eric Bervoets, and Linda Hak

1 Introduction

Every book starts with an idea. Our idea stemmed from the need to reflect on how the subject of our academic inquiry—police and security agencies—have responded to the COVID-19 crisis. At the start of COVID-19 pandemic, the security sector felt surprised and

M. Den Boer (✉)
Faculty of Military Sciences, Netherlands Defence Academy, Breda, The Netherlands
e-mail: MGW.d.Boer@mindef.nl

E. Bervoets
Netherlands Defence Academy, Breda, The Netherlands
e-mail: e.bervoets@bureaubervoets.nl

L. Hak
National Police of The Netherlands, Noord-Holland, The Netherlands
e-mail: linda.hak@upcmail.nl

M. Den Boer et al. (eds.), *Plural Policing, Security and the COVID Crisis*, Palgrave's Critical Policing Studies, https://doi.org/10.1007/978-3-031-19177-0_1

was confronted with governments that demanded them to fulfil a front-line position in monitoring and controlling compliance with the anti-COVID-19 measures (Ferwerda & Landman, 2021; Frenkel et al., 2021; Jones, 2020; Sheptycki, 2020). To us, there seemed to be a startling absence of crucial information to guide police and security organisations in their early responses to the COVID-19 pandemic (Den Boer et al., 2022). Hence, information-sharing in the early phases seemed rather unsystematic, at the level of government (administration, policy-makers, politicians), as well as in the security domain (law enforcement organisations), and the academic field (although they gathered speed rather quickly) (Newton, 2020). Initiatives such as CoroPol (see Chapter 2) were prompted by the need that was felt to bring the avalanche of news articles and social media expressions together to provide a basis to schematic analysis.[1] At the level of the NGOs (e.g. UNODC, Amnesty, etc.) robust data-gathering commenced almost immediately, and this was also the case among national and international health authorities. In any case: the epidemic/pandemic confronted us with knowledge gaps (Boin et al., 2021; Laufs & Waseem, 2020). There was no textbook on how to police (during) a pandemic.

Hence, at the basis of this book lies academic curiosity, followed by a jointly perceived eagerness to share and enrich perspectives. This jointly produced volume of comparative regional analysis is meant to provide a canon of knowledge, because we have learnt how quick our perception and reflection dissolves from our collective memory. Thus, we firmly believe that this book makes it possible to learn from one another and to share lessons, principally to be better prepared for a new pandemic that will loom on our horizon.

Throughout this book, we seek to apply the special characteristics of this pandemic to police and security responses. Our first observation is that the pandemic was not anticipated although pandemics of this size

[1] The CoroPol Monitor was to provide Dutch law enforcement agencies brief information ('headlines') on crime, (plural) policing and public order elsewhere in Europe and the world, specifically during the stages of a lockdown. Besides, the monitor was meant to indicate what to expect and what to prepare for in The Netherlands and to offer an action perspective on policing the pandemic in this country. CoroPol originates from the words "Corona and Policing".

and gravity had already been predicted for a long time, partly on the basis of previous pandemics (Karacan et al., 2021). Secondly, the COVID-19 dynamic can be characterised by its severe longevity: we are now in our second year and populations worldwide have been confronted with successive waves of new COVID-19 variants and measures that were introduced by governments around the globe (World Health Organisation (WHO), 2021). Thirdly, the scale of the pandemic is truly global in nature and vast in its scale, but different in terms of impact on mortality rates and economic resilience (Allain-Dupré et al., 2021; WHO, n.d.). Countries have been confronted with rather differentiated patterns and rates of infection, which makes the COVID-19 pandemic not merely a global issue but also a "glocal" issue with local as well as regional particularities (Aston et al., 2020). Fourth, it has been noteworthy how similar as well as dissimilar governments demonstrated response patterns, particularly when it concerned the speed with which they took to operational law enforcement services in order to conduct the front-line enforcement of anti-COVID-19 measures (Aston et al., 2020; Brown & Fleming, 2021). This has been particularly challenging in the acknowledgement that law enforcement generally rests on a scarce capacity: at least the demand always outstrips the supply. Hence, it turned out rather quickly that public police services were running short of capacity to "police" the anti-COVID-19 measures (Newiss et al., 2021; Strijker, 2020). In some countries, governments took recourse to decentral authorities and auxiliary as well as private law enforcement. Within the EU, two patterns can be observed, a modest centralisation towards the centre, in particular the Commission, and some decentralisation towards the MS, in particular France and Germany, "revitalising" the tandem, balancing controversial interests of other states. In this context, mechanisms or instruments that have the potential to "integrate" (Schomaker et al., 2021).

This brings us to the main focus in our book, namely to see how policing and security have been affected by the pandemic. In a first analysis on the basis of media reports, global health data and NGO reports, we observed that while the monopoly of violence was reinforced in first instance, it was mostly the repressive coercion of anti-COVID-19 measures in combination with scarcity of resources that "pushed" responsibility of security and policing of compliance to other actors, some of whom were public security actors other than police (e.g. paramilitary, military police, municipal wardens) (AD, 2021; Wijers, 2021), and others were private (Amnesty International, 2020a; Aston et al., 2020; Leloup & Cools, 2021; Mawby, 2020; Terpstra & Salet, 2020). Plural policing forms our central theoretical perspective, here defined as "the multiplicity of institutional forms that are now involved in the delivery of policing and security services and technologies" (Loader, 2000).

2 Leading Questions

The central argument around which the book is built is the extent to which security and governmental actors aligned with formal scripts that have been specifically designed for crisis management: they seemed ill-prepared for a long-lasting and a heavily impacting pandemic and all its consequences and safety and security aspects (van Eijken & Rijpma, 2021). Law enforcement organisations did not seem to use normative-legal frameworks, but were drifting along with the incremental (and often illogical) patchwork that gradually evolved from the hands of the governments.

The main thesis in our book is that security organisations such as police and border management organisations were not only confronted but also created the normative gap that transpired throughout the COVID-19 epidemic. The situation created ample space for professional discretion, which gave rise to documented cases of disproportionate, irresponsible, unequal, selective police conduct, leading to excessive situations in which citizens were given a fine without proper judicial redress (Boere, 2021), arrested while behaving peacefully, maltreated while not using violence or even aggression to the police (Amnesty International, 2020a).

Stop and search, arrest, the monopoly of violence: these coercive powers that are entrusted to the police and other law enforcement organisations are strictly based on the Rule of Law. If there was anything during this crisis, the Rule of Law seemed to be moved to the backburner: citizens were told to behave according to rules that had been improvised and imposed by their governments with the tendency to use administrative tools over criminal law and criminal procedure law (Aden et al., 2020; Amnesty International, 2020a, 2020b; Aston et al., 2020; Kostic & Boskovic, 2020; Tzifakis, 2020). Meanwhile, however, law enforcement organisations demanded sympathy because of the difficult and treacherous circumstances in which they had to perform their duties (Leeson, 2021). As a consequence, the whole of the COVID-19 crisis has been a form of continuous meddling-through, resulting in a precarious balance between law enforcement and communities, destroying decades of dedicated investment in police-community relations, particularly in fragile communities and poverty-stricken town districts (Jones, 2020).

We believe the book is a unique academic contribution to our common and critical understanding of security governance and policing during the COVID-19 crisis. It will no doubt be complementary to other publications that will emerge around the same topic, but we are convinced the attraction of the book is based on a combination of six different dimensions.

First, there is the empirical dimension. Our joint book departs from the so-called CoroPoL Monitor that was initiated in the early phases of the COVID-19 crisis, gathering raw data about law enforcement, police and border control authorities, and their differentiated response to non-anticipated security and safety challenges (see Chapter 2 of this book). The collection and analysis of these raw data allowed us to make a reconstruction of the security governance during the pandemic, particularly during the first phase of the pandemic. It was only in the course of the Summer of 2020 that police organisations started to get in control of the data and that they became more analytically aware of the effects of the pandemic on public order and crime patterns. The empirical dimension of this book makes it possible to compare and analyse raw data, at least to the extent that they were published by open sources.

Second, there is the international dimension: the main questions we have sought to tackle in the course of this book transgress geographical borders, jurisdictions and communities within different European regions. The European regions that are included in our analysis face law enforcement, policing and border management issues while tackling the COVID-19 epidemic, for instance in the realm of public order policing, and information & communication management. The international perspective is combined with a comparative regional dimension, comprising several contributions written from different European regional perspectives, aiming to generate a fresh reflection on the different law enforcement methods and practices that were applied throughout the pandemic, ranging from regions where police tended to be less visible than in other regions, and regions in which the police employed a top-down visible and repressive stance vis-à-vis the alignment with anti-COVID-19 rules, including the imposition of a lockdown and a curfew (Aston et al., 2020).

The academics and practitioners who co-operate in this publication enterprise originate from different disciplinary backgrounds and organisational contexts, e.g. police, border control, which strengthens the joint capacity to produce a thought-provoking volume. With an interdisciplinary dimension, this book comprises a focus on public police organisations, but also on law enforcement organisations in general. Unfortunately, for the time being, we have left border management practices outside the scope of this book. All authors have been asked to share their observations and to consider the narrative dimension, taking recourse to raw data, press coverage, but also to their personal observations of experiences with activities as performed by security providers throughout the COVID-19 crisis. What did they see and observe? How did the police exercise its competences? How did citizens respond? What was the effect on public opinion of the police? In encouraging a narrative dimension, we hope to show some elements of *couleur locale* that reach beyond mere media appreciations of policing activities. Finally, given our close liaison with operational law enforcement organisations as well as political-administrative environments, we believe this book contributes not only to a practical and operational understanding about security governance during the COVID-19 crisis, but also offers a practical perspective on lessons learnt. We also believe students of policing and law enforcement studies may find this a "must-read" addition to their reading list. At the time of writing, we were still experiencing further phases of the pandemic. Nevertheless, we did not have the luxury to wait till the end. Throughout the writing process, the authors of the chapters convened twice in the form of online workshops, where they discussed the general idea behind the book, as well as the content of their draft chapters. We believe that this form of intervision has contributed to a sound level of academic coherence and mutual comparability of findings.

3 Trends and Patterns

Throughout the COVID-19 crisis, we have witnessed several universal trends and patterns. A striking resemblance between nearly all countries in the world is that the emergence of COVID-19 has been subject to significant "crisisification" as well as "securitization": the crisis frame was applied from the very early days on, during the first months of 2020, referring to a problem that seemed to get out of hand, an uncontrollable infection that would affect the entire global population, with severe consequences for people's health and high mortality rates (Rhinard, 2019; Waever, 2007). Everyone will remember the days, weeks and ensuing months when the media continued to disseminate images of patients in IC-units, nurses and doctors wearing protective outfits, and cues of coffins carrying the deadly victims of the disease. There seemed to be no escape but to take the disease very seriously. The "crisis" as it became framed, continued to dominate the scene for several years, and at the time of writing has not come to a halt. The "crisis" also unrolled the red carpet for the centralisation of government, although there were exceptions when the responsibility was deliberately delegated to municipal, regional and international actors, or to the medical experts when invasive instruments, such as the CoronaCheck app, were introduced that needed medical argumentation (Aston et al., 2020; Coronacheck, n.d.; Schomaker et al., 2021; Terpstra & Salet, 2020; Vampa, 2021). The "crisis" unfolded the tapestry for a significant strengthening of executive power at the level of government, often at the expense of parliaments who were either marginalised to the extent that they could merely alter minor issues ex post facto, or who were greatly overshadowed in terms of timely and profound scrutiny of legislative proposals (Russack et al., 2021). In The Netherlands, for example, Prime Minister Rutte and Health Minister Hugo de Jonge performed a spate of press conferences, which greatly enhanced their visibility during election time (parliamentary elections in March 2021 and municipal elections in March 2022) and associated them with leadership and coordination of the COVID-19 pandemic.

On the security side, the framing of the pandemic as a crisis opened the door for exceptional measures that were imposed on the populations, though in varying degrees. Some countries experienced tough measures, such as complete lockdowns, which confined people to their homes for long periods. Many of these types of measures were experienced as deeply invasive into peoples' private lives, as profoundly infringing on fundamental rights, and as vastly repressive compared with normal everyday life (Gentithes & Krent, 2020; Human Rights Watch, 2021; Spadaro, 2020). Hence, what societies all over the world have experienced is that—also due to the longevity of the pandemic—exceptional measures have become subject to a gradual normalisation. For instance, this has become visible in weak legal foundations for these measures, using executive regulations and emergency orders rather than bills and laws that are passed through parliaments, often in the absence of sunset-clauses or hard expiry conditions (Russack et al., 2021). The perpetuation of the state of emergency (in several countries) has certainly not benefited parliamentary scrutiny and democratic involvement, particularly as it supplied police and law enforcement authorities with the authority to apply extraordinary coercive measures, often for non-criminal offences, such as breaking quarantine or going to work during a lockdown (Terpstra & Salet, 2020). What we have observed in the margin of all this, is that police and law enforcement organisations were largely sufficiently loyal to apply these measures, but that there were also signs of discontent and ethical objections among police officers (Newiss et al., 2021).

A trend largely shared by most countries and has been included in the regional comparison, is the observation of eroding trust in vertical governance interactions, particularly between governments and societies and between police and citizens (Adepeju & Jimoh, 2021; Krouwel et al., 2021). Police-community relationships have definitely suffered an enormous setback and will continue to be under strain for the near future. This is, for instance, due to the perception that citizens have of police performance during the COVID-19 pandemic, namely that police seemed to be prepared to exert more violence in the face of social discontent (Amnesty International, 2020a; Leung, 2020; NOS, 2021b). Strikingly enough, in the era of digitalisation and domestic confinement, the world has been marked by a significant number of public demonstrations against measures that were imposed by governments in Europe and elsewhere (Gerbaudo, 2020). Unfortunately, COVID-19 has amplified underlying social tensions and has infused deep levels of polarisation (Charron et al., 2020; Rowe et al., 2021). This has come to the surface not just in clashes between citizens and police, but also amongst citizens themselves, both in the physical and in the virtual space (Mihelj et al., 2021; NOS, 2021a). The deep grooves of polarisation are likely to have a lasting effect on the social cohesion and community textures. Hence, most authors in this book share the observation that except for tensions in vertical governance relationships, there is a significant downturn in horizontal relationships in society, which are being undermined by polarisation between citizens. This has become exemplary in the deep wedges between "the vaccinated" and "the unvaccinated", leaving little space for nuanced argument and open debate, with the effect that entire families and social relationships have been torn apart (Ellyatt, 2021). Hence, underlying patterns of social discontent have strongly perspired throughout this pandemic and have left deep traces on society (NOS, 2021a; Pleyers, 2020).

The interesting thing is that despite these deep levels of societal division, governments have in fact called on the loyalty of citizens, companies and institutions to co-operate in the enforcement of the often restrictive anti-COVID-19 measures (Aston et al., 2020). For instance, restaurants, bars and non-grocery shops were confronted with long-lasting lockdowns and had to comply with the closure rules, and if not, they would be confronted with sanctions. Another example is schools: except for complete closures they had to implement several other measures, including distance rules, face-masks, online education and self-testing. Ipso facto for the work-floor that had to comply with the rules and impose them on the workforce at the same time. Through this wide application of mostly coercive measures (e.g. fines, sanctions), citizens, companies and institutions were not only forced to comply themselves but also became a shadow security actor in the sense that they became enforcers of the law as well as supervisors of the compliance simultaneously. At the same time, despite all these commonalities, a sensitive eye should be kept at differences between populations, governments and their responses. For instance, what we have seen in the contributions to this volume, is that satisfaction rates about the anti-COVID-19 measures on basis of surveys were widely different, not just between countries, but also between citizens themselves and between periods of time (Halliday et al., 2020; Möring et al., 2021; Toshkov et al., 2021). Nevertheless, what we may be able to conclude is that, on the one hand, societies have been caught in a social treatise with their respective governments, while, on the other hand, they were subjected to a dynamic of discipline and punish.

4 Comparative Dimension

In this volume, we have developed a comparative European perspective on how the COVID-19 pandemic has impacted on policing and security. Our prime theoretical perspective is that of "plural policing", which views policing as a function within a social system that is not uniquely performed by the uniformed police force and other security actors that may exercise the monopoly of violence, but also by private actors, communities and institutions. Ian Loader for instance, analyses recent developments in the area of policing as a "shift" or "transformation" from police to policing, whereby the state is no longer the single provider of the police function, but is shared by a more diverse network of actors (see, e.g., Loader, 2000). In arguing this, Loader divides four shifts, namely the shift from public to private policing (privatisation and commodification of security), the shift from policing by police forces to policing by citizens and communities (responsibilisation and self-policing), the shift from public to private police activities (out-sourcing of police activities such as forensic accountancy) and finally the shift from local and national policing to transnational policing (internationalisation and transnationalisation).

In a previously published joint article (Den Boer et al., 2022), we summarised these developments as follows: "Governments have predominantly relied on security services, in particular public police services, for enforcing compliance with the most restrictive COVID-19 measures, including quarantine, curfew, lockdown, and to some extent also physical distancing measures". Given the apparent limits in available capacity, the public police had to rely on cooperative arrangements with auxiliary police officers (including volunteers, community police support officers and private security guards) for executing these tasks. Hence, some countries specifically promoted levels of individual responsibility and "self-policing" (e.g. Ayling, 2007). To some extent, the role of institutions and societal actors in self-policing seems to be overshadowed in the media and evaluation reports.[2] Policing, here defined as ensuring compliance with the COVID-19 measures, has been distributed among several different actors, as can be seen in the "plural policing" Fig. 1.

What can be derived from this chart is that the public police forces have specifically been tasked with imposing "tougher" coercive measures in enforcing compliance with anti-COVID-19 measures (see, e.g., Ayling & Grabosky, 2006), particularly by ordering people to go home, issuing fines and by engaging in crowd and riot control during violent manifestations. For instance, in the United Kingdom, police were given new powers to enforce the anti-COVID-19 rules, ensuring parents to do all they could to stop their children breaking the rules, issue a 60 GBP fixed penalty, lowered to 30 GBP if paid within 14 days, and issue a 120 GBP penalty for second-time offenders, doubling on each further repeat offence. Anyone who did not could be taken to court, with magistrates able to impose unlimited fines (BBC News, 2020).

Our comparative research reveals that this emergence of plural policing can particularly be observed in countries like the Netherlands and the United Kingdom, but to a lesser degree in southern European countries like Greece and Spain. To a certain extent, this may be linked

[2] However, two months prior to "Liberation Day" on 19 July 2021, former Prime Minister Johnson of Great Britain expressed the following words: "And it is thanks to your effort and sacrifice in stopping the spread of this disease that the death rate is coming down and hospital admissions are coming down. And thanks to you we have protected our NHS and saved many thousands of lives" (Prime Minister's Office., & The Rt Hon Boris Johnson MP, 2020).

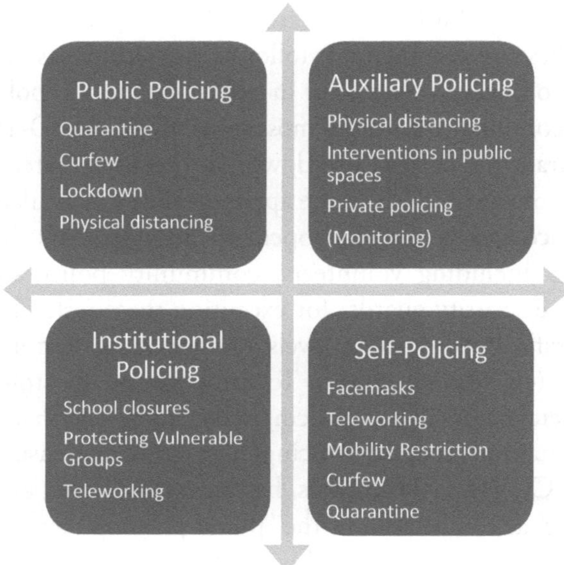

Fig. 1 Plural policing during COVID-19

to relatively high levels of professional discretion, as well as longstanding traditions of critical reflection on styles of policing. However, at the same time, we have observed rather significant levels of privatisation in Central Europe, particularly Croatia and Slovenia, as is visible in the Fig. 2.

Our regional comparison has brought authors together from different European countries (Germany, Netherlands and United Kingdom) as well as European regions (Southern Europe and Central and Eastern Europe) to mutually compare patterns and trends on policing and security as they developed during the COVID-19 pandemic, occasionally culminating in surprising outcomes. This comparison was performed on the basis of common central questions. All authors in this volume are prominent experts in policing, security, criminology and law. Most of them are academic writers but we were lucky to include practitioners. As all authors are well-versed into the domain of policing and security, they were uniquely capable of bringing on board validated knowledge, allowing them to embed their respective analysis in a long-term perspective. The writing project, which was supported by two interactive online

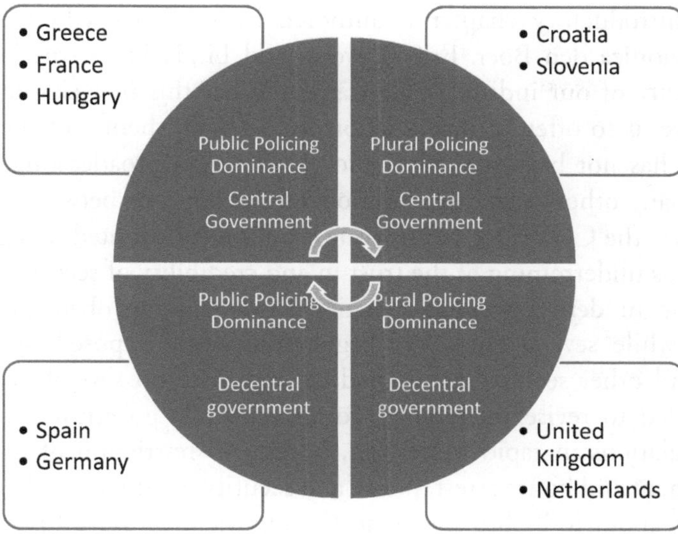

Fig. 2 Comparative spheres of policing

workshops for all authors, was mutually enriching as it has invited each author to reflect on their own observations as well as to distil insights from foreign experiences.

5 Reading Guide to the Chapters

As argued above, this book is written by experts on policing and security, who are generally well-known for their authorship and advisory roles. At the same time, all authors are citizens who themselves experienced the impact of the pandemic on their private and social lives, as fathers, mothers, sons, daughters, friends and more. Like most citizens, they felt catapulted into a new era, marked by what sometimes occurs as a large-scale social experiment. Hence, the perspectives that have been brought to the fore are not merely academic and professional, but also deeply personal. The perspective we share as authors is one of strong interest, curiosity and even passion to understand, reflect and analyse on this huge game-changer called COVID-19.

This introductory chapter is authored by the three editors of the book—Monica den Boer, Eric Bervoets and Linda Hak—the latter in the capacity of our indispensable trainee. What this first chapter seeks to achieve, is to offer an introduction to the main themes of the book. As there has not been a single radio or television broadcasting, newspaper or any other media that overlooked the tensions between citizens and police, the COVID-19 crisis seems to have contributed to a gradual but serious undermining of the trust in and credibility of security organisations in modern European societies. In demanding obedience from citizens while several rules and regulations were imposed on them, police and other security actors had to improvise on several occasions and needed to revise their moral compass. While governments issued new regulations in rapid succession, leading to restriction of mobility, confinement and house arrest, police and security organisations had to fix what was about to be broken: trust. During the COVID-19 pandemic, governments enforced rules that were—certainly in the early phases—not based on a democratically approved judicial framework. Moreover, local and regional government authorities issued rules and regulations that differed from one other, leaving citizens wondering about their rights. Due to the longevity of the pandemic, emergency laws were widely applied but seemed ill-suited as a proper basis for exceptional law enforcement powers. While citizens were confronted with extraordinary practices of policing, police and other security agencies were confronted with disappointed, angry and occasionally aggressive individuals. Given their "front-line" positions in streets, parks and land borders, security providers had to respond to shifting patterns in crime (see, e.g., Collier et al., 2020; Coomans et al., 2021; Nivette et al., 2021; Organisation for Security and Co-operation in Europe, 2021) and public order violence: although violent domestic abuse and cybercrime were on the rise, public violence went down originally due to the cancellation of many public events, such as football competitions. This took police organisations by surprise, and thus the COVID-19 crisis revealed a weakness in security organisations, namely that they seemed relatively unprepared for game changers and failed to collect timely information in a systematic fashion. Thus, security providers around Europe are traditional bureaucracies and it was a challenge to them to act in an agile fashion and steer the ship in a consistent direction. At the same time, a large amount of compliance monitoring and implementation was performed not by state police actors, but by private companies, public institutions like schools and universities, and citizens themselves.

The next chapter, entitled *Policing with the Help of Data: The Use of CoroPol in the Pandemic's Early Stages in The Netherlands,* is jointly written by Eric Bervoets, Jolijn Broekhuizen, Henk Ferwerda en Wouter Landman. In this chapter, the authors provide a reconstruction of the initial stages of the worldwide COVID-19 crisis, with a focus on related crime trends, public order trends and (plural) policing in Europe. The authors address the question: What were the most predominant challenges and (societal) topics during that period? Additionally, what were response patterns of law enforcement organisations (and security organisations)—and: What variety could be observed? For instance: Where had top-down directives been applied and what were the implications? The authors have applied the conceptual framework provided in this introductory chapter. To accomplish the reconstruction, raw open sources data and literature are analysed: news items and academic research reports on the COVID-19 pandemic. All data were collected using a search protocol resulting from a conceptual framework, different compared to this book. The original purpose of the data collection was non-academic. It was to provide Dutch law enforcement agencies brief information ('headlines') on crime, (plural) policing and public order elsewhere in Europe and the world, specifically during the stages of a lockdown. Besides, the CoroPol[3] Monitor was meant to indicate what to expect and what to prepare for in The Netherlands and to offer an action perspective on policing the pandemic in this country. Agencies were able to register to acquire periodic updates. CoroPol was independently set up by four Dutch scholars of applied science[4] to offer a (temporary) service to bridge the gap between the demand for information and the scarcity of information during the first stage of the COVID-19 crisis in The Netherlands. The authors end with a critical reflection on the CoroPol Monitors by addressing the central questions in this book in the

[3] CoroPol comes from the words "Corona and Policing".

[4] Working for privately owned research agencies.

context of a broader (critical) perspective on policing, law enforcement and police powers during extraordinary times.

The next chapter, entitled *Policing & Security in Southern Europe: How the COVID-19 pandemic reaffirms pre-existing patterns*, written by Anastassia Tsoukala, Gemma Usabart-González & Christian Mouhanna, addresses the full scope of measures and legal instruments that were imposed during the COVID-19 pandemic. Analyzing Greece, Spain and France, respectively, the authors have worked around a common assumption, namely that in all three countries there was already a prevailing mechanism by which the relationship between police and citizens was rather juxtaposed, with a sheer absence of community policing. Moreover, these three European countries showed a strong resemblance in the fact that their governments invoked the emergency situation, thereby legitimising the imposition of restrictive measures on the population. Like the other chapters, the text revolves around concepts on plural policing and the (non-)cooperation between police and other security actors. A comparative finding is that the pluralisation of policing did not genuinely get off the ground in the south of Europe, but we should not ignore the importance of the huge responsibility for compliance by citizens themselves. The authors address the question whether and how the COVID-19 pandemic contributed to the expression of social unrest and whether violence was used by and against the police. They also analyse the scale and scope of surveillance powers vis-à-vis citizens, how professional conduct of the police has been perceived by citizens and the effect these perceptions have had on trust levels in the police.

The chapter, entitled *Police and other plural policing institutions in Central and Eastern Europe facing COVID-19 pandemic*, authored by Branko Lobnikar, László Christián, József Balla, Ádám Kalmár, Irena Cajner Mraović, Krunoslav Borovec and Andrej Sotlar, revolves around concepts on plural policing and the (non-) cooperation between police and other security actors. First and foremost, there will be a mapping of the principal law enforcement actors in the selected Central and Eastern European countries and the police and security activities that were performed throughout the pandemic in managing the virus and whether they faced social discontent, in the form of public order. The authors also address the question whether plural policing in the form of cooperation between security actors, work in favour of the public support for the police. Moreover, the authors have studied the question how individual governments of selected Central and Eastern European countries have sought to govern the pandemic through a security lens, whether top-down directives were imposed, and whether surveillance powers vis-à-vis citizens were expanded. How did the pandemic affect the trust levels between society and security providers is one of the leading questions in this chapter, with surprisingly different outcomes.

The next chapter, entitled *Policing the COVID-19 Pandemic in Germany—Challenges and Learnings for Future Crises*, written by Hartmut Aden, sketches the evolution of the situation around the COVID-19 epidemic from a law enforcement and policing perspective in Germany. The main assumptions underlying this chapter are that security and law enforcement organisations in Germany were tightly embedded in the Länder, that seemed to implement anti-COVID-19 measures in a differentiated manner. The author observes that German police agencies are generally not prepared to openly evaluate the quality of policing in order to learn for future crises. Therefore, in his view, police organisations need to change into learning organisations with a culture that is open to learning from errors. This transformation may be subject to future political choices.

Last but not least, the chapter on the United Kingdom looks at plural policing from a British perspective. This chapter, entitled *Policing by Consent in a Pandemic: Security Governance and Policing of COVID-19 in the United Kingdom,* is written by Saskia Hufnagel, Rudi Fortson, Clive Walker and Megan O'Neill. In the land of Brexit and plural policing, how were police forces used by the central government to impose coercive measures on the British population, such as the lockdowns and tele-working? The chapter revolves around concepts on plural policing and the (non-)cooperation between police and other security actors. The authors analyse the distribution of governance and responsibility between public and private actors, taking into account levels of resistance that manifested themselves in public order issues. Did they follow any scripts for crisis management during a pandemic or did they apply high levels of professional discretion? And how did the state of emergency (in London) apply to the execution of extraordinary policing powers? Did levels of trust between police and society suffer a blow due to COVID-19, and if so, what lessons will be learnt for the future of policing?

6 An Introduction to the Authors

Prof. Dr. **Hartmut Aden** is a Professor of German and European Public Law, Public Policy and Public Administration at the Berlin School of Economics and Law (*Hochschule für Wirtschaft und Recht Berlin*) in the Department of Police and Security Management. In 2013, he co-founded the university's Berlin Institute for Safety and Security Research (FÖPS Berlin) which he co-directed from 2016 to 2020. Since 2020, he has been the Vice President for Research at HWR Berlin. Before his appointment as a professor at HWR Berlin in 2009, he was a Senior Audit Manager at the German Federal Court of Auditors (*Bundesrechnungshof*) at Bonn and an Assistant Professor at Leibniz University Hanover where he obtained his PhD in 1997, based on his research on police cooperation in the European Union. His research and teaching cover transdisciplinary and comparative questions related to internal security, policing, technology governance, human rights, data protection and environmental policy with a special focus on accountability issues. He has published widely on these topics. Recently he was co-editor of the edited volumes "Financial Accountability in the European Union. Institutions, Policy and Practice" (2021) and "Cybersecurity in Humanities and Social Sciences. A Research Methods Approach" (ISTE/Wiley 2020).

Pol. Col. Dr. **József Balla** is Head of the border policing department at Ludovika-University of Public Service (Ludovika-UPS). He is a police colonel and police high councillor. He started his professional career at the Border Guard in 1993 and continued at the National Headquarters of the Border Guard and National Headquarters of the Hungarian National Police, General Policing Directorate Border Policing Department in Documentation, as Head of Border Policing and Compensation Division head till 2015, for ten years. Associate professor, because has also been to teaching in higher education since

2003. He is the editor-in-chief of *Határrendészeti Tanulmányok* (Border Police Studies Scientific Journal), and the author about 80 publications. His research interest includes Schengen-compatible border guard training and education, integrated border management and biometric personal data in police control (biometric identification).

Dr. **Eric Bervoets** is Research Fellow at the Netherlands Defence Academy (NLDA). He is a Police Scientist and Criminologist. Since 1997 he has been an active researcher, after obtaining a Master's degree in Public Administration at Erasmus University Rotterdam. In 2006 he obtained his doctorate on Policing troubled neighbourhoods. Between 2000 and 2007 he worked at the Netherlands Police Academy. Since 2009 he has worked as a self-employed researcher, mostly co-operating with universities, polytechnics and research institutes. Organised crime, drugs, criminality and plural policing draw his academic attention. He was co-author of a book on the judicial leadership of chief detectives, published regularly on local policing and criminal investigation, and edited a collection on street-level bureaucracy. He also conducted a study on neighbourhood watch and private security guards and published on militarisation of the police(function) and military assistance. He lectures in public administration at several universities of applied sciences and is an officially recognised expert for the Netherlands National Police.

Prof. Dr. **Monica den Boer** was appointed Professor of Military Policing Operations at the Netherlands Defence Academy in June 2020, after serving as a member of parliament. Her research focuses on military policing, as well as border policing, international policing, urban policing and policing in the Caribbean. She fulfilled several functions, including Director of SeQure Research and Consultancy, Adjunct Professor at the Department of Security & Criminology at Macquarie University, and Director of Research and Knowledge Development at the Netherlands Police Academy, in conjunction with a Chair of Comparative Public Administration at the VU University Amsterdam. Prior, after obtaining a PhD from the European University Institute in 1990, she worked at Edinburgh University, the Netherlands Study Centre for Crime and Law Enforcement, the European Institute of Public Administration, Tilburg University, and the European Institute of Law Enforcement Co-operation (EULEC). She has published on European police co-operation, terrorism and organised crime, including "Comparative Policing from a Legal Perspective" (2018).

Dr. **Krunoslav Borovec**, PhD, is the Dean of the Police College at Police Academy Zagreb and a police scientist. Dr Borovec is a native of Zagreb, Croatia, and he received his PhD in Prevention Science at the Faculty of Special Education and Rehabilitation, University of Zagreb. Throughout his 30-year-long police career, he obtained many different leading positions within the police system, among which Assistant Director-General and Head of the Police Directorates, Advisor to the Croatian Minister of the Interior and many others. His primary research interest includes the area of community policing, public perception and confidence in police, police integrity and legitimacy. He is the author of numerous scholarly articles in the field of policing.

Jolijn Broekhuizen MA is a Sociologist. She has worked at various research bureaus since 2003 and has her own research bureau, Bureau Broekhuizen, since 2018. In the past decades, she conducted investigations for various (mostly) public organisations, such as the police, municipalities and provinces. Her investigations focused on security, (subversive) crime and the police. For example, she has authored a report on drug crime in the municipality of Utrecht in 2021. And in 2022 she investigated the role that the province of Noord-Brabant plays in combating subversive crime.

Dr. **Irena Cajner Mraović**, PhD, is an Associate Professor at the Faculty of Croatian Studies, University of Zagreb, Croatia, and a Representative at the City Assembly of the City of Zagreb. She graduated from the University of Zagreb and received a PhD in Special Education Sciences. She was the Dean of the Police College, an Advisor on Community Policing to the Minister of the Interior, and the Head of the Police Academy. Her research interests include sociology of policing, criminology of juvenile crime and violence, and sociology of social control. She has authored numerous scholarly papers, books and manuals. She has also mentored students who have received international awards for their work.

Pol. Brig. Gen. Dr. **László Christián** is Vice-Rector for Education of Ludovika-University of Public Service. He has the rank of police brigadier general and is a lawyer by profession. He has been the Head of the Department of Private Security and Local Governmental Law Enforcement of the Faculty of Law Enforcement of Ludovika-UPS since 2013. He is a habilitated Associate Professor and has been teaching in higher education since 2002. He started his professional career at the Customs and Finance Guard in 2002, then continued at the National Tax and Customs Office in various management positions. Since 2016 he has been a regular member of the Police. He is the Editor-in-Chief of *Magyar Rendészet (Hungarian Law Enforcement)* and the author of 130 publications. He is also the leader of a National Laboratory of Security Technologies. He is the holder of several awards, he has participated in 30 study trips abroad on several continents, and he regularly gives lectures at national and international conferences. His main field of research is public administration, law enforcement, private security, municipal policing.

Dr. **Henk Ferwerda** is a Criminologist. He studied social sciences and law at the University of Groningen. Henk got his PhD for a thesis on juvenile delinquency. He is Director and Researcher at Bureau Beke in Arnhem, the Netherlands. Bureau Beke is a criminological bureau that researches criminological phenomena and advises on crime and security measures for the government, police and municipalities. He published several books and articles on crime and security measures. Research topics he worked on, include juvenile delinquency, criminal networks, policing, undermining crime, hooligans and riots and violence against the police.

Professor **Rudi Fortson** QC, is an independent practising Barrister-at-law in London and Visiting Professor of Law, Queen Mary University of London. He is noted for his work in relation to serious crime, including economic crime, weapons and drug law. He has written and lectured extensively on a wide range of issues relating to the criminal law (as it applies in the United Kingdom and in the EU). He is a contributing author (two chapters) to "*Blackstone's Criminal Practice*" and he regularly writes for "*Criminal Law Review*".

Linda Hak is a Detective-Assistant for the National Police of the Netherlands. She obtained her BSc in Criminology at Erasmus University and a Master's degree in Legal Psychology at Maastricht University. She also served as a research intern at Bureau Bervoets.

Dr. **Saskia Hufnagel** is a Reader in Criminal Law at Queen Mary University of London. Previously, she worked as a Research Fellow at the Australian Research Council Centre of Excellence in Policing and Security (CEPS), Griffith University, Australia, and was a Leverhulme Fellow at the University of Leeds. She taught at the ANU College of Law and held a permanent teaching position at the University of Canberra. Her main research areas encompass law enforcement cooperation in Asia, North America, the EU and Australasia, comparative constitutional and human rights law with a focus on terrorism legislation and the policing of art crime. She has widely published on national and international police cooperation, security, comparative constitutional law and art crime. She is a qualified German legal professional and accredited specialist in criminal law.

Pol. Lt-Col. **Ádám Kalmár** is Head of the Aliens policing Division of the Baranya County Police Headquarters. He is a police lieutenant-colonel and police councillor. He started his professional career as border guard officer at the Border Guard in 1997, then continued at the National Police as border police officer in various management positions. He is PhD student at the Doctoral School of Police Studies at the National University of Public Service in Budapest. He is a member of the National Association of Doctoral Students as the international referent of the Department of Law Enforcement. His research interests include integrated border management, international police cooperation, border and aliens policing, fighting against illegal immigration, and Schengen evaluations.

Dr. **Wouter Landman** works as an independent researcher and advisor. Until 2019 he worked at the Dutch research and consultancy company Twynstra Gudde. His (action) research focuses on change and innovation in policing. He publishes mainly on police culture and behaviour, criminal investigation and impact of technology on policing.

Prof. Dr. **Branko Lobnikar**, PhD, is a Full Professor of Security Studies and Head of the Policing and Security Studies Department at the Faculty of Criminal Justice and Security, University of Maribor, Slovenia. His areas of expertise comprise issues of contemporary policing, human resource management, and deviant behaviour within organisations. He has authored several papers on various aspects of policing and police deviance management and co-edited Handbook on Policing in Central and Eastern Europe for Springer and the book Improving Frontline Responses to Domestic Violence in Europe (University of Maribor Press; open access). At the time of writing, he was involved in the studies of police integrity, domestic violence (H2020 project IMPRODOVA) and (de) radicalisation.

Dr. **Christian Mouhanna (CESDIP, France)**, sociologist (PhD), is permanent Researcher at the CNRS (French National Center for Scientific Research) and at the University of Paris-Saclay, Member and former Director of the CESDIP (*Centre de Recherches Sociologiques sur le Droit et les Institutions Pénales*/Center for Sociological Research on Law and Criminal Justice Institutions), a major venue for the study of criminal justice and deviance in France, and one of the leading research organisations dedicated to the study of crime and law organisations. He works for more than 20 years on the French Police Forces, including the French Gendarmerie, the courts and security policies. Among others, he published: "Reforms and Unexpected Events: The influence of Terrorist Attacks on Policing Strategies" in *Policing: A Journal of Policy and Practice* (2021), "Police Centralization and its Pathologies", in De Maillard and Skogan (eds), *Policing in France,* 2021; "Local governance in the centralized French system of policing: From co-production to conflict of legitimacy", *European Journal of Criminology*, 2019; and "Theories on Policing and Communities", in Bruinsma & Weisburd (eds) *Encyclopedia of Criminology and Criminal Justice*, 2014.

Dr. **Megan O'Neill** is a Reader in Human Geography at the University of Dundee and an Associate Director of the Scottish Institute for Policing Research (SIPR). Her work focuses on aspects of police culture, community policing, public sector pluralisation in policing, private policing and surveillance practices of the state. Her research is primarily qualitative, with in-depth ethnographies of football policing in Scotland (*Policing Football*, 2005) and the work of Police Community Support Officers (PCSOs) (*Police Community Support Officers*, 2019) in England. She has studied policing across the United Kingdom and in the EU. In recent work, she was co-leader of a work package in the Horizon 2020 project "Unity" (which examined community policing), was the Principal Investigator for the NordForsk-funded project "Eyes Online" (which studied online state surveillance) and is a co-leader of a working group in the COST Action "PolStops", which considers the practice of police stops in the EU.

Dr. **Andrej Sotlar**, PhD, is Associate Professor of security sciences and from 2015 on Dean of the Faculty of Criminal Justice and Security, University of Maribor, Slovenia. He has a Ph.D. in defence studies (University of Ljubljana). His pedagogic and research interests include national security systems, security policy, private security and private detective activity, and plural policing. He has recently participated in research projects on safety in local communities; international comparison of private security; plural policing; radicalisation and deradicalisation; and has directed research on the development of private detective activity in Slovenia; on reshaping of municipal warden service in Ljubljana; and on appeal mechanisms overwork of private security officers, municipal wardens and private detectives in Slovenia.

Dr. **Anastassia Tsoukala**, PhD in Law and Criminal Sciences, is Associate Professor of Criminology at the University Paris-Saclay, Senior Researcher at the University Paris-Cité and Research Associate at the Centre for Conflict, Liberty and Security (France). She works on the design and implementation of European security policies in relation to counter-terrorism, immigration, football crowd violence, and on the social construction of threat. She is author of: *Lutte armée grecque contemporaine. Des stratégies discursives de (dé)légitimation* (2021); *Football Hooliganism in Europe: Security and Civil Liberties in the Balance*, (2009); she is co-editor of: *Legal Responses to Football "Hooliganism" in Europe* (2016); *Terror, Insecurity and Liberty: Illiberal Practices of Liberal Regimes after 9/11* (2008).

Dr. **Gemma Ubasart-González** is Associate Professor of Political Science at University of Girona. Currently also visiting professor at Université Lumiére Lyon 2. Her areas of interest revolve around public policy analysis and political conflict, especially in Southern Europe and Latin America. In recent times, she has developed research on welfare regimes and social policies; conflicts and the criminal system; local government and politics; Spanish and Catalan politics. She has published in JCR and SJR indexed journals such as *Social and Legal Studies*; *CIDOB Journal of International Affairs*; *International Journal of Sociology and*

Social Policy; *Crime Law and Social Change*; *Social Compass*: *Revista de Pensamiento e Investigación Social* and several others. She has recently co-coordinated three books: *"Política y Govern a Catalunya: des de la transició a l'actualitat"* with Salvador Martí. *"Manual del Estado del Bienestar y las politiques sociolaborales"* with Ferran Camas at Huygens Editorial and *"Vidas en transición. (Re)construir la ciudadania social"* with Ricard Gomà. She also cooperates as a political analyst in various media.

Prof. Em. Dr. **Clive Walker** is Professor Emeritus of Criminal Justice Studies at the School of Law, University of Leeds, where he served as the Director of the Centre for Criminal Justice Studies (1987-2000) and as Head of School (2000-2005, 2010). He was awarded a Ph.D in 1982 and an LL.D in 2015 by the University of Manchester. He became a Solicitor in 1978 and a Queen's Counsel (Hon) in 2016. He has written extensively on constitutional, terrorism and internet issues and frequently given advice to the UK Government and UK Parliament. In 2003, he was appointed as a special adviser to the UK Parliamentary select committee which scrutinised what became the Civil Contingencies Act 2004, following which he published *The Civil Contingencies Act 2004: Risk, Resilience and the Law in the United Kingdom* (2006). His research on the internet produced the book (with Akdeniz and Wall), *The Internet, Law and Society* (2001) as well as many papers on specialised aspects such as virtual democracy and cyberterrorism. His books on terrorism are recognised and cited widely and include *Terrorism and the Law* (2011), *The Anti-Terrorism Legislation*, (3rd ed., 2014), the *Routledge Handbook of Law and Terrorism* (2015), (with Gurulé and King) The *Palgrave Handbook of Criminal and Terrorism Financing Law* (2018) and (with Llobet Anglí and Cancio Meliá) *Precursor Crimes of Terrorism: The Criminalisation of Terrorism Risk in Comparative Perspective* (2022). In 2010, he was appointed in 2010 by the Home Office as Senior Adviser to the Independent Reviewer of Terrorism Legislation.

References

Aden, H., Arzt, C., & Fährmann, J. (2020). Gefährdete Freiheitsrechte in Krisenzeiten – Lehren aus der COVID-19-Pandemie. *Zeitschrift für Bürgerrechte und Gesellschaftspolitik Nr. 230, 59*(2), 99–111.

Adepeju, M., & Jimoh, F. (2021). An analytical framework for measuring inequality in the public opinions on policing-assessing the impacts of COVID-19 pandemic using Twitter Data. *Journal of Geographic Information System, 13*(2), 122–147. https://doi.org/10.4236/jgis.2021.132008.

Algemeen Dagblad. (2021). *Politie: inzet leger onvermijdelijk bij code zwart in ziekenhuizen.* Accessed on 22 December 2021, from https://www.ad.nl/politiek/politie-inzet-leger-onvermijdelijk-bij-code-zwart-in-ziekenhuizen~a6a76177/.

Allain-Dupré, D., Chatry, I., Komprobst, A., Michalun, M., Wheeler, C. (2021). *The territorial impact of COVID-19: Managing the crisis and recovery across levels of government.* Organisation for Economic Co-operation and Development (OECD).

Amnesty International. (2020a). *COVID-19 Crackdowns: Police abuse and the global pandemic.* Accessed on 4 March 2021, from https://www.amnesty.org/en/documents/act30/3443/2020a/en/.

Amnesty International. (2020b). *Policing the pandemic. Human rights violations in the enforcement of COVID-19 measures in Europe.* Accessed on 9 February 2021, from https://www.amnesty.org/en/documents/eur01/2511/2020b/en/.

Aston, L., Brandariz, J. A., Czerwinska, D., De Kimpe, S., Maillard, J. de, Hoffman, I., O'Neil, M., Rowe, M., & Solhjell, R. (2020). *Policing the pandemic.* Horizon 2020 Framework Programme of the European Union. Accessed on 4 March 2021, from https://livrepository.liverpool.ac.uk/3105581/1/White%20Paper%20-%20Policing%20the%20Pandemic.pdf.

Ayling, J. (2007). Force multiplier: People as a policing resource. *International Journal of Comparative and Applied Criminal Justice, 31*(1), 73–100. https://doi.org/10.1080/01924036.2007.9678761.

Ayling, J., & Grabosky, P. (2006). Policing by command: Enhancing law enforcement capacity through coercion. *Law & Policy, 28*(4), 420–443. https://doi.org/10.1111/j.1467-9930.2006.00233.x.

BBC News. (2020). *Coronavirus: Police get new powers to enforce protection.* Accessed on 8 July 2022, from https://www.bbc.com/news/uk-52053527.

Boer, M., Bervoets, E., & Hak, L. (2022). Preparing for future pandemic policing. *European Law Enforcement Research Bulletin, (SCE 5)*, 261–271. https://doi.org/10.7725/eulerb.v0iSCE%205.491.

Boere, R. (2021). *Massaal bezwaar gemaakt bij opleggen coronaboetes.* Het Parool. Accessed on 22 December 2021, from https://www.parool.nl/nederland/massaal-bezwaar-gemaakt-bij-opleggen-coronaboetes~b21f5d0f/?referrer=https%3A%2F%2Fwww.google.nl%2F.

Boin, A., McConnell, A., & 't Hart, P. (2021). *Governing the pandemic: The politics of navigating a mega-crisis.* Palgrave Macmillan.

Brown, J., & Fleming, J. (2021). Exploration of individual and work-related impacts on police officers and police staff working in support or front-line roles during the UK's first COVID lockdown. *The Police Journal,* 1–23. https://doi.org/10.1177/0032258X211052891.

Charron, N., Lapuente, V., & Rodriguez-Pose, A. (2020). *Uncooperative society, uncooperative politics or both? How trust, polarization and populism explain excess mortality for COVID-19 across European regions.* University of Götheborg. Accessed on 9 March 2021, from https://gupea.ub.gu.se/bitstream/handle/2077/67189/gupea_2077_67189_1.pdf?sequence=1&isAllowed=y.

Collier, B., Horgan, S., Jones, R., & Shepherd, L. (2020). *The implications of the COVID-19 pandemic for cybercrime policing in Scotland: A rapid review of the evidence and future considerations.* Scottish Institute for Policing Research. Accessed on 9 February 2021, from https://www.researchgate.net/profile/Ben-Collier-3/publication/341742472_Issue_No_1_The_implications_of_the_COVID-19_pandemic_for_cybercrime_policing_in_Scotland_A_rapid_review_of_the_evidence_and_future_considerations/links/5ed4f73a458515294527b273/Issue-No-1-The-implications-of-the-COVID-19-pandemic-for-cybercrime-policing-in-Scotland-A-rapid-review-of-the-evidence-and-future-considerations.pdf.

Coomans, A., van Deuren, S., van Dijk, M., van de Weijer, S., Blokland, A., van Baak, C., Kühling, D., Bombeld, R., & Eichelsheim, V. (2021). Stay home, stay safe? *Justitiele Verkenningen, 47*(3), 35–53. https://doi.org/10.5553/JV/016758502021047003003.

Coronacheck. (n.d.). *Veilig op reis met je coronabewijs.* Ministerie van Volksgezondheid, Welzijn en Sport. Accessed on 31 December 2021, from https://coronacheck.nl/nl.

Eijken, H. van, & Rijpma, J. J. (2021). Stopping a virus from moving freely: Border controls and travel restrictions in times of Corona. *Utrecht Law Review*, 17(3), 34–50. https://doi.org/10.36633/ulr.686.

Ellyatt, H. (2021). *As many return to the office, tensions flare between the "vaxxed and unvaxxed"*. CNBC. Accessed on 27 December 2021, from https://www.cnbc.com/2021/09/13/office-tensions-rise-between-the-vaccinated-and-unvaccinated-.html.

Ferwerda, H., & Landman, W. (2021). *Wat nemen we mee? Blauwe vakontwikkeling in de basisteams tijdens Covid-19 en lessen voor de toekomst.* Politie Nederland, Bureau Beke, Bureau Landman. Accessed on 31 December 2021, from https://bureaubeke.nl/wp-content/uploads/2021/01/Wat-nemen-we-mee.pdf.

Frenkel, M. O., Giessing, L., Egger-Lampl, S., Hutter, V., Oudejans, R. R. D., Kleygrewe, L., Jaspaert, E., & Plessner, H. (2021). The impact of the COVID-19 pandemic on European police officers: Stress, demands, and coping resources. *Journal of Criminal Justice, 72*, 1–14. https://doi.org/10.1016/j.jcrimjus.2020.101756.

Gentithes, M., & Krent, H. J. (2020). *Pandemic Surveillance-the New Predictive Policing. Conlawnow, 12*(1), 57–74.

Gerbaudo, P. (2020). The pandemic crowd: Protest in the time of COVID-19. *Journal of International Affairs, 73*(2), 61–76.

Halliday, S., Meers, J., & Tomlinson, J. (2020). *Public Attitudes on Compliance with COVID-19 Lockdown Restrictions.* University of New York, Nuffield Foundation. Accessed on 31 December 2021, from https://www.nuffieldfoundation.org/project/law-and-compliance-during-covid-19.

Human Rights Watch. (2021). *Covid-19 Triggers Wave of Free Speech Abuse.* HRW. Accessed on 15 February 2021, from https://www.hrw.org/node/377786/printable/print.

Jones, D. J. (2020). The potential impacts of pandemic policing on police legitimacy: planning past the COVID-19 crisis. *Policing: A journal of policy and practice, 14*(3), 579–586. https://doi.org/10.1093/police/paaa026.

Karacan, O., Luesink, M., & Wijkhuis, V. (2021). *De coronacrisis: voorbereiding en improvisatie.* Instituut Fysieke Veiligheid (IVF). Accessed on 31 December 2021, from https://nipv.nl/wp-content/uploads/2022/02/20210722-IFV-De-coronacrisis-voorbereiding-en-improvisatie.pdf.

Kostic, J., & Boskovic, M. M. (2020). How COVID-19 pandemic influences rule of law backsliding in Europe. *Regional Law Review*, 77–90. https://doi.org/10.18485/iup_rlr.2020.ch6.

Krouwel, A., Vries, O. de, Heck, L. van, Kutiyski, Y., & Étienne, T. (2021). *COVID-19 en institutioneel vertrouwen.* Accessed on 18 November 2021, from https://www.impactcorona.nl/wp-content/uploads/2021/10/Institutioneelvertrouwen_KL01.pdf.

Laufs, J., & Waseem, Z. (2020). Policing in pandemics: A systematic review and best practices for police response to COVID-19. *International Journal of Disaster Risk Reduction, 5*, 1–17. https://doi.org/10.1016/j.ijdrr.2020.101812.

Leeson, L. (2021) *Yorkshire's police forces respond to criticism of pandemic policing following Sarah Everard vigil*. Yorkshire Post. Accessed on 16 March 2021, from https://www.yorkshirepost.co.uk/news/crime/yorkshires-police-forces-respond-to-criticism-of-pandemic-policing-following-sarah-everard-vigil-3166875.

Leloup, P., & Cools, M. (2021). (Post-)crisis policing, public health and private security: The COVID-19 pandemic and the private security sector. *Policing and Society, 1–16*. https://doi.org/10.1080/10439463.2021.1970159.

Leung, M. (2020). *Concerns raised about extreme measures, power abuse during virus lockdowns.* CTV. Accessed on 27 December 2021, from https://www.ctvnews.ca/health/coronavirus/concerns-raised-about-extreme-measures-power-abuse-during-virus-lockdowns-1.4877776.

Loader, I. (2000). Plural policing and democratic governance. *Social & Legal Studies, 9*(3), 323–345.

Mawby, R. (2020). Coronavirus, Crime and Policing: Thought on the implications of the lockdown rollercoaster. *European Police Science and Research Bulletin, 20*, 13–30.

Mihelj, S., Kondor, K., & Štětka, V. (2021). Audience engagement with COVID-19 news: The impact of lockdown and live coverage, and the role of polarization. *Journalism Studies, 1–19.* https://doi.org/10.1080/1461670X.2021.1931410.

Möhring, K., Naumann, E., Reifenscheid, M., Wenz, A., Rettig, T., Krieger, U., Friedel, S., Finkel, M., Cornesse, C., & Blom, A. G. (2021). The COVID-19 pandemic and subjective well-being: Longitudinal evidence on satisfaction with work and family. *European Societies, 23*(sup1), 601–617. https://doi.org/10.1080/14616696.2020.1833066.

Newiss, G., Charman, S., Ilett, C., Bennett, S., Ghaemmaghami, A., Smith, P., & Inkpen, R. (2021). Taking the strain? Police well-being in the COVID-19 era. *The Police Journal,* 1–12. https://doi.org/10.1177/0032258X211044702.

Newton, K. (2020). Government communications, political trust and compliant social behaviour: The politics of Covid-19 in Britain. *The Political Quarterly, 91*(3), 502–513. https://doi.org/10.1111/1467-923X.12901.

Nivette, A. E., Zahnow, R., Aguilar, R., Ahven, A., Amram, S., Ariel, B., Arosemena Burbano, M. J., Astolfi, R., Baier, D., Bark, H. M., Beijers, J. E.

H., Bergman, M., Breetzke, G., Concha-Eastman, I. A., Curtis-Ham, S., Davenport, R., Diaz, C., Fleitas, D., Gerell, M., … & Eisner, M. P. (2021). A global analysis of the impact of COVID-19 stay-at-home restrictions on crime. *Nature Human Behaviour, 5*(7), 868–877.

NOS. (2021a). *NCTV: harde coronaprotesten breken met vroegere protestcultuur.* Accessed on 20 April 2021a, from https://nos.nl/artikel/2376718-nctv-harde-coronaprotesten-breken-met-vroegere-protestcultuur.

NOS. (2021b). *Politie registreerde meer geweld en kreeg meer klachten.* Accessed on 29 December 2021b, from https://nos.nl/artikel/2381365-politie-registreerde-meer-geweld-en-kreeg-meer-klachten.

Organization for Security and Co-operation in Europe. (2021). *Civil society: Building trust and peace during the COVID-19 pandemic.* Accessed on 31 August 2021, from https://www.osce.org/mission-to-moldova/494464.

Pleyers, G. (2020). The pandemic is a battlefield. Social movements in the COVID-19 lockdown. *Journal of Civil Society, 16*(4), 295–312. https://doi.org/10.1080/17448689.2020.1794398.

Prime Minister's Office., & The Rt Hon Boris Johnson MP. (2020). *Prime Minister's statement on coronavirus (COVID-19): 10 May 2020.* GOV.UK. Accessed on 19 July 2021, from https://www.gov.uk/government/speeches/pm-address-to-the-nation-on-coronavirus-10-may-2020.

Rhinard, M. (2019). The crisisification of policy-making in the European Union. *Journal of Common Market Studies, 57*(3), 616–633. https://doi.org/10.1111/jcms.12838.

Rowe, M., O'Neill, M., de Kimpe, S., & Hoffman, I. (2021). Policing during a pandemic—for the public health or against the usual suspects? *European Law Enforcement Research Bulletin, 5*, 1–5.

Russack, S., Bodson, B., Primatarova, A., Kovár, J., Kvorning Lassen, C., Wind, M., Due, X., Kuusik, P., Ketola, J., Chopin, T., Gauvin, L., Alander, M., K, A. L., Rehbaum, D., Chatzistavrou, F., Wolford, Z., Poli, E., Bukovskis, K., Palkova, A. … Wetter-Ryde, A. (2021). *The effect of Covid on EU democracies.* European Policy Institutes Network (EPIN). Accessed on 31 December 2021, from https://epin.org/wp-content/uploads/2021/04/EPIN-REPORT_The-effect-of-Covid-on-EU-democracies-1.pdf.

Schomaker, R. M., Hack, M., & Mandry, A. K. (2021). The EU's reaction in the first wave of the Covid-19 pandemic between centralisation and decentralisation, formality and informality. *Journal of European Public Policy, 28*(8), 1278–1298. https://doi.org/10.1080/13501763.2021.1942153.

Sheptycki, J. (2020). The politics of policing a pandemic panic. *Australian & New Zealand Journal of Criminology, 53*(2), 157–173. https://doi.org/10.1177/0004865820925861.

Spadaro, A. (2020). COVID-19: Testing the limits of human rights. *European Journal of Risk Regulation, 11*(2), 317–325. https://doi.org/10.1017/err.2020.27.

Strijker, R. (2020). *Nijpend tekort aan agenten door coronamaatregelen, dagelijks werk in gevaar.* RTL Nieuws. Accessed on 20 July 2022, from https://www.rtlnieuws.nl/nieuws/artikel/5185659/politie-testen-corona-agenten-capaciteit.

Terpstra, J., & Salet, R. (2020). *Politie in tijden van Corona: Over haar maatschappelijke opdracht in buitengewone omstandigheden.* Landelijke Portefeuille GGP van de Nationale Politie. Accessed on 31 December 2022, from https://www.ru.nl/rechten/alumni/%401292693/publicatie-politie-tijden-corona-renzesalet-jan/.

Toshkov, D., Carroll, B., & Yesilkagit, K. (2021). Government capacity, societal trust or party preferences: what accounts for the variety of national policy responses to the COVID-19 pandemic in Europe?. *Journal of European Public Policy, 29*(7), 1–20.https://doi.org/10.1080/13501763.2021.1928270.

Tzifakis, N. (2020). The Western Balkans during the pandemic: Democracy and rule of law in quarantine? *European View, 19*(2), 197–205. https://doi.org/10.1177/1781685820963333.

Vampa, D. (2021). COVID-19 and territorial policy dynamics in Western Europe: Comparing France, Spain, Italy, Germany, and the United Kingdom. *Publius, the Journal of Federalism, 51*(4), 601–626. https://doi.org/10.1093/publius/pjab017.

Waever, O. (2007). Securitisation and desecuritisation. In B. Buzan & L. Hansen (Red.), *International security: Widening the agenda of international security* (pp. 66–99). Sage.

Wijers, M. (2021). *Australië zet leger in om lockdown te handhaven.* Accessed on 22 December 2021, from https://nos.nl/artikel/2391675-australie-zet-leger-in-om-lockdown-te-handhaven.

World Health Organization. (2021). *Tracking SARS-CoV-2 variants.* WHO. Accessed on 27 December 2021, from https://www.who.int/en/activities/tracking-SARS-CoV-2-variants/.

World Health Organization. (n.d.). *WHO Coronavirus (COVID-19) dashboard data table.* WHO. Accessed on 28 December 2022, from https://covid19.who.int.

2

Policing with the Help of Data: The Use of CoroPol in the Pandemic's Early Stages in The Netherlands

Eric Bervoets, Jolijn Broekhuizen, Henk Ferwerda, and Wouter Landman

1 Introduction

A pandemic is simultaneously a health and safety issue, as was already stated in the introductory chapter of this book. To manage a pandemic, governmental response is required to reduce the chance of large-scale infection and social malfunctioning. In many countries lockdowns,

E. Bervoets (✉)
Netherlands Defence Academy, Breda, The Netherlands
e-mail: e.bervoets@bureaubervoets.nl

J. Broekhuizen · H. Ferwerda · W. Landman
Bureau Beke, Arnhem, The Netherlands
e-mail: info@bureaubroekhuizen.nl

H. Ferwerda
e-mail: h.ferwerda@beke.nl

W. Landman
e-mail: wouter@bureaulandman.nl

M. Den Boer et al. (eds.), *Plural Policing, Security and the COVID Crisis*, Palgrave's Critical Policing Studies, https://doi.org/10.1007/978-3-031-19177-0_2

curfews and the closing of public facilities like schools, shops, restaurants and the cancelling of events were regarded as necessary during the COVID-19 pandemic (Aston et al., 2020). The safety measures to manage the pandemic enhance the potential for social tensions and violence, as had been observed in many countries across the world in 2020 and 2021 (Charron et al., 2020; Den Boer et al., 2022). The focus of this chapter is on the initial stages ('first wave') of the pandemic in The Netherlands. Unlike most other European countries, in the early stages, there was no significant politically engaged anti-government or anti-police sentiment, at least not until the riots that took place during the Summer of 2020, eventually culminating in 'the curfew riots' in January 2021.

In this chapter, we discuss whether a pandemic like COVID-19 may invoke social disorder, which, is best be explained theoretically by 'anomie' (Merton, 1968) and sometimes even by the concept of a 'moral holiday' (Weenink, 2013). The concept moral holiday was coined by psychologist and philosopher James, to denote situations in which individuals regale themselves with a temporary relaxation of the rules of conduct, "treating" themselves to an enjoyable moment.

From a criminological point of view, it is also useful to analyse the effect of a pandemic on crime and crime trends. The assumption is that social disorder and crime may overlap, for example in the case of public violence. Moreover, a pandemic may directly or indirectly affect criminal opportunities, targets and perpetrators (Clarke & Cornish, 1986; Wilcox et al., 2018). During the pandemic, social surveillance has been increased. In many countries, the police organisation lacked capacity to enforce the measures that were required to enforce the safety issues that came along with COVID-19 (Politie Eenheid Amsterdam, 2021; Stogner et al., 2020). Many police departments experienced a lack of capacity, because the coronavirus influenced the sick leave within the police forces.

J. Broekhuizen
Bureau Broekhuizen, Amersfoort, The Netherlands

W. Landman
Bureau Landman, Hengelo, The Netherlands

Additionally, other public and private institutions sometimes had better resources to implement and enforce measures to fight and prevent further social disorder (Aston et al., 2020; Mawby, 2020). That is why, in many European countries, plural policing seemed a viable response to control the pandemic-related security.

Knowledge, information and intelligence are crucial to support informed (plural) policing, because they offer the security actors insight to challenges and the mode and timing of potential interventions (James, 2013; Ratcliffe, 2016). In this chapter, "intelligence" is defined as action-oriented information (and knowledge) in police data systems, knowledge derived from scientific publications as well as information that originates from open sources like the news media, websites etc. From the body of knowledge on crisis management, we know that intelligence is simultaneously strongly needed and scarcely available during the initial stages of a crisis such as a pandemic (Boin & Overdijk, 2020).

Similar to other countries, the Dutch police forces had to adapt to the extraordinary circumstances for the performance of law enforcement in the course of a pandemic. The information and intelligence departments within the police had a hard time, initially, to offer the needed information and knowledge. This is why the authors of this chapter, all applied scientists, developed a monitor and a research project aiming to supply open source intelligence as well as research findings to the police and other governmental actors in order to improve their understanding of policing COVID-19. This service was a private and non-commercial initiative, based on societal commitment. The intended purpose was to assist Dutch safety and security actors with knowledge to being able to prepare and forecast, and not having to react on an ad hoc and improvising basis. Helping the police and other security actors is not obvious in many countries. It is, however, a bit more common in countries like The Netherlands with a profound tradition of Community Policing in which the police tends to be receptive to (applied) scientific research. The information and knowledge products were used in police briefings and turned out to be one of the sources that complemented the knowledge deficit during the early stages of the pandemic in The Netherlands.

In this chapter, we focus on the main findings and outcomes of the Dutch CoroPol Monitor and Research Project. "CoroPol" is an amalgamation of the words 'corona' and 'policing'. We will discuss the process of information-supply and methodology as well as the substantive results of the monitor. Three central questions are addressed in this chapter:

What were the predominant challenges and (societal) topics during the initial stages of the worldwide COVID-19-crisis, concerning crime trends, public order and (plural) policing, with a focus on The Netherlands?

Additionally, what were response patterns of law enforcement organisations (and security organisations), and which levels of variety could be observed?

How has CoroPol contributed to the provision of information for law enforcement and other public actors during the first phase of the pandemic?

1.1 Plural Policing

In line with the general conceptual framework of this book, in this chapter, we apply the theoretical concept of 'plural policing', which we define as a range of policing activities carried out by a multiplicity of actors, steered and controlled by their specific (or at least different) authorities (Loader, 2000). In The Netherlands, this includes both public police actors as well as private actors, and national as well as local and regional actors. The plural policing scope in The Netherlands includes the National Police and the municipal officers ('*gemeentelijke handhaving*') and the Royal Marechaussee (military constabulary), as well as non-police actors, such as local government actors, youth workers and private security actors. Police actors formally enforce the law, while non-police actors contribute to influencing public conduct by exercising (more or less formal) social control.

To answer the third central question, we further elaborate on the background of the CoroPol Monitor and Research Project, and we briefly discuss the methodology of the monitor and research designs. To respond to the questions on substantive results, key observations and predictions on (international) crime developments are discussed in the third paragraph. In the fourth paragraph, we expand on predominant challenges and societal topics such as the link between social disorder and policing. In paragraph five, we present key observations on enforcing and policing measures on COVID-19 in The Netherlands. The chapter is wrapped up with conclusions by putting them into a critical theoretical perspective.[1]

2 CoroPol: Collating Information During the Initial Stages of the Pandemic

Throughout the globe, during the first weeks of the pandemic uncertainty prevailed. This definitely also applied to the Dutch security actors, including the National Police. Questions included what would the expected effects of this crisis on crime and public order be and what would be a sensible strategy to enforce the law during these extraordinary circumstances? With this in mind, a police chief in our professional network approached us with a request, namely how the National Police could gain systematic access of international trends on policing the pandemic based on news media, and how we could assist in a systematic analysis of publicly available research on the matter. According to the chief officer, the National Police was not yet in the position to make an inventory and analysis of the information. Moreover, research findings on policing COVID-19 were still rare at the time. As the pandemic evolved, information gradually became available in a more systematic fashion, providing police forces with a fundament to stage evidence-based policing. In sum: the National Police acknowledged the need to bridge the gap between the demand for information and its scarcity during the first stages of the COVID-19 crisis in The Netherlands.

The authors of this chapter started to collect, analyse and interpret knowledge about the impact of COVID-19 on crime, safety and enforcement. With the aim to share the acquired knowledge with law enforcement, local authorities and other public actors concerned with safety and security. Agencies were facilitated to receive periodic updates by e-mail.[2] Eventually, the Monitor gained 384 subscriptions, amongst

[1] Strictly speaking, in this chapter we focus on the first stages of the pandemic (in the Netherlands). Although, when essential to put the CoroPol data in perspective, we incidentally focus as well on consecutive stages of the pandemic.

[2] Eventually, in 2020 we produced a Basic source document on March 27th and five updates on, respectively, March 31st, April, 3rd, April 11th, April 21st and May 18th of that year. The

these National Police, Royal Marechaussee, and other law enforcement agencies such as Europol and Dutch municipalities.

The Monitor relied on the collecting of international open sources data: news items and academic research reports on the COVID-19 pandemic. All data were selected using a search protocol.[3]

In the meantime, the researchers were requested by the National Police and local government to engage into two small-scale research projects for local governments (Amsterdam and Arnhem), as well as two research projects for the Dutch Police (Broekhuizen et al., 2020). The research for the police was focused on both the effects of the pandemic on criminal investigation and working on the beat. The research in Amsterdam and Arnhem had a different scope. It was focused on plural policing public order and interventions of youth work, induced by perceived tensions and risk of youngsters causing disorder, because of the strict anti-COVID-19 measures that had been taken (e.g. closing of schools, sporting clubs and youth clubs).[4]

So much for a background on CoroPol.[5] The remaining empirical section of this chapter will be addressing the substantive findings of CoroPol on crime, disorder and policing the pandemic during the first wave in The Netherlands. In order to put findings into perspective, we will, when useful, compare the Dutch findings with international developments and trends.

---

basic document and the updates all had a 'point by point' and 'to-the-point' character, for we wanted to take into account the needs of the target audience.

[3] Further details about CoroPol and its methodology can be obtained from the authors.

[4] Because of the mentioned projects in Amsterdam and Arnhem, the analysis in this chapter is slightly more focused on policing *youths*.

[5] To provide an idea of the usefulness of the CoroPol documents, we sent an e-mail on 13 July 2021 to the 384 subscribers of CoroPol in 2020, asking them to participate in a mini-poll on the usefulness of this initiative during the first months of the pandemic. Eventually, a total of 48 respondents responded. In general, the respondents indicate that they consider the documents as very valuable and useful. Many respondents responded that at the beginning of the crisis the need for information was very urgent and that the CoroPol documents fulfilled this need. In addition, the documents were used to convert national trends and developments into local and regional relevance. The information has also proved valuable in developing various scenarios with regard to the pandemic, whether or not in combination with issues such as (organised) crime. According to the respondents, the intelligence supply amongst various organizations was not optimal, especially at the start of the pandemic. The average rating assigned to CoroPol by respondents is an 8.3. The lowest number given is a 7.0, but a 10 or a 9 has also occurred a few times.

3 Key Observations: Crime Shifts During the Initial Stages of the Pandemic

To find out what crime trends could be expected in The Netherlands throughout the pandemic, in CoroPol, we relied on both theoretical predictions and actual observations abroad. Specifically, for theoretical predictions, we relied on the criminological theory on opportunity structures (Wilcox et al., 2018). To provide insight into the situation, we studied available publications on the situation during the first COVID-19 wave in The Netherlands. Sometimes this concerned a precise comparison (comparing the period before and during the first wave), and on other occasions a less precise comparison (e.g. between 2020 and 2019).

3.1 Opportunities as an Issue

Decrease in Classic Property Crime

From foreign reports, it was clearly understood that various forms of classic crime originally declined spectacularly, particularly during the first wave of COVID-19. Home isolation, more social control, decreased mobility within public spaces and the closing of shops resulted in a decrease in domestic burglary, shoplifting and theft, simply because the opportunity to engage in this kind of crime decreased significantly (Europol, 2020a, 2020c).

> OBSERVATION: The opportunity structure for committing crimes - exposure with (potential) offenders, the relationship between offender and victim and formal and informal social control - are strongly influenced by the covid measures taken (home isolation, less movement in public spaces and less group formation). It is therefore considerably more difficult for offenders to commit 'classic' offences. Concerning this argumentation, a decrease in 'classic' offences can therefore be expected. This decrease

has already been observed in some countries.[6] (CoroPol basic document, translated, 27 March 20)

At the beginning of March 2021, The Netherlands Central Bureau of Statistics (CBS) reported—in line with the above development—a sharp decline in traditional forms of crime in The Netherlands. In 2020, there was a decrease in registered pickpocketing crimes (−47%), domestic burglary (−23%), street robbery (−16%) and shoplifting (−13%), compared to 2019 (CBS, 2021). Kruisbergen et al. (2021) compared the first corona year with the previous year and observed a 34% reduction in domestic burglaries (and 48% in the first lockdown period) as well as a 62% reduction in pickpocketing.

Increase in Online Crime

Due to the lockdowns, online interaction had increased significantly. Work-related interaction, social contact, studying and shopping took place online more often than ever. The risk of common crime offences decreased whereas the online opportunities for criminals increased enormously. Indeed, international reports (Europol, 2020a, 2020c) established a strong increase in various forms of cybercrime (a category of crime that had already been on the rise in the last decade). For example, online shopping fraud rose sharply in the UK and WhatsApp fraud increased: 'relatives' ask for money when in fact they turn out to be cyber criminals. In addition, cyber-attacks with malware on medical organisations took place in Spain and England. Organisations that were extraordinary vulnerable due to the corona crisis. It involved a hospital in Madrid as well as an English company that was in the process of testing a vaccine. Moreover, cyber-attacks were staged at the World Health Organization (WHO).

OBSERVATION: "Ransomware attacks on hospitals seem to be a growing threat. For example, employees receive a message 'information

[6] For instance, Belgium (De Morgen, 24 March 2020) and Spain (The Olive Press, 21 March 2020).

> about COVID-19' in their email. It contains ransomware 'Netwalker'. It blocks computers and demands a ransom for unlocking. Such an attack has already taken place in Madrid (Inspanje, 2020). The Center for Cybersecurity and the Belgian government warn hospitals about ransomware." (CoroPol Update, translated, 31 March 20)

In The Netherlands, the number of registered online crimes (forgery, online fraud and hacking) increased by 54% between 2019 and 2020, in line with the above-mentioned development in foreign countries (CBS, 2021), while Kruisbergen et al. (2021) described that in the 'Covid year 2020' there had been a 64% increase in online crimes. During the first lockdown, this percentage even amounted to 112%. Although the researchers had some caveats—such as registration effects and the fact that online crime has already been on the rise—they concluded that '*the increase in the number of online crimes, especially during the first lockdown, is that of a real increase seems to be the case*' (Kruisbergen et al., 2021). The same impression emerged from our observations in the CoroPol studies in Arnhem and Amsterdam we briefly referred to in the second paragraph. The professionals that were interviewed within these studies indicated during the first COVID-19 wave that there was an increase in the online provision of drugs and prostitution (Bervoets et al., 2020).

Fraud Due to Scarcity of Goods

In The Netherlands, the initial stages of COVID-19 offered criminals an opportunity to monetise crime targeting scarce goods: medical items, (illegal) medicines, food and hygiene products. For example, they went out to steal such goods and sell them dearly. For example, in Italy and Japan, there had been reports to the police of disappearing stocks of new expensive face-masks and disinfectants. Criminals could also make parties pay for scarce goods that they did happen not to own at all or that did certainly not meet with the necessary qualifications. For example, there were reports of scams related to face masks and hand sanitisers.

> OBSERVATION: Europol (2020b) reports new forms of crime namely the 'Corona crimes'. This concerns, for example, fraud from Asia and

> Europe (in the order and magnitude of millions of euros) in relation to face masks and hand disinfectants. (CoroPol, translated, 31 March 20)

Looking at crime developments in The Netherlands, one large-scale scam with face-masks has come to the fore, in which Dutch perpetrators were involved. It concerns two men who had been suspected of having defrauded the German government for 880.000 euro in April 2020.[7] They sold eleven million face-masks to two German companies, but failed to deliver them (RTL Nieuws, 2020a). In addition, approximately four hundred reports of possible pandemic-related fraud were identified, three quarters of which were about face-masks and other protective medical equipment (Waterval, 2021).

3.2 How Vulnerable Persons Turn into Victims

Increasing Vulnerability of Civilians

In other countries, an increase in the abuse of vulnerable citizens was observed in various ways. In Spain, for example, burglars disguised themselves as 'covid doctors' (to carry out medical checks). The elderly also became a target for minor 'door-to-door' crime: offering to buy groceries, then stealing the money that was obtained. In addition, an increase was seen in sex scams and exposure of children to online abuse and exploitation.

Indeed, in line with what was predicted in CoroPol, frail elderly fell victim to scams (RTL Nieuws, 2020b; Spetter, 2021; Voskuil, 2020). There are indications of an increase in online child abuse due to the opportunities the pandemic offered to that kind of crime and there had been more paid webcam sex (Ministerie van Volksgezondheid, Welzijn en Sport, 2020). The National Rapporteur on Trafficking in Human Beings and Sexual Violence against Children described in the Offender Monitor

[7] At the beginning of this year, it turned out that a Dutch political activist and lobbyist generated considerable profit in the Spring of 2020 through his so-called non-profit organisation *Stichting Hulptroepen Alliantie* on a face-mask deal with the government (where he himself had indicated that he would do this selflessly).

sexual violence against children 2015–2019 (2021) that various organisations had observed an increase in reports of online sexual abuse, such as "sextortion" (NOS, 2021a). In addition, sexual violence against children had become less visible because these children could not take part in public life and school activities due to the corona measures.

Domestic Violence

Several countries also anticipated an increase in domestic violence (CoroPol Basic Document, 2020; Piquero et al., 2021). Previous research had also shown that domestic violence has a tendency to increase in times of crisis and disaster (Koppen et al., 2021). However, the ultimately emerging pattern seemed rather diverse.

For example, the Dutch Ministry of Health, Welfare and Sport (VWS) (2020) mentioned in a news item (that the expected increase in domestic violence had not been reflected in relevant statistics). In the same report, the Dutch National Network Safe at Home stated that the lack of an increase could be explained by the fact that professionals are usually the ones who report domestic violence and not the victims themselves. They were temporarily absent from the office and had less contact with vulnerable families. Self-report studies of families that previously had experienced domestic violence neither reported an increase in domestic violence (Koppen et al., 2021).

At the same time, the Child Telephone[8] received more calls about domestic violence, incest and neglect in April, May and June 2020 and the demand for help at Chat with Fier[9] also increased between 1 March and 30 April 2020, especially regarding child abuse. In addition, professionals—asked to estimate the size of the problem—reported an increase (Koppen et al., 2021). An international systematic review (of 32 studies) also demonstrated an increase in domestic violence in the first period (Kourti et al., 2021).

---

[8] The *Kindertelefoon* is a Dutch telephone helpline for children, to which children and young people up to the age of 18 who need a conversation about a subject can call for free (or chat). They are answered by trained volunteers.

[9] This chat is part of the organisation "Fier", which offers help to children, adolescents and adults who experience violence, abuse or exploitation.

In short, it is plausible that domestic violence increased, but that this did not manifest itself in the statistics.

Hate Groups

Various media reported on the increase in (activities of) hate groups. In England, for example, Chinese people were suffering from violence because of their ethnicity, with the source of the coronavirus (most probably) originating in Wuhan Province (BBC News, 2020). In Australia, extremist platforms took advantage of the situation by questioning the legitimacy of government, the identification of groups to blame, and the mobilisation of people against 'outsiders', thereby inciting violence (CoroPol Basic Document, 2020).

With regard to the expectation of the increase in hate groups, the National Coordinator on Terrorism and Security ("NCTV") published its Netherlands Terrorism Threat Assessment in April 2021. The Assessment reported that since March 2020 there had been close encounters between activists who demonstrated in public space and a radical undercurrent which agitated against the governmental COVID-19 measures (NOS, 2021b).

Adaptation of Organised Crime

During the COVID-19 pandemic, the adaptive capacity of organised crime appeared to be rather strong (Europol, 2020b). Alternative routes for drug trafficking opened up rather quickly, for instance by re-using old smuggling routes. New opportunities were quickly identified, such as hiding drugs in bulk transports of face masks. News reports from Italy contained information that the Italian mafia (*Cosa Nostra*) jumped at the momentum to offer money or food to citizens in need and act as a benefactor. It was expected that mafia bosses with a lot of liquid assets would supply these assets in exchange for the option to money launder their criminal profits in the future. In The Netherlands, it was anticipated that organised crime would adapt similarly, by taking recourse to its agility and flexibility, and by showing resistance against potential negative effects from the COVID-19 pandemic. Moreover, there was considerable anxiety about the possibility that organised crime would become even more deeply rooted in Dutch society than before (CoroPol update, April 11 2020).

Moreover, in the first CoroPol Update, it was expected that the opportunities for organised drug crime in The Netherlands would decrease due to the changed logistical situation: Schiphol Airport virtually reached at a standstill (CoroPol Basic Document, 2020).

Hence, organised crime, including drug trafficking, was not hindered by the pandemic in The Netherlands. The National Police, for example, observed that the illicit drug economy appeared to be resistant to the pandemic (Politie Eenheid Amsterdam, 2021). It expressed serious concerns about growing violence amongst adolescents and observed disturbing signs concerning the involvement of juveniles in violent activities while having access to or even possessing a (lethal) weapon. Various recent studies show that illicit drug traffickers adjusted their modus operandi (van Laar et al., 2021). Trade predominantly took place via social media such as WhatsApp, Instagram and Telegram and via online orders sent by mail (a development that already started prior to the pandemic). In May 2020, the Street Value(s) programme of the Central Netherlands Security Coalition described that drug trafficking seemed to continue as usual (Team Straatwaarde(n), 2020).

3.3 Reflection

Hence, it seemed that developments abroad were mirrored in The Netherlands to a significant extent. Foreign developments contained a strongly predictive value for domestic developments that resulted from the COVID-19 pandemic. The trends could be observed in The Netherlands as well as abroad, including a strong decrease in community crime, a (temporary) transition from offline to online (particularly in property crimes) and the emergence of "new crimes" that were specifically related to the pandemic ('corona-related crime'). All predictions based on foreign developments had become true. Studies on the actual development only show a diffuse picture with the expected increase in domestic violence. In addition, organised (drug) crime has experienced virtually no blow from the pandemic: it has managed to adapt and to seize new opportunities.

4 Social Disorder

Except for the potential effect of a pandemic on crime trends, it is likely to have an impact on public order as well. Below, we seek to focus on the actual tensions that were identified by the CoroPol project, with more fundamental links to the social context.

4.1 Actual Tensions and Disorder in The Netherlands During First Pandemic Wave

From the end of March 2020 onward, the CoroPol Updates included warnings about growing dissatisfaction, especially amongst juveniles. As the anti-pandemic measures were subject to extension, news reports from Spain revealed a growing frustration amongst younger people, as they started to show public resistance against the lockdown measures and began to engage in public order offences.

> OBSERVATION: Reports from Spain indicating growing resistance of youth against COVID-19-measures. Young people have blocked ambulance vehicles. They are frustrated because they are not allowed to leave their house. (CoroPol Update, translated March 31 2020)

In The Netherlands, during that particular period some young people were observed as failing to comply with the anti-COVID-19 measures. News media reported partying activities amongst higher education and university students. According to our CoroPol Updates, adolescents experienced great difficulty with the acceptance of anti-COVID-19 measures, particularly because their social lives were deeply affected while the virus itself seemed to have little or no harm for their health. Subsequently, cat and mouse games were created around parties, where young people were on guard to keep an eye on the potential arrival of the police (NOS, 2020; Omroep Flevoland, 2020).

Looking at these phenomena from a theoretical perspective, at the beginning of April 2020 larger-scale social unrest may have been the expression of moral panic (collective emotion) and—exceptionally—infused panic (collective violence). The safety of law enforcement officers became an additional point of concern (Algemeen Dagblad, 2020). Later that month, the so-called Covid Trend Monitor of the National Police revealed a trend that disorder, especially caused by adolescents, was on the increase. This was confirmed by law enforcement and social workers. Frictions between adolescents and governmental actors were also on the increase, especially in weak neighbourhoods. It was anticipated that perhaps the Ramadan and Islamic fasting month would contribute to social unrest amongst young Muslim people. However, this did not materialise. At the end, Ramadan did not turn out to be the biggest public order issue at all.

In the CoroPol Update of early May 2020, the attitude of citizens was expected to change gradually. A simultaneous decrease in support and an increase in resistance were observed, especially amongst young people and not only in The Netherlands (Duursma, 2021). In the course of 2020, a growing segment of the population participated in various protests against the governmental policy, while occasionally taking recourse to significant violence. In the initial phase, we observed the first signs of a broader social unrest, which was no longer limited to young people. During the first half of 2020, this broader social resistance was not yet abundantly apparent.

4.2 Background: Decrease in Support (of Measures) and 'Moral Holiday'

On the basis of international reports, in the Basic Document of CoroPol, it was predicted that:

> 'PREDICTION: Good to note: in the longer term - if one no longer sees the usefulness and/or very bored – can maintaining measures against the

> coronavirus become a challenge. What is important here is the attitude of the enforcers towards the citizens, not too draconian, militaristic or aggressive, this affects the relationship/trust between police and citizen not good. It is important to act fairly (hopefully with rules that are clear are what legitimate exceptions are) and act consistently. (Base document, March 31, p. 6, translated)

During the first wave of the pandemic, the majority of the Dutch citizens were primarily law abiding and complied with behavioural instructions. Especially during the initial stages, most citizens complied with the anti-COVID-19 rules, based on the widespread anxiety due to the obscurity of the coronavirus.

Increasing Opposition by Economically, Politically and Socially Disadvantaged

However, a resistant minority of the public grew increasingly resistant and became more difficult for the police to handle. While the pandemic further progressed and took longer than originally anticipated, the government policy and measures to control this crisis became more controversial. Amongst this minority were the economically disadvantaged, like shop owners, restaurant owners and (other) kinds of professional categories who directly suffered by missing income because of the lockdowns. Moreover, the group of persons who considered themselves as politically disadvantaged by the government policy and ensuing enforcement, like antivax people and conspiracy thinkers, was growing. This group feared that the government used the pandemic to control and suppress the public and—thus—undermine their freedom. Several individuals belonging to this group were convinced of the fact that the Coronavirus was not real and made up by (mainly) governments (Bierwiaczonek et al., 2020).

Hence, a growing part of the public questioned the government policy, for fearing 'anti-democratic' tendencies in society enhanced by top-down government measures, strict surveillance measures (e.g. the corona-app) and the limitation of the freedom of movement (Den Boer et al., 2022;

Van Brakel et al., 2022). The fear of autocratic tendencies had not been unfounded:

> OBSERVATION- To contain the COVID-19-pandemic, many countries around the world have restrictions imposed on the population. This seems effective, but may also have a downside, namely that some governments abuse the situation to promote human rights suppress and exercise excessive power. (Update, 11 April, translated)

The group of the socially disadvantaged largely consisted of people who experienced a significant narrowing of their lifestyle. Examples of this category are students because of the closed universities and colleges, elderly people in quarantine and adolescents experiencing boredom as almost all facilities were closed (like sporting clubs, schools, bars). Illegal parties in homes, buildings, sheds and in the open air were expressions for how particularly young people tried to maintain a social life during the pandemic (Team Straatwaarde(n) (2020). These different subgroups required a different influencing strategy.

However, it was often extremely difficult to distinguish the different categories of people who felt economically, politically or socially deprived because of the anti-COVID-19 measures.

> OBSERVATION – The prolonged persistence of the corona measures and the uncertainty about their further development means that the unrest among certain parts of the population is spreading. In the Netherlands, but certainly also abroad, there are now mainly concerns about young people. Street workers and local police officers in our network are wary of an increase in nuisance and vandalism. Police officers and municipal enforcers have great difficulty to maintain the corona measures among youth in public space. For this reason, riots have already started in France (see relevant cases of supervision and enforcement, point 5). There is always the danger of 'copycat. (Update 21 April, translated)

Vulnerable Youths on a Moral Holiday

The social cleavages before the pandemic had only been strengthened by the pandemic. Youths, often with low or no income, sometimes with a multi-ethnic urban background had already been a target of (over)policing before the pandemic. They experienced low trust in police (Charron et al., 2020; Den Boer et al., 2022).

From our CoroPol Updates, it can be concluded that vulnerable juveniles were one of the first categories that resisted to the government policy and lockdowns that eventually in the (late) Summer of 2020 culminated in urban violence in several Dutch cities and towns. In January 2021, when curfews were introduced in The Netherlands, this led to urban violence in several cities and neighbourhoods. However, political analysts observed that the urban violence had in fact been committed by a cocktail of groups and individuals who opposed to the lockdowns and curfews or (like many youngsters) preferred to riot with no other reason than challenging the authorities (Van Ham et al., 2021). Except for the CoroPol data and research projects in Amsterdam and Arnhem, we concluded that vulnerable youths were not so much (or not exclusively) showing opposition on the basis of political ideas. Police officers, youth workers and youngsters observed that youngsters often deployed violence because they wanted to oppose to entertain themselves and 'riot-to-riot'. Specifically, from these observations one could notice that youngsters were experiencing anomie and a moral holiday (Merton, 1968; Weenink, 2013). The urban violence by youngsters during the first wave of the pandemic showed striking similarities to 'regular', 'recreative' hooliganism where other opponents who took recourse to violent protests against the anti-COVID-19 measures seemed more politically inspired.

4.3 Trust in Police

On the basis of population surveys, an increase in trust in the Dutch police could be identified during the first corona wave, which is the period on which this chapter is focused. After that, social trust in the police dropped again to pre-pandemic levels (Krouwel et al., 2021). During 2020, trust in the police was higher than in 2019 (CBS, 2022). Altogether a decrease in support (of measures and for the policing) and an increasing (risk of) violence could be observed. The first signs came to the fore in the first phase of the pandemic:

> 'Despite the global observations [...] (which could lead to a prediction of relatively little unrest and insurrection in the Netherlands, given that there is relatively high confidence in the police here and a fairly serious health situation), violence against the police in the Netherlands has increased in the corona crisis. In the first weeks after the introduction of the corona measures, in March, the number of violent incidents against police officers was still about 10 percent lower than at the end of February. The number of incidents increased sharply from April. In the week of April 6, the number of times police encountered violence was 40 percent higher than the last week before the corona crisis. In the weeks that followed, officers also had to deal with an above-average amount of violence. According to the police, examples of this are the 'corona spitters', people who spit or coughed in the face of officers and threatened with corona infection. Meanwhile, the number of incidents seems to be decreasing again. At the beginning of May, the number of incidents was still 4 percent higher than before the crisis.' (CoroPol Update Document, May 18, 2020, translated)

In the first months of the pandemic in The Netherlands, we observed the first signs of social unrest, but it was not yet manifest. Frictions between young people and the police increased, especially in the subsequent period, certainly in the summer of 2020, resulting in riots. It is also noticeable that in the first phase, we occasionally report the presence of disinformation and conspiracy theories. This became a much more dominant theme in the later phases of the pandemic, not merely in The Netherlands.

5 Key Observations on Plural Policing and Security

5.1 Introduction: Observations and Predictions

In this paragraph, we present key observations based on CoroPol on enforcement and plural policing COVID-19 in The Netherlands. In the previous paragraph, the changing support given by the public was already addressed. Further, our collected data offer a view on the specific circumstances in which (plural) policing was implemented and on a classic dilemma in policing that touches on police legitimacy. Police work is shaped by street-level bureaucrats with their own moral compass (Landman, 2015; Lipsky, 2010; Reiner, 1991). It is precisely during exceptional circumstances that police work presents dire dilemmas, especially during crises and disasters.

5.2 Circumstances: Little Pluralism, No Protocols, Little Intel, Lack of Proximity

Taking our data into consideration, four specific elements stand out related to the circumstances in which policing activities were conducted, specifically during the initial stages of the pandemic in The Netherlands. These include the relative absence of pluralism, the virtual absence of protocols, the lack of relevant intelligence and obstacles to community policing.

First, like in many other countries, policing COVID-19 in The Netherlands was expected to be conducted along the lines of plural policing, which is the prevailing model in The Netherlands. However, a full plural deployment did not happen as several agencies in the police network in The Netherlands were not operative (at all), due to the fact that their employees were (tele)working from home or were on sick leave due to the coronavirus. Police agencies could largely count on municipal officers ('*gemeentelijke handhavers*')[10] and incidentally on youth workers. Police officers we interviewed, therefore, felt quite lonely in the first phase of the pandemic. In certain cases, the previously mentioned professionals shared a WhatsApp group with the local police to fine-tune police response to ill-compliance by youngsters. The police and the municipal officers worked together to enforce the anti-pandemic rules and regulations. Generally, the public would be issued with a warning first and subsequently get fined if they still failed to comply with the rules. For example, restaurant and pub owners would first get informed and be advised by (police and municipal) officers about the sometimes complex anti-pandemic measures.[11]

Second, law enforcement and (other) government agencies lacked suitable protocols to police a pandemic and to implement other necessary safety measures (Broekhuizen et al., 2020). This resulted in a situation in which many actors had to improvise, 'muddle through' and respond to new and unknown (operational) challenges. Before 2020, the possibility of a pandemic had rarely, if ever, been addressed in police training. Neither did government organisations have ready-made scenarios at their disposal. In sum, public administration and security actors were ill-prepared for the COVID-19 pandemic.

Third, already referred to, agencies experienced a lack of relevant intelligence on how to police COVID-19 and potential social tensions and disorder. According to the respondents of our mini-poll, the gap between the demand for intelligence and the scarcity of intelligence persisted for a considerable period.

Fourth and finally, a lack of proximity policing turned out to be one of the key issues. Many professionals were unable to establish contact with their target groups, because of COVID-19 and because they had work from home. As a result, interventions on domestic violence, psychiatric

[10] In The Netherlands, municipal officers have the task to check on licenses and permits and can be compared with the so-called administrative policing agencies like the *Police Municipale* in France.

[11] During the first stage, pubs and restaurants had to be closed and later on could be opened under specific conditions.

patients and youth at-risk encountered became considerably more difficult for district police officers and street-level bureaucrats. In the first CoroPol Update, it was advised that:

> Make contact and communicate, if that is (still) possible:
> 1. As the police and municipal officers, continue to make and maintain contact with citizens (by telephone, digitally and safe distance on the street). (CoroPol Basic Document, March 31st , p. 4, translated)

5.3 A Classic Police Dilemma in Extraordinary Times

Police work is shaped by street-level bureaucrats on the basis of their own moral compass. During exceptional circumstances police work goes along with dire dilemmas, especially during crises and disasters.

Tough Measures on (Normally) Unproblematic Social Conduct

For example, the COVID-19 pandemic has fundamental consequences for the freedom of movement of people. In the past period, intensive social control aimed at compliance with the corona measures, resulting in strongly curtailed freedom. Think of the lockdowns, the limitation of passenger traffic at national borders and quarantine measures in the initial stages. Consider as well the curfews and corona apps in later stages of the pandemic in 2020 and 2021. To combat the pandemic, measures were required to reduce passenger traffic to avert the risk of contamination. According to Kupferschmidt and Cohen (2020), several countries had resorted to a series of extreme measures, as they forced almost their entire population to stay within their houses. In late January 2020, China demanded more than 50 million people in Hubei Province to stay at home. Some experts argued that Western countries could never enforce such draconian measures—curtailing human rights and economies—but Italy, which suffered a huge shock by the strain on the health care system in the north of the country, initiated very similar measures on 9 March

2020. In France, 100,000 police officers started patrolling the streets on March 17 to ensure that citizens would stay indoors, except for essential travel. On 31 March 2020, the CoroPol Monitor phrased this as follows:

> Prepare for misunderstanding, quarrels, people who refuse to go into isolation and tensions in prisons. Reports show that enforcement authorities are thinking about the most optimal way of dealing with citizens in this new situation. For example by using humor (Spain) or by not giving a fine immediately, but first start a conversation (US). This is not only important for this tense situation, but also for the longer term - aimed at a good relationship and trust between citizens and government. Countries pay specific attention to communication with citizens: indicating what the citizen can or cannot expect in this special situation and it is so consistent possible implement and enforce the measures. Regarding communication with hard-to-reach communities do use key figures and role models in the existing network (in the Dutch City of Arnhem and in Canada). (CoroPol Basic document, March 31, p. 5, translated)

Policing Styles: Coping with Dilemmas

Social conduct that is considered as non-problematic by law enforcers prior to the pandemic suddenly fell subject to prohibition and criminalisation. National as well as international research indicates that individual police officers occasionally experienced considerable difficulties in enforcing the anti-COVID-19 measures (see other chapters of this book, specifically those on the UK and Germany). Law enforcement officials experienced that (emergency) regulations and measures were often open to various, sometimes regional or local interpretations. Furthermore, officers at times felt burdened to enforce measures, regarding fines and penalties "disproportionate" and unjust. An example is the 400 euro fine in The Netherlands imposed on members of the public that failed to comply with anti-COVID-19 measures, for instance public gathering on the streets and the absence of social distancing.

From one of our two CoroPol research projects for the National Police, on patrol work, it emerged that some officers started with warning and eventually fined (repeated) offenders, while others imposed a fine from the very first moment (to be clear about the rules) and yet other enforcers were reluctant to give any fines at all. Essentially, the multiplicity of reactions and behaviour of law enforcers can be understood by referring to the different styles of policing that are distinguished in the theoretical literature on police sociology, such as Reiner and Broderick on police culture and categories of working/coping styles (Broderick, 1973; Landman, 2015; Reiner, 1991). The dilemmas caused by the pandemic (e.g. having to criminalise otherwise non-deviant social conduct) were certainly not merely a Dutch issue:

> In the US (New York), police first try to talk to offenders. Not immediately a fine: 'education over enforcement'. (basic doc CoroPol, p. 9, translated)

5.4 Summary and Reflection: A Quest for Balance

Altogether, law enforcers experienced a hard time enforcing the anti-COVID-19 rules: throughout the country, there was a debate amongst those preferring a more strict model (immediate fine, 'control') and a 'consultation model' (explain, stepped, policing by 'consent'). Additionally, there were strong regional as well as differences between precincts and departments, which is traditionally intertwined with the public administration model in The Netherlands. The Dutch police were well aware that already overpoliced groups like the vulnerable youths could easily be provoked by strict enforcement. Also, in other European countries, it seemed a quest for balance between necessity of strict enforcement (to further prevent the spreading of the virus) and public acceptance of enforcement actions:

> OBSERVATION - In a number of countries (including Italy, France and Spain) there was talk of strict lockdowns, which led to relatively many fines and tensions. Sweden chose (certainly initially) for much less far-reaching measures. (CoroPol Update, May 18th 2020)

Some authoritarian regimes (e.g. the Philippines) and (less developed) democracies exploited the pandemic to tighten their grip on their citizens. However, during the first stages of the pandemic, repressive reflexes could also be observed in parliamentary democracies (Onderzoeksraad voor Veiligheid, 2022).

6 Conclusions and Critical Assessment

The CoroPol Monitor and Research Project was based on the identification of an information gap within The Netherlands National Police regarding the strategy of how to police the pandemic. During the initial stages of COVID-19, governmental actors experienced a strong need to bridge the gap between the demand for information and its scarcity. With CoroPol, international knowledge about the impact of the pandemic on crime, safety and enforcement was collected, analysed, interpreted and disseminated. Moreover, CoroPol provided normative guidance about potential ways to tackle policing issues. Apparently, the documents were regarded as useful to professionals, certainly in the initial stages of the pandemic, as it helped them to quickly gain awareness of developments and broader trends regarding COVID-19.

Developments observed abroad held a strongly predictive value for COVID-19-related developments in The Netherlands. In the field of criminality, the main trends included a strong decrease in common crime, a shift from offline to online criminality and the emergence of specific corona-related criminal activity.

All predictions in our monitor based on foreign developments were replicated in The Netherlands. Studies on the actual development only show a diffuse image when it concerns the then expected increase in domestic violence. Above all, the observation that organised (drug) crime was not hampered by the corona crisis was a rather striking one: the world or organised crime quickly adapted and seized new opportunities.

In the area of public order, empirical and theoretical predictions were made for the Dutch situation. Many international news reports pointed out that adolescents started to resist the lockdowns and caused public order problems. Interpreting these developments, we were inspired by social theory about anomie and moral holidays. Social disorder seemed eventually on the increase in The Netherlands, where during the first weeks the great majority of the public were law abiding and not (openly) opposing the anti-pandemic measures. More specifically, we outlined the following phenomena: more disorder by youths, social tensions between young people and law enforcement officers, more friction between citizens regarding compliance with measures. We observed that youngsters not always had a deeper, fundamental political reason to rebel and riot. Later in 2020, more people started to protest against the governmental policy (sometimes with significant violence). In the first phase, the first signs of a broader social unrest, not limited to young people, but this was not yet a clearly delineated pattern during the first half of 2020.

Additionally, what were response patterns of Dutch law enforcement and security organisations, and what was the level of variety that could be observed? In general, law enforcers faced a hard time enforcing the anti-COVID-19 rules: there was a rank-and-file debate throughout the country amongst those preferring a more strict enforcement and a 'consultation model' (explaining rules to the public, warning first, policing by 'consent'), with strong regional as well as local differences between precincts and departments. The chiefs of the regional units of the Dutch National Police were well aware some groups were already subject to over-policing, and that they could easily be provoked by strict enforcement. Hence, strategically, the "management cops" tended to prefer "policing by consent" to strict, repressive and disciplinary policing as long as possible.

Further, enforcement professionals were confronted with social conduct that was considered normal and non-problematic prior to COVID-19 but was prohibited during the pandemic. Both national and international research indicates that individual law enforcement officers sometimes experienced great (moral) difficulties in enforcing the COVID-19 measures. The Netherlands law enforcement community did not deviate from this pattern. Essentially, the multiplicity of responses of law enforcers can be understood by referring to the different styles of policing that have been identified in the theory on police sociology. The strict enforcers deduced additional legitimacy in the anti-pandemic measures, while the consent-driven professionals found it hard how to react properly in line with their moral standards.

We assumed that policing COVID-19 in The Netherlands would unravel how plural policing was conducted during the early phases of the pandemic, which we define as the performance of a range of policing activities by a multiplicity of actors, each on their own initiative and steered and controlled by their specific (or at least different) authorities (Loader, 2000). Our data show that the actual implementation was much less "plural" than expected during the initial stages of the pandemic. Plural policing was limited to the (regular) public police departments (including Dutch Royal Marechaussee for border policing), the municipal officers and youth workers in case of (treating) youth violence. The rest of the policing network was mostly confined to teleworking. However, at the same time, it was observed that policing was also conducted by private actors as well as institutions and citizens themselves (private policing, auxiliary policing and self-policing) (Den Boer et al., 2022).

To control the coronavirus and its impact, the government of The Netherlands created a temporary social order, which definitely left its mark on the texture of society, with new rules for interactions, impacting on almost every domain of our lives (Terpstra et al., 2020). The permanently changing rules and regulations, which were very detailed and announced shortly before entering into force, had to be policed some way or another, by public police and other security actors. Due to these circumstances, the police was placed in an unknown situation regarding enforcing social order (Terpstra & Salet, 2020). Social conduct that was previously considered legal and non-problematic by the law enforcement community fell subject to criminalisation for the purpose of public health, with significant consequences for human rights.

On a more fundamental level, the relationship between state and citizens was under significant strain. The state curtailed human rights in a way that most citizens had never experienced before. Inevitably, this had consequences for the position of the police. From a theoretical perspective, the police can take at least two positions. These positions are based on the work of Weber, on the one hand, and Durkheim, on the other

(Terpstra, 2011). In Weber's perspective, the police appears as an instrument of state that may legitimately use force (instrumental perspective, related to high policing). Emphasis is placed on a vertical and negative relationship between state and citizens (risk of citizens for the state) (Brodeur, 1983). Normative legitimacy is key: action that complies with the rules. From the perspective of Durkheim, the moral-symbolic role of the police in society is deemed to be a central one, with emphasis on a horizontal relationship and shared values between the state and its citizens. Social legitimacy is the principal yardstick for acceptance of police action by citizens. These theoretical perspectives are complementary but may also clash with one another.

In The Netherlands, a great deal of emphasis is traditionally put on the social integration of the police, namely a police force that stands between citizens, supported by public consent and thereby enjoying social legitimacy (Adang et al., 2010). There turned out to be different reasons, one of them being the relational style of policing in alignment with the dominant model of Community Policing (Adang et al., 2010). This relational style of policing, with emphasis on consultation and consent, was evident in the first months of the corona crisis (Terpstra et al., 2020). This style was practically implemented under the condition of mainly rule-abiding citizens and a high degree of social stability. In other words, the horizontal, relational perspective of Durkheim was dominant in the position of the police between state and citizens.

After the first months of the COVID-19 pandemic, the condition for policing changed gradually. This is evident in the behavioural research of the National Institute for Public Health and Environment (Rijksinstituut voor Volksgezondheid en Milieu, 2022). Social confidence in the anti-COVID-19 decreased gradually. In the Summer of 2020, more than 70% had (high) confidence in policing. Towards the end of 2021, this level had decreased to a low point of 15% (RIVM, 2022). Since the Summer of 2020, protests and riots became more widespread. The first signs of this change became visible in our CoroPol Monitor, but substantial change took place after the period in which we collected the data.

Against this background, the position of the police changed too. More often, they were (inevitably) positioned as state instrument. Weber's perspective became more dominant. The implementation of the curfew (January 2021) can be regarded as an important turning point: during the press conference the government stated 'there will be enforcement' and the police received the order of a stricter enforcement (Adang, 2021). This changing social condition for policing the COVID-19 pandemic increased the amount of pressure on the relationship between the police and (part of) citizens. Even though the relational model still holds today, there is some concern that the corona crisis has fundamentally altered the relationship between the police and citizens. The high level of trust in the police is a revenue of Dutch policing that has to be cherished now and in the future, regardless of pandemic situations.

References

Adang, O. (2021). *Zijn we nog anders? Over de rellen van afgelopen week*. Politieacademie. Accessed 21 May 2022, from https://www.politieacademie.nl/actueel/Paginas/Zijn-we-nog-anders.aspx

Adang, O., Quint, H., & van der Wal, R. (2010). *Zijn wij anders? Waarom Nederland geen grootschalige etnische rellen heeft*. Politieacademie.

Algemeen Dagblad. (2020). Boa naar ziekenhuis na mishandeling bij strand IJmuiden. *AD.nl*. Accessed 30 of March 2020, from https://www.ad.nl/binnenland/boa-naar-ziekenhuis-na-mishandeling-bij-strand-ijmuiden~a3605a8d/

Aston, L., Brandariz, J. A., Czerwinska, D., De Kimpe, S., de Maillard, J., Hoffman, I., O'Neil, M., Rowe, M., & Solhjell, R. (2020). *Policing the pandemic*. Horizon 2020 Framework Programme of the European Union.

BBC News. (2020). *Coronavirus: Hate crime reports rise in Exeter*. Accessed 26 March 2020, from https://www.bbc.com/news/uk-england-devon-51773774

Bervoets, E., Ferwerda, H., Broekhuizen, J., & Landman, W. (2020). *Openbare orde en veiligheid bespiegelingen COVID-19 lokaal voor gemeenten, politie en justitie*. Team CoroPol. Accessed 25 August 2021, from https://www.bureaubroekhuizen.nl/downloads/CoroPol-Openbare-orde-en-veiligheid-bespiegelingen-lokaal-niveau.pdf

Bierwiaczonek, K., Kunst, J. R., & Pich, O. (2020). Belief in COVID-19 conspiracy theories reduces social distancing over time. *Applied Psychology, 2*(4), 1270–1285. https://doi.org/10.1111/aphw.12223

Boin, A., & Overdijk, W. (2020). *Handboek voor strategisch crisismanagement*. Crisis University Press.

Brakel, R. van, Kudina, O., Fonio, C., & Boersma, K. (2022). Bridging values: Finding a balance between privacy and control. The case of Corona apps in Belgium and the Netherlands. *Journal of Contingencies and Crisis Management, 30*(1), 50–58. https://doi.org/10.1111/1468-5973.12395

Broderick, J. (1973). *Police in a time of change*. General Learning Press.

Brodeur, J. (1983). High policing and low policing: Remarks about the policing of political activities. *Social Problems, 30*(5), 507–520.

Broekhuizen, J., Bervoets, E., Ferwerda, H., & Landman, W. (2020). Lessen uit een onverwacht experiment. *Het Tijdschrift Voor De Politie, 6*, 10–16.

Centraal Bureau voor de Statistiek. (2021). *Scherpe daling traditionele vormen van criminaliteit*. Accessed 20 August 2021, from https://www.cbs.nl/nl-nl/nieuws/2021/09/scherpe-daling-traditionele-vormen-van-criminaliteit

Centraal Bureau voor de Statistiek. (2022). *Vertrouwen in mensen en in organisaties; persoonskenmerken*. Accessed 8 December 2021, from https://www.cbs.nl/nlnl/cijfers/detail/82378ned?dl=1B45F

Charron, N., Lapuente, V., & Rodriguez-Pose, A. (2020). *Uncooperative society, uncooperative politics or both? How trust, polarization and populism explain excess mortality for COVID-19 across European regions*. University of Götheborg.

Clarke, D. B., & Cornish, R. V. (1986). *The reasoning criminal: Rational choice perspectives on offending*. Springer.

Coropol Basic Document. (2020). Amersfoort: The Netherlands.

De Morgen. (2020). *Criminaliteit daalt met 30 procent dankzij corona*. Accessed 25 March 2020, from https://www.demorgen.be/nieuws/criminaliteit-daalt-met-30-procent-dankzij-corona~b15343f21/?utm_campaign=shared_earned&utm_medium=social&utm_sourc%20e=email

Den Boer, M., Bervoets, E., & Hak, L. (2022). Preparing for future pandemic policing first lessons learnt on policing and surveillance during the COVID-19 pandemic. *European Law Enforcement Research Bulletin, (SCE 5)*, 261–271. https://doi.org/10.7725/eulerb.v0iSCE%205.491

Dutch Ministry of Health, Welfare and Sport. (2020). June 24th 2020.

Duursma, M. (2021). *Europese regeringsleiders balanceren tussen harde maatregelen en morrende burgers*. NRC. Accessed 16 April 2022, from https://www.nrc.nl/nieuws/2021/02/25/europese-regeringsleiders-balanceren-tussen-harde-maatregelen-en-morrende-burgers-a4033272

Europol. (2020a). *Beyond the pandemic: How COVID-19 will shape the serious and organised crime landscape in the EU*. Accessed 27 August 2021, from https://www.europol.europa.eu/cms/sites/default/files/documents/report_beyond_thepandemic.pdf

Europol. (2020b). *How criminals profit from the COVID-19 pandemic.* Accessed 27 August 2021, from https://www.europol.europa.eu/media-press/newsroom/news/how-criminals-profit-covid-19-pandemic

Europol. (2020c). *How COVID-19-related crime infected Europe during 2020.* Accessed 27 August 2021, from https://www.europol.europa.eu/sites/default/files/documents/how_covid-19-related_crime_infected_europe_during_2020.pdf

INSpanje. (2020). *Hackers gebruiken coronacrisis bij cyberaanval op ziekenhuizen in spanje*. INSpanje.nl. Accessed 30 March 2020, from https://inspanje.nl/algemeen/13047/hackers-gebruiken-coronacrisis-bij-cyberaanval-op-ziekenhuizen-in-spanje/

James, A. (2013). *Examining intelligence-led policing: Developments in research, policy and practice*. Palgrave Macmillan.

Koppen, V., van ter Weiden, C., & Harte, J. (2021). Het vermeende effect van de coronacrisis op de prevalentie en aard van huiselijk geweld: Een overzicht van veronderstellingen en empirische feiten. *Proces: Tijdschrift voor strafrechtspleging, 100*(4), 194–211.

Krouwel, A., de Vries, O., Van Heck, L., Kutiyski, Y., & Étienne, T. (2021). *COVID-19 en institutioneel vertrouwen.* Accessed 27 August 2021, from https://www.impactcorona.nl/wp-content/uploads/2021/10/Institutioneelvertrouwen_KL01.pdf

Kruisbergen, E., Haas, M., Van Es, L., & Snijders, J. (2021). De pandemie als criminologisch experiment. *Justitiële Verkenningen, 47*(3), 9–34.

Kupferschmidt, K., & Cohen, J. (2020). Can China's COVID-19 strategy work elsewhere? *Science, 367*(6482), 1061–1062. https://doi.org/10.1126/science.367.6482.10

Landman, W. (2015). *Blauwe patronen: Betekenisgeving in politiewerk.* Boom Lemma Uitgevers.

Lipsky, M. (2010). *Street-level bureaucracy: Dilemma's of the individual in public services*. Russel Sage Foundation.

Loader, I. (2000). Plural policing and democratic governance. *Social and Legal Studies, 9*(3), 323–345. https://doi.org/10.1177/09646639000900301

Mawby, R. (2020). Coronavirus, crime and policing: Thoughts on the implications of the lockdown rollercoaster. *European Law Enforcement Research Bulletin, 20*, 13–30.

Merton, R. (1968). *Social theory and social structure* (Enlarged ed.). The Free Press.

Ministerie van Volksgezondheid, Welzijn en Sport. (2020). *Niet méér meldingen huiselijk geweld tijdens coronacrisis*. Accessed 26 August 2021, from https://www.huiselijkgeweld.nl/actueel/nieuws/2020/06/24/niet-meer-meldingen-huiselijk-geweld-tijdens-coronacrisis

Nationaal Rapporteur Mensenhandel en Seksueel Geweld tegen Kinderen. (2021). *Dadermonitor Mensenhandel 2015–2019*. Accessed 27 August 2021, from https://www.nationaalrapporteur.nl/publicaties/rapporten/2021/01/21/dadermonitor-mensenhandel-2015-2019

NOS. (2020). *Aboutaleb sluit hotel waar jongeren feest vierden*. Accessed 27 August 2021, from https://nos.nl/artikel/2328643-aboutaleb-sluit-hotel-waar-jongeren-feest-vierden.html

NOS. (2021a). *Meer meldingen van slachtoffers van sextortion tijdens lockdown*. Accessed 25 August 2021, from https://nos.nl/artikel/2371435-meer-meldingen-van-slachtoffers-van-sextortion-tijdens-lockdown

NOS. (2021b). *NCTV: harde coronaprotesten breken met vroegere protestcultuur*. Accessed 15 mei 2022, from https://nos.nl/artikel/2376718-nctv-harde-coronaprotesten-breken-met-vroegere-protestcultuur

Omroep Flevoland. (2020). *Politie beëindigt anti-coronafeest in Urkerbos*. Accessed 28 March 2021, from, van https://www.omroepflevoland.nl/nieuws/179662/politie-beeindigt-anti-coronafeest-in-urkerbos

Onderzoeksraad voor Veiligheid. (2022). *Aanpak coronacrisis (deel 1)*. Accessed 30 March 2020, from https://www.google.nl/url?sa=t&rct=j&q=&esrc=s&source=web&cd=&ved=2ahUKEwia3Lah6PP3AhWSG-wKHQcPC-cQFnoECAMQAQ&url=https%3A%2F%2Fwww.onderzoeksraad.nl%2Fnl%2Fmedia%2Fattachment%2F2022%2F2%2F16%2Faanpak_coronacrisis_deel_1.pdf&usg=AOvVaw1TTxiFpgGloVJkllOTBSEO

Piquero, A. R., Jennings, W. G., Jemison, E., Kaukinen, C., & Knaul, F. M. (2021). Domestic violence during the COVID-19 pandemic-evidence from a systematic review and meta-analysis. *Journal of Criminal Justice, 74*. https://doi.org/10.1016/j.jcrimjus.2021.101806

Politie Eenheid Amsterdam. (2021). *Trendbeeld 2021: Politiewerk in coronatijd*. Nationale Politie Eenheid Amsterdam Dienst Regionale Informatie Organisatie Team Analyse & Onderzoek. Accessed 27 August

2021, from https://www.politie.nl/binaries/content/assets/politie/nieuws/2021/maart/tb2021def.pdf

Ratcliffe, J. H. (2016). *Intelligence-led policing*. Routledge.

Reiner, R. (1991). *The politics of the police* (2nd ed.). Harvester Wheatsheaf.

Rijksinstituut voor Volksgezondheid en Milieu. (2022). *Communicatie en vertrouwen*. RIVM. Accessed 20 August, from https://www.rivm.nl/gedragsonderzoek/maatregelen-welbevinden/communicatie-en-vertrouwen

RTL Nieuws. (2020a). *Fraude met 11 miljoen mondkapjes, verdachten langer vast*. Accessed on 20 August 2021, from https://www.rtlnieuws.nl/nieuws/nederland/artikel/5099281/oplichting-mondkapjes-fraude-nederlands-duo-duitse-overheid

RTL Nieuws. (2020b). *Ouderen opgelicht met corona-babbeltruc: "Trap er niet in"*. Accessed on 25 August 2021, from https://www.rtlnieuws.nl/editienl/artikel/5035721/corona-babbeltruc-ouderen

Sergentanis, T. N., & Tsitsika, A. (2021). Domestic violence during the COVID-19 pandemic: A systematic review. *Trauma, Violence, & Abuse*, 1–27. https://doi.org/10.1177/15248380211038690

Spetter, E. (2021). *Amsterdamse ouderen opgelicht met corona-babbeltruc, elders in de regio geen signalen*. NH Nieuws. Accessed 25 August 2021, from https://www.nhnieuws.nl/nieuws/279914/amsterdamse-ouderen-opgelicht-met-corona-babbeltruc-elders-in-de-regio-geen-signalen

Stogner, J., Miller, B. L., & McLean, K. (2020). Police stress, mental health, and resiliency during the COVID-19 pandemic. *American Journal of Criminal Justice, 45*(4), 718–730. https://doi.org/10.1007/s12103-020-09548-y

Team Straatwaarden. (2020). *Corona, Coke & jonge aanwas*. Accessed on 27 August 2020, from https://veiligheidscoalitie.nl/action/?action=download&id=2523

Terpstra, J. (2011). Two theories on the police. The relevance of Max Weber and Emile Durkheim to the study of the police. *International Journal of Law, Crime and Justice, 39*, 1–11. https://doi.org/10.1016/j.ijlcj.2011.01.009

Terpstra, J., de Maillard, J., Salet, R., & Roche, S. (2020). Policing the corona crisis: A comparison between France and the Netherlands. *International Journal of Police Science & Management, 23*(2), 1–14. https://doi.org/10.1177/1461355720980772

Terpstra, J., & Salet, R. (2020). *Politie in tijden van Corona. Over haar maatschappelijke opdracht in buitengewone omstandigheden*. Moduliprint.

van Ham, T., Rovers, M., & den Boer, M. (2021). 'Wisdom of the crowds': Crowd control and intelligence gaps during the COVID-19 pandemic. *Journal of European and American Intelligence Studies, 4*(1), 11–30.

van Laar, M. W., Beenakkers, E. M. T., Cruts, A. A. N., Ketelaars, A. P. M., Kuin, M. C., Meijer, R. F., Miltenburg, C. J. A., Mujcic, A., & Strada, L. (2021). *Nationale Drugmonitor Jaarbericht 2020.* Trimbos-instituut, Wetenschappelijk Onderzoek- en Documentatiecentrum (WODC) & Ministerie van Justitie & Veiligheid. Accessed 27 August 2021, from https://www.trimbos.nl/wp-content/uploads/2021/11/AF1862-Nationale-Drug-Monitor-2020.pdf

Voskuil, K. (2020). *Schaamteloos: bejaarden opgelicht met corona-babbeltruc*. AD.nl. Accessed 25 August 2021, from https://www.ad.nl/binnenland/schaamteloos-bejaarden-opgelicht-met-corona-babbeltruc~abd549d1/

Waterval, D. (2021). Illegale mondkapjes en sjoemelen met steun: 400 meldingen van coronafraude. *Trouw*. Accessed 26 August 2021, from https://www.trouw.nl/economie/illegale-mondkapjes-en-sjoemelen-met-steun-400-meldingen-van-coronafraude~b4fc3efd/

Weenink, D. (2013). Decontrolled by solidarity: Understanding recreational violence in moral holiday. *Human Figurations*, *2*(3). http://hdl.handle.net/2027/spo.11217607.0002.305

Wilcox, P., Land, K. C., & Hunt, S. A. (2018). *Criminal circumstance: A dynamic multi-contextual criminal opportunity theory*. Taylor and Francis.

3

Policing and Security in Southern Europe: How the COVID-19 Pandemic Reaffirms Pre-existing Patterns

Christian Mouhanna, Anastassia Tsoukala, and Gemma Ubasart-González

1 Introduction

Was there a Southern European model for managing the pandemic? The analysis of three countries presented here, Spain, France, and Greece, shows that this idea does not stand up to evaluation. Admittedly, there are certain similarities in all three cases, but these are widely shared across the European continent, including the labelling of the pandemic as a

C. Mouhanna (✉)
Paris, France
e-mail: mouhanna@hotmail.com

A. Tsoukala
Athènes, Greece
e-mail: tsoukala.anastassia@gmail.com

G. Ubasart-González
Girona, Spain
e-mail: gemma.ubasart@udg.edu

M. Den Boer et al. (eds.), *Plural Policing, Security and the COVID Crisis*, Palgrave's Critical Policing Studies, https://doi.org/10.1007/978-3-031-19177-0_3

security problem, and the use of coercion and punishment as the main strategy of managing the population (Amnesty International, 2020a). For the three countries selected for the purpose of this chapter, domestic contexts turn out to be quite different, before and during the pandemic.

In Spain, the outbreak of COVID-19 impacted on a government that had just been formed. The use of the *state of alarm*, which restricted fundamental rights and halted productive activity, was unprecedented in the country's democratic history. This measure was paired with the implementation of expansive social and economic policies. A process of centralisation in decision-making took place in a highly decentralised country, creating tensions and dysfunctions (Ridao, 2021). Broad powers conferred to the policing apparatus produced episodes of arbitrary and indiscriminate use of force. Despite this, due to fear or solidarity, a majority accepted the restrictions. France responded with an already impressive legal and repressive arsenal. Intended to fight against terrorism, against a real or imagined rise in insecurity that was omnipresent in public debates for a while, but also against growing anti-government street protests, this arsenal was naturally used to respond to the new crisis. It has not, however, succeeded in completely stifling the protest movements. In Greece, the government was heavily criticised by large segments of the population for exploiting the fear of the pandemic to strengthen its grip on society through increasingly harsh policing. Selective controversial bans and crack-down on targeted demonstrations clearly demonstrate the instrumentalisation of the crisis, in particular the authoritarian strengthening of the government's powers of punishment and use of force. In the latter case, counterpowers struggled to emerge and contest state violence.

In order to study the development of public policies on policing and security during the COVID-19 crisis, a comparative research strategy has been adopted. We departed from the premise that the political context prior to the pandemic to a large extent impacted on the modalities of response to the unexpected and poorly anticipated crisis that resulted from the outbreak of COVID-19. We have included three European Mediterranean countries in a combined case study, structured around certain key issues, namely the legal architecture enabling the implementation of emergency law, restrictions on fundamental rights, communication strategies and their impact on public opinion, governance of law enforcement policies and the management of prisons and migrant detention centres.

Our analysis has uncovered significant (dis)similarities in the three domestic studies. Spain, France and Greece share, in a more or less comparable way, a police tradition characterised by hierarchy, discipline and punish in the management of public order. In Spain and France, public order is maintained by ordinary police as well as by police forces of a military nature (Guardia Civil and Gendarmerie respectively). It is also relevant to note that in all three cases there is the possibility to implement emergency law, *de jure* or de facto, in exceptional situations, while the police organisations enjoy wide margins of action and discretion.

More precisely, key similarities refer to police traditions and the state of emergency.

Police traditions. Spain and Greece experienced respectively fascist and authoritarian dictatorships until the mid-1970s, during which the police were granted wide-reaching powers (Jaime Jiménez, 2001). Despite carrying out profound reforms during ensuing democratic transitions, an internal culture of authoritarian tendencies is still present. Additionally, they have a hard power approach to public order management, with Greek police forces being notorious for their heavy-handed tactics while, when prosecuted, are usually acquitted or receive disproportionate light sentences. Notwithstanding its dissimilar historical evolution, the French police is not significantly different. Furthermore, as mentioned above, Spain and France maintain police forces that are military in their origins, the Civil Guard and the Gendarmerie, respectively, though their military status does not necessarily mean that they are more authoritarian that civilian ones (Mouhanna, 2011).

The state of emergency/alarm. In all three countries, emergency legislation is foreseen in their respective constitutional system, although it is variably used in each case. Spain had not activated this legislation since its return to democracy, with the exception of its partial and limited use in 2010. Since 1955, France has declared the state of emergency six times, but never at the scale of 2020. In the post-dictatorial era, Greece never declared a state of emergency but successive governments passed many fast-tracked bills, especially during times of crisis, as was the case of the debt crisis from 2010 on. Dissimilarities are related to the government's political orientation and the domestic form of territorial organisation in political and administrative terms.

The government's political orientation. Since the beginning of 2020, Spain has been the country with the most left-leaning executive branch in Europe. Pedro Sánchez has presided a coalition government between PSOE-Podemos: social democracy with a progressive left-wing party. France has had a centre-right government, driven by a newly created political formation (La *République En Marche*) since 2017. Emmanuel Macron has exercised his leadership with a strong personalist component and with many opponents from Left and Right. Greece has been ruled by the New Democracy's right-wing party since 2019. Kyriakos Mitsotakis' decision-making tends to be heavily influenced by the powerful ultra-right wing of his party.

Territorial organisation. Spain's domestic public administration is based on autonomous communities and political decentralisation (both the police and the prison system in Catalonia and the Euskadi are dependent on regional governments). The national-territorial matter is strongly politicised. France is a highly centralised state with formal administrative de-concentration in regions and provinces. Greece is a unitary state organised on a decentralised basis, both from the political and administrative points of view, and has thirteen administrative regions.

In considering the above-mentioned (dis)similarities, the analysis that follows seeks to show that each domestic context impacts on and explains political calculation, public policies and social practices that took place or were enacted during the management of the pandemic, and, more specifically, policing politics.

2 Spain in the Face of COVID-19: State of Alarm and Decentralised Police Response

Spain was the second EU country affected by the COVID-19 pandemic, after Italy. The first wave was enormously lethal (from March to May of 2020), accounting for approximately 45,000 deaths according to the National Statistics Institute (MedicalXPress, 2020). Its effects were particularly devastating in cities with significant international interconnections like Madrid and Barcelona, among others. After the World Health Organization (WHO) elevated the COVID-19 crisis to pandemic status on 11 March 2020, some autonomous communities (regions) enacted measures (e.g. school closures). The intervention by the Spanish government intervention did not commence until Saturday, 14 March 2020, when President Pedro Sánchez, declared the state of alarm and announced the beginning of a total lockdown, which totally laid down public life. Similar to Italy, the pandemic has reinforced the personalisation of national politics—as well as regional politics. A double trend could be identified: a reinforcement of executive power as well as an iconisation of the figure of president (Fittipaldi, 2021).

Profound debates within the executive branch delayed the declaration of the state of alarm. The main difference occurred around the closure of non-essential activities of the economy. But the whole of the executive shared the idea that the population should be confined for public health reasons. The pro-neoliberal part of the executive branch was suspicious of a total economic shutdown while the social democratic sector (all of Podemos cabinet members and several PSOE members) advocated for a targeted exclusion of economic sectors from a general shutdown. Finally, on 14 March 2020, the State Official Gazette Agency published Royal Decree 463/2020 establishing a nationwide movement ban and home confinement, with limited exceptions for essential activities (work, food and medicine purchases, doctor's appointments, and care provision). Moreover, the Decree issued school closures and restrictions on non-essential commerce and leisure activities, as well as a mandate to prioritise remote working. These measures were gradually revised throughout the three-month-long state of alarm.

2.1 State of Alarm

The state of alarm is a legal measure applicable to crisis situations, established in article 116.2 of Spain's 1978 Constitution. It is ruled by Organic Law 4/1981, which also regulates the state of emergency and the state of siege. Article 4b of this law defines "health crises, such as epidemics and serious contamination situations" as serious disturbances that enable the declaration of a state of alarm. The government activates the state of alarm through a decree that must be approved by the Cabinet and informs the Congress of Deputies (lower chamber). After a maximum of fifteen days in effect, the legislative branch has to vote to ratify the measure, allowing it to negotiate its contents and extent.[1] The Congress of Deputies authorised the state of alarm with 321 yes votes and 28 abstentions from the nationalist and secessionist Catalan and Basque parties, whose legislators were concerned about the consequences this would have in terms of excessive centralisation. The Congress of Deputies sanctioned the measure six times during plenary sessions held on March 25, April 9, May 20, and June 3, 2020. Nevertheless, the volume of legislative support gradually dwindled in each vote.

It is possible to identify two distinct moments of the state of alarm with different reach: one based on strict lockdown and centralisation of power within the state government (the competent authority) that spanned from March 14 to June 21, 2020; and another one based on more moderate measures that limited social interaction and decentralised pandemic governance that spanned from 25 October 2020 to 9 May 2021. The first period has been previously outlined. The second, designed by regional governments, consisted of a series of combined measures applied according to the evolution of the pandemic: some

[1] In Spain, the state of alarm had only been partially declared in 2010 to counter a strike by air traffic controllers. There is an ongoing debate among constitutional experts over the legal instrument that should be employed to limit movement and mandate lockdowns: ordinary law (e.g. public health law, national security law, regional legislation) or special law (e.g. state of alarm or state of emergency).

implemented in the second state of alarm (restrictions on fundamental rights through perimeter lockdowns, night-time curfews, and limited right to assembly) and others enshrined in ordinary regional law (regulation of commercial activity and leisure).

Political and public support for the measures to curb COVID-19 throughout the pandemic has been comparatively high in Spain. On the one hand, and despite partisan noise, most political forces supported (sometimes hesitantly) the measures promoted by the state government and a majority of regional executives. The fact that most parties in parliament are represented in some level of government (state or regional) facilitated this relative multi-level co-responsibility.[2] Regional executives of different political ideologies ended up adopting similar measures. In some cases, they created expert committees (basically from the field of medicine and economics) to accompany and legitimise decision-making. On the other hand, as a result of a combination of public anxiety and solidarity, a high number of respondents in different surveys studies voiced a favourable attitude to the temporary limitation of fundamental rights and activities to curtail the pandemic.[3] The emergence and spike in solidarity and mutual aid initiatives within civil society are factors that supported social cohesion and interpersonal trust (Ubasart-González, 2020).[4] The implementation of a series of social and economic policies, under the name "social shield", also worked in this direction seeking to be a neo-Keynesian response to the crisis, unlike the

---

[2] Except for the extreme right-wing of VOX and the conservative PP of Madrid Community, who flirt with a rather libertarian discourse as a form of opposition to the state government. During the first state of alarm, the only contentious challenges to anti-pandemic measures came from the wealthy Salamanca neighbourhood of Madrid and later some Castilian cities that deployed an anti-science pandemic-denier discourse based on negative freedoms inspired in Trump or Bolsonaro. In these demonstrations there were cases of obstruction of work of journalist (Wiseman, 2020). Parliamentary opposition of the anti-capitalist and pro-Catalan independence Popular Unity Candidacy was different: they responded to what they labeled as insufficient economic, labor and social policies.

[3] According to a Pew Research Center survey, in Spain, only 6% of those who position themselves on the left, 10% of those in the center, and 21% of those in the right think there should have been fewer restrictions on public activity throughout the pandemic (Connaughton, 2021).

[4] According to Harari (2020), a choice had to be made between facing the crisis from a perspective of totalitarian surveillance or a type of citizen empowerment perspective. The second requires large doses of trust that can be nurtured with fraternal practices that stem from the equal recognition of the other.

economic crisis of 2008 that was responded to with austerity policies. For example, economic subsidies to companies affected by the restrictions, the Temporary Employment Regulation (ERTO) that secures occupational guarantees, the Minimum Vital Income or the measures adopted that stop evictions.

2.2 Policing the Lockdown

The Spanish police forces are organised in a complex and multi-level fashion. During the pandemic, policing guidelines and procedures required coordination between agencies and territorial levels of government. Cooperation has not always been harmonious: at the political level, there was always friction while at the technical level it tended to work much better. On the one hand, as a result of recent history, there are two police forces with a national scope: the National Police and the Civil Guard (halfway between the police and the military, similar to the French Gendarmerie or the Italian Carabinieri). On the other hand, due to the pluri-national nature of the state, in Catalonia and the Basque Country regional police forces have most of the policing powers (*Mossos d'Esquadra* and the *Ertzaintza*). In addition, there are other regional police forces with fewer powers and functions, and a large number of local police forces. Within the context of the COVID-19 pandemic, the Armed Forces were factored in as an additional "agent of authority", as stipulated by the fifth additional provision in the State of Alarm Decree.

The first state of alarm had a centralising character in several fields of public policy where competencies were mostly transferred (health care, education, social protection, and policing—the last only in Catalonia and the Basque Country). This caused notable imbalances (Ridao, 2021). Ministries were tardy in implementing various sectorial public policies for decades. Thus, the central government had to continue trusting regional implementation and reaching agreements with regional administrations for the development of its public policy. In the sphere of policing, the State of Alarm Decree provided in its article 5.1 that "members of the State Security Forces, regional Police Agencies, and local corporations will be under the direct orders of the Ministry of Interior...". However, it also stipulated that regional governments that have security forces will serve in the Follow-up and Coordination Commissions established in the respective Security Boards. The government also decreed the authority of the Interior Ministry over private security (Article 5.5 of the State Alarm Decree).

Concerning fines and penalties for non-compliance with the adopted measures, article 20 of the Royal Decree established a penalty system. Still, due to a lack of prior legislative development, significant dysfunctions we can identify. Two existing means (despite not being originally designed for pandemic and lockdown contexts) were used to sanction lack of compliance with the anti-COVID-19 rules, namely the violation of article 36.6 of Organic Law 4/2015, for the protection of citizen security (popularly known as "gag law"), for disobedience or resisting authority; and the violation of article 68.b of Law 18/2009, on public health. During the first state of alarm over 1.1 million sanctions were imposed and 9,000 people were arrested (Defender a quien defiende, 2020). Furthermore, the lack of protocol and specification of the exceptions to home confinement (i.e. what essential services allowed a person to leave their home) and the means to prove them in some cases (e.g. informal workers, care provision, etc.) resulted in legal insecurity that alerted human rights organisations and associations (Defender a quien defiende, 2020).

Additionally, special emphasis should be laid on the occurrence of institutional violence as a result of abusing the broad powers that were granted to the police authorities by the decree. Of the 330 incidents recorded by the organisation *Defender a quien defiende* (Defending defenders), 70 accounted for police mistreatment also with a clear racist, ageist, or class bias.

2.3 Restriction on Fundamental Rights and Deprivation of Liberty Management

Restriction on fundamental rights affected the normal development of political action. On the one hand, due to the evolution of the pandemic, electoral processes were subject to adaptation, limiting in some cases the right of certain citizens. The Galician and Basque regional elections, scheduled for 5 April 2020, were postponed until July 12, 2020 (unprecedented in four decades of democratic rule). Additionally, when the elections were finally held, people who tested positive for COVID-19 and their immediate contacts were exempted from their right to vote and were not offered an alternative such as e-voting. To avoid this from happening during the Catalonian elections of February 14, 2021, the regional government promoted voting by mail and enabled a specific time frame during which extraordinary protection measures were implemented at poll centres allowing voters who tested positive for COVID-19 or contacts to exercise their democratic rights.

On the other hand, unconventional politics has been vastly conditioned. Social movements usually make an intensive use of public space. And the presence in the public space is limited during the first state of alarm. In these first few months, the appropriateness of organising rallies and demonstrations became a matter of debate within social movements (like anti-racist, ecologist or pro-housing) and progressive political actors. Some intellectuals and activists of social movements argued: it is time to create new repertoires of action and postpone the return to the streets (Della Porta, 2020). Others argued that the use of the public space could not be the sole patrimony of the right wing and that, with pertinent protection measures, they should return to the streets (Alabao, 2020). Be that as it may, it was not until the first downturn in contamination cases that authorised rallies were held that adhered to social distancing measures.

Religious worship, as a fundamental right, has been limited by state and regional governments' regulation but it has not been suppressed. Article 11 of the State of Alarm Decree allows attendance to places of worship and civil and religious ceremonies, including funerals, with the condition of adopting measures to prevent large crowds, limiting the number of attenders.

Regarding deprivation of liberty, during the first state of alarm, border closures made impossible for Spain to forcefully return migrants to their countries of origin. The government decided release all immigrants from detention centres. When the first state of alarm ends, human rights groups demanded the continuation of this policy throughout the pandemic, but state authorities rejected this. The same did not happen in prisons, where inmates are doubly affected: firstly, being closed settings, prisons pose an extreme risk of contagion, especially during the outset of the second wave; secondly, prisoners' interaction with the outside world was further restricted by the visitation limitations and a reduced capacity to move and interact within prisons (Centre de Recerca Observatori del Sistema Penal i Drets Humans, 2021). Greater isolation for the prison population has been accompanied by a deterioration of inmates' mental health and an increase in suicides within prisons (García Bueno, 2021; La Vanguardia, 2021).

In conclusion, from a plural policing approach, the governability of the exceptional measures fell on the public (state, autonomous, and local) and with a very minor role for private policy bodies. From a theoretical point of view, the direction of public security policy subject to centralisation during the first state of alarm, but the autonomous police of Catalonia and the Basque Country continued to play an important role at the decentralised level. Although the decree of the state of alarm enabled the activation of the Army, it finally did not assume police functions, it was limited to providing logistical support (and a symbolic presence in government press conferences during the first state of alarm). A limited number of surveys have measured the degree of citizen trust in the police apparatus during the period. The Spanish Sociological Research Center (CIS) asked in October 2020 about the opinion regarding institutions and essential professional groups, whether this had improved or worsened. The national police, the civil guard, and the army led the improvement data with 54.8, 54.8 and 52%, similar data than teachers (54.6%) and health workers (49%). On the contrary, citizens worsened their opinion regarding governments (central, regional, municipal) and media.

During the pandemic, fundamental rights have been limited: the most damaging restrictions have been those of movement and assembly. This occurs severely during the first alarm state but also during the second (although more moderately). Despite this, citizen dissatisfaction with the pandemic control measures was relatively low and social mobilisations were few and in minority. Several factors may explain this limited dissatisfaction: the normalisation of the exercise of political rights after the first wave; the permanent opening of schools from September 2020; the accompaniment of the restrictions with socio-economic policies; judicial counterweights; multi-level governance; and the development of social and solidarity initiatives.

3 France: A Permanent State of Emergency, With or Without COVID-19

Having initially underestimated the seriousness of the pandemic, the French government subsequently embarked on the adoption of very harsh measures restricting civil liberties (Bergeron et al., 2020). Faced with the rapid increase in the number of mortalities, the President of the Republic ordered, by a decree of 16 March 2020,[5] the setting up of a lockdown, and two days later, by another decree, to introduce sanctions in the case of non-compliance with the measures. On 23 March 2020,[6] the French parliament passed a law creating a *state of health emergency* that endowed the government with exceptional powers to make decisions in all areas, ranging from economic measures to civil liberties: the possibility of requisitioning people—i.e. forcing them to work—(carers among others), imposing teleworking in companies and decreeing lockdowns. Many fundamental rights were thus put in question: the right to move freely, the right to demonstrate, or the right to consume whatever one wants. In their majority, decisions were taken in the form of decrees by the government, with a posterior validation by the parliament, in which the opponents have little weight. The French police forces were made primarily responsible for enforcing them, through a proliferation of street controls and surveillance measures.

[5] Décret n° 2020-260 du 16 mars 2020 portant réglementation des déplacements dans le cadre de la lutte contre la propagation du virus covid-19.

[6] Loi n° 2020-290 du 23 mars 2020 d'urgence pour faire face à l'épidémie de covid-19.

3.1 A Permanent State of Emergency

While the notion of *health emergency* is new, the *state of emergency* has been used increasingly in France over time. This term refers to a law passed in 1955, during the Algerian War, a period particularly troubled by attacks on national soil. This law allowed France to avoid declaring war and thereby giving Algerian rebels the status of combatants (Thénault, 2007). Since 1955, this state of emergency has been declared six times: three times during the Algerian period; once in 1985 but only in New Caledonia; at the time of the 2005 riots in the suburbs (for the duration of two months); and following the Paris attacks on 13 November 2015. In the latter case, the state of emergency lasted two years, until 30 October 2017. The seriousness of the 2015 attacks that left 130 dead and 413 injured in the Bataclan theatre and on the Parisian terraces is obviously not questionable, but the extended use of this notion of a state of emergency has given rise to serious controversy (Mastor & Saint-Bonnet, 2016), particularly when compared with the wave of attacks in Paris in 1986—14 explosive devices in one year, 14 dead and 303 injured—or that of the Islamic extremists in 1995—nine attacks, ten dead, 190 injured, when the state of emergency was not declared. On the one hand, this has not prevented, in the latter two cases, the strengthening of anti-terrorist legislation or the resources made available to the services engaged in the fight against these forms of violence. On the other hand, it can hardly be contested that the 2015 state of emergency was used for purposes other than the struggle against terrorism. Indeed, the period following 13 November 2015 was marked by an instrumentalisation of the state of emergency. While the latter has been used to increase the number of house arrests or to facilitate searches, measures whose legitimacy some may question but which are at least partly justifiable, the use of the tools provided by the state of emergency to limit democratic expression is much more debatable (Rousseau, 2006). Thus, the government banned the demonstrations planned for the COP21 climate conference on 18 November 2015, and then limited those against the labour law in March 2016. The socialist government thought that the stupefaction and fear from terrorist attacks would block any form of protest, especially in the streets. Advantage was taken of this situation by passing unpopular laws. Surprised by the resistance of the street and the perseverance of the demonstrators, more violent police response strategies were adopted (Tartakowsky, 2020).

Hence, when the COVID-19 pandemic occurred, French citizens were already used to emergency situations. Since November 2015, they had experienced two years of a state of emergency. Three relevant laws have strengthened the government's powers over public freedoms, including outside state of emergency. A *Vigipirate* anti-attack plan is in effect almost continuously since September 1995, which now allows for the presence of military patrols in the streets. And the successive governments have adopted strategies that favour increasing repression of street protests and security measures, with, for example, the closure of shops in many streets of Paris and other major cities during the Yellow Vests demonstrations—from October 2018 to July 2019. Without denying the entirely unprecedented nature of the pandemic-related state of emergency, it constitutes more of an extension of governing by emergency than a revolution that marks a break with the past.

3.2 Police Practices Towards Hesitant Governmental Strategies

The increasingly restrictive legal framework, and the political will to impose a lockdown by force that was initially relatively uncontested, resulted in a major mobilisation of the police forces. It was out of question to seduce or convince, but to impose. In keeping with a tradition of coercion strongly anchored in the government culture, the President declared on 15 March 2020 that France "is at war with the virus" and that "any breach of the rules will be punished" (Le Monde, 2020). The use of the military to ensure compliance with the lockdown was considered, but not implemented in the end, because they were involved in external military operations and also because the previous experiences of military troops in the streets were not regarded as very successful. Indeed, they were deployed in the French cities after the terrorists attacks of January 2015, but many soldiers did not favour these domestic missions while "real fighting" was going on abroad (Oldra, 2021). In the end, the civil police organisations and gendarmes were in charge of the concrete application of the measures and controls.

Initially, improvisation by the authorities prevailed. The face masks, denounced a few weeks prior by ministers who described them as useless, became compulsory in public space. Above all, going out into the street was made dependent on the possession of a travel certificate, which citizens filled in on a sheet of paper or on their smartphone. In effect, they authorised themselves to go out, by ticking the boxes provided for: essential work; purchase of basic necessities; medical care; walking their dog; or practising one hour of daily sport. Failure to present this certificate or obvious errors in filling it in are subject to punishment with a fine of 38 and later 135 euros, 1500 in the event of a repeat offence. Seashores, parks, and forests were totally forbidden, as are the banks of the Seine in Paris. Drones were deployed to ensure that these bans are respected. The Ministry of the Interior announced 12.6 million stops and control as well as 760,000 fines during the first month of confinement, that lasted from 17 March until 15 April 2020.[7] Later, the introduction of a curfew generated similar types of surveillance.

Several of these measures culminated in abuses by the police and gendarmes, endorsed by a Ministry of the Interior determined to show its strength. Checking several boxes was considered an offence. Police officers who discovered that some people's shopping baskets did not contain "basic necessities" handed out fines, assuming the discretion to decide which foodstuffs fall into this category. The certificate filled in with a black pencil instead of a pen, in order to be able to reuse the sheet and not waste paper, was considered null and void. Walkers who did not run were considered "non-sporty" and subject to punishment. The incomprehension grew when people walked alone in the countryside, without being able to contaminate anyone, and were also punished. Accustomed to carrying out mass identity checks, the police and gendarmes increased the sanctions to demonstrate their efficiency to their hierarchy. The result was a perception of police arbitrariness, worsened by the fact that the police officers who carry out the stop and control are not masked at the

[7] Response of the Minister of the Interior during a hearing by the control mission on the measures related to the COVID-19 epidemic set up by the Senate Law Commission.

start of the pandemic. Their superiors even forbid them to wear masks on duty, so as "not to frighten the population" (Mouhanna, 2020).

Another source of misunderstanding arises from the confrontation between, on the one hand, territories very differently affected by the virus and, on the other hand, the centralised policies followed by French governments, in terms of both health and security (Lorino & Mottis, 2020). The above-mentioned rules apply uniformly throughout the country. The imposed confinement created even more irritation in the southern regions of the country, which remained randomly affected by COVID-19 but were subject to the same restrictions of freedom as the Parisian agglomeration or the east of France, which were severely hit. Moreover, there has also been a strong discrepancy between the rural environment and the urban centres. The restrictions are the same in the middle of the countryside as in the centre of Paris, while the population density is incomparable. One is obliged to have a mask, alone in the middle of the countryside. Home confinement is more tolerable in houses with a garden than in cramped flats in cities. While the richest inhabitants of urban areas leave their main home to take refuge in a second home or a relative's house at the countryside, the poorest inhabitants of districts that are more controlled by the police cannot leave and are subject to greater pressure. Because police patrols and especially special squads dedicated to fight drug trafficking and consumption have the habit to control more young adults with an ethnic minority background (Defenseur des Droits, 2017), they continue to target them, using the new rules against COVID-19 to do so, which raises the question whether this was a case of systematic ethnic profiling. Here again, as far as the practices of the police are concerned, COVID-19 marks more of an accentuation than a revolution in policing and law enforcement. Disadvantaged suburban neighbourhoods remain a target for repression, even though they already have experienced high mortality rates due to poor housing and lack of alternative resources. These disadvantaged neighbourhoods have also been disproportionately affected by the unemployment generated by the paralysis of the economy (Mariette & Pitti, 2020), even if their position seems to be better in 2022.

Excessive centralisation of freedom-restricting rules (Renaudie, 2020), the obvious improvisation in the face of a new health challenge, the arbitrariness found in police practices, restrictions on the means of political contestation—parliament, demonstration—of a government and a president already unpopular in a significant part of society, gave rise to anger to from many citizens, leading to a further deterioration of the image of the police. Indeed, with the choice of a primarily authoritarian and security-based management of the consequences of COVID-19, the police, and the gendarmerie in the countryside, find themselves in the front line. As in the aftermath of the 2015 terrorist crisis, as in the face of the Yellow Vests crisis, the room for debate has been reduced and replaced by police authoritarianism and punishment. The French National Police has abandoned community-oriented policing (COP) strategy since 2002 (Roché, 2005). Since then, all successive governments have resisted to relaunch a real policy in this direction, because they are anxious of being accused of tolerance of crime by the extreme right, and because they prefer to keep a police force at the service of the protection of the state—high policing (Brodeur, 1983)—and its interests rather than at the service of citizens. The COVID-19 crisis has thus represented a new opportunity to reinforce centralised and authoritarian style of governance.

3.3 Public Opinion Still Keen to Oppose

However, it would be simplistic to think that French public opinion has remained inert in the face of these restrictions. There was no "rally-round-the-flag" effect in France (Kritzinger et al., 2021). Controversially, many people were very critical about the government. A high degree of distrust still remained during this crisis, as it was during the previous ones.

After the attacks of 2015, the fear of terrorist murders did not succeed in anaesthetising opponents of labour reform laws or supporters of more effective environmental policies who continued to demonstrate (Mouhanna, 2021). The threats brandished by the Prefect of Police of Paris, the head of the police force, and by ministers during the Yellow Vests demonstrations did not succeed in curbing them either. The state of health emergency will also come up against the inalienable nature of the right to demonstrate.

Thus, a decree of 31 May 2020 that banned gatherings of more than ten people on the public highway was suspended by the *Council of State*, the highest administrative court, on 13 June. This decision reaffirmed a right to demonstrate that was underlined by the Constitutional Council—i.e. the French supreme court—on 4 April 2019 by refusing to approve the individual ban on demonstrations as was proposed by the government. Trade unions and the Human Rights League were quick to circulate notices to add the right to demonstrate as a reason for travel in travel permit forms. Mobilisations against climate inaction continued throughout 2020, especially from the Autumn onward. There were also a few demonstrations by Yellow Vests, as well as rallies against police violence. Demonstrations against the Global Security Law were of interest: initiated in January 2020, this law provides for strengthening of police powers, large-scale use of drones to monitor populations, and greater control of the press related to images concerning police action in public places. Numerous demonstrations against this bill took place in November and December 2020, and in January 2021 (in 70 cities in France on 28 November 2020, in the middle of the second lockdown). In December 2020, the *Council of State* ruled against the use of drones for the purpose of filming demonstrators. The Global Security Law would finally be adopted in April 2021, but with limits set by the Constitutional Council. In addition to all this, from 2021 onwards, numerous demonstrations were held against the containment measures and then against compulsory vaccination.[8]

Although it is difficult to assess the impact of these demonstrations, three observations stand out. Firstly, despite its use of the security argument and the police force, the government has not managed to curb the right to demonstrate in the public space, due to the support of administrative judges but also to the mobilisation of citizens on various subjects. Secondly, the instrumentalisation of events, be it COVID-19 or terrorism, to strengthen police powers is becoming unacceptable to a growing number of citizens. It undermines the legitimacy of political power more than it serves it. When combined with improvisations

[8] Between 17 July 2021 and 21 August 2021, each Saturday, between 100,000 and 240,000 people participated in demonstrations.

and constant changes of direction, this weakening of the legitimacy of law enforcement becomes even more pronounced. Thirdly, by making itself the instrument of these policies without reflecting on the concrete application modalities, the police is subject to a weakening of its social legitimacy, which should be seen in the context of a failure to implement neighbourhood policing and the consolidation of contact with the community.

The COVID-19 crisis has also underlined the paradox of a police force that is perceived as irritating or even hated in some segments of the population—diverse minorities, protesters against government policies, be they right-wing, left-wing, or environmentalists. On the one hand, the police who control authorisations or repress demonstrations are perceived as an obstacle to individual freedom. For people who are already targeted by the police patrols, like youngsters in poor suburbs, the new measures adopted during the pandemic were another source of confrontation with the police. For demonstrators, the pandemic could have formed a pretext for the police to reduce their movements, but legal authorities reaffirmed their right to public protest. Thanks to this, more tensions with the riot police forces could be avoided.

Nevertheless, on the other hand, the police have been regarded as indispensable by the same citizens in others circumstances. The management of the pandemic has shown the need for a police force not only focused on control, but also focused on protecting the citizens and taking more time to respond to the needs of the public. For example, during the lockdown, because of the confinement of families in their homes, problems multiplied: during the first lockdown—17 March to 11 May 2020—the hospitalisation of children under five years of age increased by 50% due to physical violence, the number of calls to 3919 (a national call number for victims of sexist and sexual violence) tripled compared to the same period in 2019. Ushered by the MeToo movement, many women wanted to file a complaint for sexual assaults or harassment. But these needs were not satisfied, partly because police forces were primarily used to control.

This social demand for a police force that listens to the problems of the population is not always honoured, particularly because control activity is a priority imposed by the hierarchy and the government (Defenseur des droits, 2017; Mouhanna, 2011; Roché, 2005). As Dominique Monjardet underlined 25 years ago (Monjardet, 1995), the French police forces—whether it be the Police Nationale or the Gendarmerie—still serve firstly the State, and secondly the citizens (Brodeur, 1983). The implementation of the community policing model in France still faces some challenges. In conclusion, in France the COVID-19 crisis reinforced a trend that was already in existence prior to the pandemic.

4 Greece: Authoritarian Modes of Policing

In February 2020, a few days after Greece's first confirmed COVID-19 case, the Greek conservative government progressively took precautionary measures, ranging from closure of schools and universities to closing down cafes, museums, restaurants, and retail shops, that culminated in a national lockdown from 23 March until 4 May 2020. Severe limitations imposed on public mobility and travelling were originally not contested by opposition parties or the people. Yet, broad consensus rapidly withered away during the second national lockdown, from 7 November 2020 until 3 May 2021, when the government, which had been elected in July 2019 on a law-and-order agenda, was gradually perceived as sliding into authoritarianism with regard to protection of civil rights and liberties as well as press freedom (Reporters Without Borders, n.d.a). Opposition parties and human rights organisations heavily criticised the authorities for instrumentalising the pandemic to legitimise both introduction of illiberal rules and reinforcement of executive power (Amnesty International, 2021a; Stamouli, 2021). They also denounced the authorities for being reluctant to effectively protect public health as it did not strengthen public health and education systems, improve public transport and slow down the production rhythms of heavy and small industry (Athens News Agency—Macedonian Press Agency (ANA-MPA), 2021; Human Rights Watch, 2021).

In retrospect, in the absence of efficient counter-pandemic measures, it is plausible to consider that crisis management relied strongly on the instrument of law enforcement. Moreover, the pandemic management rested upon a governmental communication strategy that sought to justify and normalise police controls and bans or restrictions of public outdoor assemblies. As will be shown below, these measures aroused serious controversy about their (un)constitutionality.

4.1 Governmental Communication Strategy on Policing and Security

Following the COVID-19 outbreak, the government allocated €20 million to media outlets to broadcast specific public health messages. This public information campaign became controversial when it was revealed that critical media were either excluded or given a disproportionately small share of the advertising while significant amounts had been allocated even to non-existent news websites (Safety of Journalists Platform, 2020). (In)direct control of the flow of pandemic-related information and subsequent sharp rise in misinformation have been denounced by the opposition parties that eventually imposed a Parliamentary Inquiry Committee to investigate the funding of media outlets. For its part, the International Press Institute considered that "scrutiny over how the government would meet the challenge of building up a public healthcare system devastated by years of cuts was absent from the majority of the media. Questions over the government's implementation of safety protocols for travellers from abroad were largely unasked" (International Press Institute, 2020) and "press conferences heavily favoured pro-government media" (Wiseman, 2020).[9]

This large-scale pro-government media landscape allowed the deployment of communication tactics that aimed both at redefining responsibility with regard to (in)efficient pandemic management and overshadowing relevant criticism. The government was backed by the National Committee for the Protection of Public Health against COVID-19 (National Committee), which however never disclosed the extracts of its meetings and from April 2021 on benefited from legal impunity for all opinions and votes of its members, the latter having been granted

[9] Close control of information entailed a downgrading of Greece's international ranking as regards press freedom, with the country ranking 108th out of 180 countries in 2021 (Reporters Without Borders, n.d.b).

immunity so that they did not have to testify in court. Notwithstanding this opacity, the government positioned itself from the very beginning as the responsible leader of the decision-making process and citizens were expected to accept its decisions as well-intended and scientifically motivated. For instance, bookshops and retail stores had to shut down, despite the fact that they were respecting sanitary protocols, while everyday working people were more or less forced to travel on crowded public transport. Meanwhile, the government followed a blame avoidance strategy (Zahariadis et al., 2020) that implied denial of responsibility for any undesirable outcome of its policy. The blame was almost always shoved onto citizens who were perceived as failing to comply with the rules, especially juveniles and protesters. Public discourses were depicting people as fully accountable for the (in)efficient control of the pandemic and guilty for potentially threatening other people's life due to their alleged irresponsible and even antisocial stance. The poor disciplining of the spatial distribution of the bodies, in the Foucauldian sense, was punishable as such even if, as will be shown below, it did not endanger public health. Criticism of public health measures was dealt with hegemonic anxiety discourses that exploited fear as a tool to generate consensus, if not submission (Tsoukala, 2021). Juvenile outdoor gatherings were thus repeatedly qualified as "covid-spread bombs" (Kotronakis, 2020) or "hygienic bombs [likely to entail] disastrous consequences" (Newsbreak, 2020). Hence, they were invariably dispersed by the police that used excessive force to youngsters even when they were not infringing public health rules (Apostolopoulou & Liodaki, 2021). Media amplification of the threat created by allegedly indisciplined conduct went along with unreserved acceptance of measures that were in fact scientifically ill-grounded and opposed to common sense, such as imposing curfew at the first stages of the pandemic and suspending it when the pandemic reached a peak. This media representation of the issue was resting upon broad coverage of omnipresent harsh punishment of non-compliance.

4.2 Maintaining Law and Order During the COVID-19 Crisis

Once framed in these terms, the pandemic management relied heavily on multifaceted policing. Regarding everyday policing, people's discipline was obtained through intensive COVID-19 document checks conducted by a public police motorcycle unit entitled "special guards" (SG). Largely composed by male law enforcers who completed their military service in army special forces units, SG-members are generally recruited without attending Police Academy, and they assume their police responsibilities after three-month training. Inherent militarisation and lack of police ethics led to sharp rise in brutality during checks and subsequent complaints by citizens who criticised police violence or contested their fines. As administrative fines were excessively high—€300 with minimum wage amounting to €650 and about 1.5 million people living with €534 lockdown grants—COVID-19 document checks were rapidly perceived as disproportionate, cruel, class-oriented dissuasive measure rather than fair public health-oriented policy, thus fuelling discontent and hostility to SG. In breaking down civil expectations about fair policing, over-policing of usually law-abiding people ended up producing the opposite effect of what it was intended to. While complaints of brutality and fines soared, footage in March 2021 illustrated the unlawful use of force against a peaceful young man by a police officer during an SG-patrol that performed a COVID-19 document check in a quiet, middle-class neighbourhood in Athens, subsequently sparking a public protest against police violence (Smith, 2021). The demonstration was marked by clashes with riot police in the course of which one SG was seriously injured, SG incompetently left behind their injured colleague and fired stun grenades against journalists and riot police (in.gr, 2021). Following public outrage about the initial incident and exposure of risk generated by insufficiently trained SG, the COVID-19 document checks were immediately called to a halt.

Enhanced law enforcement powers were accompanied by restrictions and even bans of assemblies (Kouroundis, 2021). On 10 July 2020, the Greek government passed Law 4703/2020 regulating public outdoor assemblies that were followed by implementing legislation in September

2020.[10] Opposition parties and human rights organisations criticised the law for introducing a mandatory notification regime, thus allowing riot police to disperse peaceful assemblies if unnotified (Amnesty International, 2021b; Hellenic League for Human Rights, 2020), and providing that the organiser of an assembly would be held accountable for any damage caused by the protesters. This provision would deter individuals or organisations to convene public meetings due to the significant financial impact in the event of material damage. Thus far, this provision failed to materialise due to its multi-interpretable nature and the difficulty to identify "the organiser".

The Greek Constitution (art. 11§2) provides for restrictions on peaceful assembly only for public safety reasons or to avoid disproportionate disturbance of social and economic life. Public outdoor assemblies may be banned (art. 48§1) only if the government has declared a state of emergency and the ban has been approved by the parliament. Yet, in early November 2020, following a Decision of the Head of Greek Police, all assemblies of four or more individuals were banned from 15 to 18 November for public health reasons. It was stated that this Decision had taken into account the undisclosed relevant opinion of the National Committee. There was no parliamentary debate because the government evoked emergency to prevent a vote. The Hellenic League for Human Rights and left-wing party MeRA25 challenged the ban before the Council of State as unconstitutional, and demanded suspension and annulment of the Decision. Regarding the suspension, the Court referred to the above-mentioned opinion of the National Committee and rejected the injunction citing the public interest and protection of public health. Yet, disclosure of the extracts of the relevant meeting revealed that the National Committee had not proposed a ban as implied in the Decision (Emfiredia ton Syntakton, 2021), thus raising serious questions about the ethics of the Committee and impartiality of the judiciary. As of today, there is no Court ruling about the demand for annulment of the Decision.

[10] Presidential Decree 73/2020.

Several citizens refused to comply with measures they regarded as unconstitutional and subsequently sought to challenge them by organising a public protest on 17 November. This date is a traditional protest day to commemorate the 1973 student revolt against the military dictatorship. On that day, a socially distanced group of seven left-wing MPs was unlawfully prevented from demonstrating on the pavement; a socially distanced assembly of 1,500 communists was tear-gassed and protesters were beaten by riot police for allegedly breaching public health rules. It is noteworthy that these police operations in fact potentially contributed to an increase of health risks as several members of riot police were patrolling without properly wearing face masks or respecting social distancing rules, while arrested citizens were held in very poor detention conditions likely to expose them to COVID-19 (Stamouli, 2021). On 25 November 2020, assemblies were not banned but nine women, who briefly unfolded a banner outside of parliament to mark the Day of the Elimination of Violence Against Women, were arrested and handed fines for allegedly breaching public health rules. As this caused (inter)national outcry (Amnesty International, 2020b), the Minister of Citizen Protection apologised over the incident but the charges against the activists were not dropped. Following another Decision of the Head of Greek Police, on 6 December 2020, which is a protest day to commemorate a teenager's murder by a police agent, assemblies of more than three people were banned and 374 people were eventually arrested and handed fines for allegedly breaching public health rules, in spite of the fact that they were respecting social distancing and wearing masks (Bali, 2020). In late January 2021, amidst a wave of students' protests against an education bill providing for the creation of a university police force, the Head of the Greek Police introduced another ban on assemblies of more than 100 people from 26 January until 1 February 2021. Once again, opposition parties and human rights organisations vehemently criticised these bans as being unconstitutional. Moreover, the bans were considered as constituting "disproportionate restrictions to the rights to freedom of expression and peaceful assembly and violated Greece's obligations under international human rights law" (Amnesty International, 2021b).

Since January 2021, many pandemic-law-abiding peaceful assemblies expressing concern over problems in public health system, police violence or other important issues have been dispersed by riot police allegedly to protect public health. Peaceful protesters, be they human rights defenders, members of political parties or trade-unionists, have been subject to arbitrary criminalisation. In addition, they were handed fines for allegedly breaching public health rules and for not providing the police with required documentation. In fact, until March 2021, public outdoor assemblies were not formally included as a legitimate reason for movement, thus allowing the police to impose fines on citizens who exercised their constitutional right to freedom of peaceful assembly.

While Greece never declared a state of emergency and continued to implement ordinary legislation, Greek authorities continued to restrict civil rights and liberties, and to disperse peaceful assemblies in a violent manner. At the same time, the Greek authorities remained extremely tolerant to religious ceremonies and gatherings. Long after the COVID-19 outbreak, both the government and the National Committee were reluctant to oblige Orthodox Church clerics to stop using a shared spoon to administer the Holy Communion to the entire congregation (Kitsantonis, 2020). A member of the National Committee even stated twice that this ritual implied no risk of contamination. Similar tolerance was displayed when the Church defied government orders by allowing huge worshippers' gatherings during the celebration of St. Dimitris in Thessaloniki, on 26 October 2020, and the celebration of Epiphany across the country, on 6 January 2021 (Bali, 2021). Hence, equity of justice was not guaranteed.

Tolerance to indictable religious ceremonies and gatherings, in sharp contrast to unconstitutional bans and unlawful dispersal of public outdoor assemblies even by resorting to excessive use of force likely to jeopardise public health, as well as criminalisation of peaceful protesters, vindicate criticism made by human rights organisations and opposition parties denouncing the government for taking advantage of the pandemic as a pretext to restrict civil rights and liberties. In this authoritarian drift, the government was backed by part of the judiciary, the overwhelming majority of mass media, beneficiaries of its generous allocations, and the National Committee that avoided transparency, obtained legal impunity and instrumentalised the banning of public assemblies.

Turning policing, law enforcement and security into key instruments of pandemic management were paralleled by the absence of efficient public health measures, which entailed a further erosion of public legitimacy of police forces that already enjoyed a reputation for their violent and undemocratic tactics in dealing with demonstrations (Amnesty International, 2011, 2012, 2014a, 2014b; Hellenic League for Human Rights, 2011a, 2011b, 2011c; 2020; Pressenza, 2020). As these police tactics traditionally targeted left-wing protesters, anti-authoritarian people and anarchists, prior to the outbreak of COVID-19 police forces were significantly discredited within these political milieus. Over-policing and especially expansion of these tactics to the whole population during the pandemic entailed a significant new loss of legitimacy that nowadays characterises broad parts of civil society regardless of the political convictions of their members. A poll conducted on 11–12 March 2021 established that 61% of those polled sere of the opinion that police officers use excessive force when managing public order issues. A poll conducted on 24 March 2021 showed that 77% of respondents considered use of police force to be excessive. These findings stand in sharp contrast to prior polling findings. On 27 January 2020, use of police force was seen as excessive by only 34% of the sample.

5 Discussion

The review of the three countries provides a varied picture of the strategies that have been adopted in response to the outbreak of COVID-19. More than a revolution or a fundamental transformation, the pandemic has further accentuated previously prevailing trends, thus confirming formerly established security governance. It is not COVID-19 that implies specific policies, but a pre-existing political and administrative system that reasserts itself on the basis of a large-scale sanitary crisis that legitimised, amplified and updated underlying patterns. The reproduction of formerly existing security governance confirms the continuity of an inner dynamic in governing strategies and practices. Amidst an unstable and ever-changing socio-economic and political frame of action, this continuity reflects in fact prior domestic balance of power between the executive power, the judiciary and civil society. At the same time, it uncovers the real substance of domestic governing models as the crisis management exhorted governments to classify their value system and subsequent political priorities in an unambiguous way.

In this context, resorting to policing and coercion is an ordinary response, a reflex of the governments in place that will also be used in the case of COVID-19. This trend in Europe initially led to scepticism about what appeared to be just a form of flu, and then, under the threat of public panic, provoked a strong reaction in all three countries. The COVID-19 case illustrates a trend: in the face of unpredictable events, governments tend to revert to traditional habits and previous plans (Graham, 1971). In the absence of upstream reflection and preparation in the face of a risk that was nonetheless largely foreseeable, particularly after the SARS crisis of 2002, governments, confronted with the risk of losing their legitimacy, preferred to "secure" the issue by resorting to the rhetoric of war—the French "defence council", the symbolic role played by the army in Spain, the state of emergency de jure or de facto—and by deploying police forces in the frontline to manage a public health issue. These prevailing political reflexes, especially in the early days of the pandemic, entailed the introduction of familiar policies.

Over time, this evolution will reveal the profound nature of security governance in the respective countries, depending on their domestic balance of power. While in Spain and to some extent in France there is a certain rebalancing, or at least a limitation of the prohibitions imposed by the government, in Greece nothing seems to counteract the strengthening of governmental authoritarianism, which highlights the instrumentalisation of COVID-19 to justify the security management of society.

After analysing some similarities among the three countries, the second part of our discussion examines the impact of the factors that have influenced divergent domestic developments.

5.1 An Emergency Adaptation

The lack of anticipation to a full-blown epidemic situation culminated in an immediate decision to manage the pandemic primarily from a security perspective. During an emergency, the executive powers decide on the measures to be taken throughout the national territory. Even in Spain, a decentralised country, decision-making processes were subject to centralisation. The declaration of a state of emergency, formally in France and Spain, and informally in Greece, grants legal justification to the operation, while allowing the use of coercive means—police, army. The pandemic-generated fear, aggravated by the relative lack of scientific knowledge due to the unknown virus and the uncertainty of the situation, was thus recuperated by the central governments, presenting themselves as the exclusive and trustworthy managers of the crisis. Central authorities, therefore, felt legitimised to reassert and even expand their authority.

Consequently, citizens accepted unprecedented restrictions on civil rights and liberties. In all three countries, a severe lockdown was instituted, limiting movement in space and time, monitored by public police forces and enforced by sanctions such as fines. Prohibition of public interactions also included gatherings or demonstrations of protest allegedly to reduce the spread of the virus. Without questioning the usefulness of these liberty-restricting measures, they were introduced at the right time for governments that were subject to criticism and contestation before the pandemic. The sanitary crisis was subject to instrumentalisation in order to justify a strong central executive, making decisions without lengthy legislative or consultative processes that are regarded as responsible for slowing down necessary reforms. Draconian measures have thus been imposed with little or no parliamentary or public consultation. The governmental objective has been focused on zero risk, which stands in stark contrast to, for example, environmental threats that could also be considered an emergency. Governments exploited the full range of arguments to avoid any negotiation and limit the possibilities of planning.

This is reflected in police performance. The woefully familiar register of emergency and the threat of death, frequently used in response to terrorist attacks, are mobilised to prohibit but also to avoid any discussion with people who disagree with, or have a different interpretation of, rules that have been adopted very quickly, without them necessarily being clear, explicit, scientifically grounded, and even rational. The recommended—by the governments—severity of the police combined with their professional discretion has involved the performance of fastidious, indiscriminate, and sometimes brutal police measures. This has led to over- and under-policing, but also to the arbitrary punishment of people who were walking alone in the words or at the beach, on the pretext that they failed to comply with the curfew. Police officers without face masks demanded citizens to lower theirs to check their identity provoked a twofold reaction. On the one side, the image of above-the-law police forces called into question the reliability of the constitutional balance of power between police and the people. On the other side, this practice has been perceived as multiplying the risks of contamination, thus leading to substantial public irritation and criticism.

Implementation of imperfect, improvised and contradictory rules, that are constantly questioned by the evolution of knowledge about the virus, along with the reinforcement of police powers, gradually led to irritation and growing contestation among the population. This discontent has arguably a twofold origin. Firstly, it stems from the very conditions of the application of the pandemic-related prohibitions. People, individually and then collectively, contest the measures. While the vast majority of citizens accept the restrictions, or even confine themselves, as shown by the images of Paris, Madrid or Athens with empty streets, the harshness and the abusive and illogical nature of certain bans arouse opposition. In any case, it should be noted that the impact in each country was diverse. Greece and Spain draw two extreme cases. Greece is marked by many mobilisations, most of them with a transversal composition; in Spain only punctual and small mobilisations are organised, and those that did take place were mainly led by the far-right. Secondly, protests will also denounce the opportunism of governments that take advantage of the lockdown to prevent democratic debate. This is illustrated in France, with the demonstrations against climate inaction or pension reform, or the laws strengthening the powers of the police; in Spain, with the political resistances against centralisation; in Greece, with the demonstrations against the authoritarian drift of power.

If a part of the population, subjected to fear, accepts the restrictions without protest, another part mobilises to oppose the instrumentalisation of the pandemic in order to strengthen the executive power and to control public assemblies. Thus, in conclusion, one could argue that the alignment with the anti-covid measures has resulted in increased polarisation within the relevant societies.

However, there are differences from one country to another, related both to the degree of repression/contestation and to the nature of counter-pandemic policies.

5.2 Limits to COVID-19 Policing Vary from Country to Country

While support for COVID-19 security management has gradually decreased in all three countries, the attempted shift in power away from the executive varies in each country. In Greece, citizen mobilisation failed to counter the reaffirmation of authoritarianism. Public dissent was stifled by reference to the pandemic. In the other two countries, counterpowers have been put in place and reduced the government's potential to rule exclusively by executive power.

Several variables will come into play. The effectiveness of the restriction of civil rights and freedoms depends first of all on the readiness of the respective governments to continue the rationale of reinforcing police control on the occasion of COVID-19. The Spanish government, composed of an alliance of the left and the extreme left, has already turned towards a less repressive stance on compliance with the anti-COVID-19 measures. France, governed by the centre-right, with strong opposition to the structural reforms proposed by the state—the Yellow Vests, for example—was engaged in a tendency to tighten up security and police controls of compliance with anti-COVID-19 measures. Similar to Greece, France was de facto confronted with the establishment of an increasingly authoritarian right-wing regime. The reaffirmation of authoritarianism is more likely to materialise in centralised regimes—France, Greece—than in decentralised countries, such as Spain.

The second important variable is the weight of judicial counter-power, mainly under the form of administrative justice. The Spanish and French governments saw their measures come rapidly under the control of the judicial authorities that annulled several provisions. In France, for example, the right to demonstrate is clearly preserved, even if the police authorities sometimes try to circumvent relevant court rulings. In Greece, on the other hand, this judicial counterweight appears to be very weak or even non-existent. The judiciary, therefore, played a determining role in controlling the exercise of police powers.

A third variable is the intervention of human and social scientists—psychologists, psychiatrists, and sociologists—who have been able to show the harmful effect of certain measures on particular groups. In Spain, the intervention on the public debate of experts in social sciences and social actors attenuated some liberty-restricting measures (e.g. in relation to the relaxation of the prohibition of minors from going out into the street). In Greece, overarching pro-government media position greatly hindered the establishment of similar debates.

We can also question the role of medical experts on the pandemic, epidemiologists and virologists, who are omnipresent in the media and often call for ever more restrictive measures to prevent the spread of the virus, without integrating ethical, political, legal and social consequences of their prescriptions into this technical reasoning. Some may have indirectly encouraged the authoritarian stance of governments, as was the case in Greece or Spain. At other times, however, the government refrains from following their advice and even opposes them, as was the case in France, where the government declared itself against extending the lockdown demanded by some medical experts, and especially the ones appointed to the scientific council set by the government itself.

The three countries analysed in this chapter cover a broad range of the liberal democratic spectrum, with Spain and Greece standing at the opposite poles as regards authoritarianism and France evolving in-between. Domestic (dis)similarities end then by illustrating the origin and form of contemporary threats posed on liberal democratic regimes as well as the institutional instruments and civil reactions likely to efficiently counter governments' propensity to illiberal modes of governance.

One key issue remains: What has been the impact of the COVID-19 crisis and its management on police forces? The diversity of situations presented here does not allow to present a simple answer to this question. The fact that the management of this crisis refers to patterns of police use—a tool used to face any kind of unexpected and exceptional circumstances—and the more or less successful instrumentalisation of the crisis to improve the government's position against its critics are likely to have provoked contradictory reactions within the police forces. On the one hand, as is the case whenever the police are used to respond to a crisis, they take pride in it. They were recognised, along with doctors and nurses, as essential pillars in the fight against COVID-19. This shows how indispensable police forces seem to be to the current functioning of our countries. On the other hand, police officers found themselves in the position of applying these regulations, which they themselves sometimes found irrelevant. This may lead to the widening of professional self-discretion, which may add to the uneven application of rules in different districts or areas.

In conclusion, it may be assumed that relations between police and population have suffered a blow throughout the COVID-19 pandemic. Even citizens who traditionally have a positive relationship with the police may have felt that they were victim of the abuse of power. This may call into question whether the governmental use of these forces and the strengthening of citizen control requires reconsideration. This intensive use of the police may also incite some to believe that force in general, and public force in particular, are normal means of imposing rules, norms, and regulations. The polarisation in the political discourse in Spain, France, and Greece arguably finds one of its sources here.

References

Alabao, N. (2020). *Cuando protestar no es un lujo*. CTXT. Accessed on 30 March 2021, from https://ctxt.es/es/20200601/Firmas/32516/manifestaciones-racismo-migrantes-derechos-fundamentales-Nuria-Alabao.htm

Amnesty International. (2011). *Greece urged not to use excessive force during protests*. Accessed on 11 December 2021, from https://www.amnesty.org/en/documents/pre01/301/2011/en/

Amnesty International. (2012). *Greece: Police violence in Greece: Not just 'isolated incidents'*. Accessed on 11 December 2021, from https://www.amnesty.org/en/documents/eur25/005/2012/en/

Amnesty International. (2014a). *Greece: A law unto themselves: A culture of abuse and impunity in the Greek police*. Accessed on 11 December 2021, from https://www.amnesty.org/en/documents/eur25/005/2014/en/

Amnesty International. (2014b). *Amnesty International Public Statement: Greece: Unlawful police violence during protests must end and perpetrators held accountable*. Accessed on 11 December 2021, from https://www.amnesty.eu/wp-content/uploads/2018/10/Greece_public_statement.pdf

Amnesty International. (2020a). *COVID-19 crackdowns. Police abuse and the global pandemic*. Accessed on 1 December 2021, from https://www.amnesty.org/en/wp-content/uploads/2021/05/ACT3034432020ENGLISH.pdf

Amnesty International. (2020b). *Greece: Charges against women's rights activists—Including Amnesty staff—Must be dropped*. Accessed on 27 September 2021, from https://www.amnesty.org/en/latest/news/2020/11/greece-charges-against-womens-rights-activists-including-amnesty-staff-must-be-dropped/

Amnesty International. (2021a). *Greece: Authorities abusing power to trample on right to protest*. Accessed on 11 December 2021a, from https://www.amnesty.org/en/latest/news/2021/07/greece-authorities-abusing-power-to-trample-on-right-to-protest/

Amnesty International. (2021b). *Greece: Freedom of Assembly at risk and unlawful use of force in the era of COVID-19*. Accessed on 11 December 2021b, from https://www.amnesty.gr/sites/default/files/greece_freedom_of_assembly_at_risk_and_unlawful_use_of_force_in_the_era_of_covid-19.pdf

Apostolopoulou, E., & Liodaki, D. (2021). The right to public space during the COVID-19 pandemic: A tale of rising inequality and authoritarianism in Athens, Greece. *City, 25*(5–6), 764–784. https://doi.org/10.1080/13604813.2021.1989157

Athens News Agency—Macedonian Press Agency (ANA-MPA). (2021). *Tsipras highlights dangers of ' tragic overcrowding' on public transport.* Accessed on 11 December 2021, from https://www.amna.gr/en/article/606919/Tsipras-highlights-dangers-of-tragic-overcrowding-on-public-transport

Bali, K. (2020). *Greek government uses pandemic to justify police violence.* Deutsche Welle. Accessed on 9 December 2021, from https://www.dw.com/en/greek-government-uses-pandemic-to-justify-police-violence/a-55884958

Bali, K. (2021). *Greek Orthodox Church undermines COVID measures.* Deutsche Welle. Accessed on 1 January 2021, from https://www.dw.com/en/orthodox-church-undermines-greeces-covid-pandemic-measures/a-56251674

Bergeron, H., Borraz, O., Castel, P., & Dedieu, F. (2020). *Covid-19: une crise organisationnelle.* Presses de Sciences Po.

Brodeur, J. P. (1983). High policing and low policing: Remarks about the policing of political activities. *Social Problems, 30*(5), 507–520. https://doi.org/10.2307/800268

Centre de Recerca Observatori del Sistema Penal i Drets Humans (OSPDH). (2021). *Final Report on the management of coronavirus in Spanish and Catalan Penitentiary Centers: Monitoring the deprivation of liberty and the police activity during the emergency of COVID-19.* Accessed on 30 March 2022, from https://www.ub.edu/portal/documents/10080835/0/informe+final+carcel+ingles/81afaac1-3cac-256b-4a10-a500e4435d78

Connaughton, A. (2021). *Those on ideological right favor fewer COVID-19 restrictions in most advanced economies.* Pew Research Center. Accessed on 10 February 2021, from https://www.pewresearch.org/fact-tank/2021/07/30/those-on-ideological-right-favor-fewer-covid-19-restrictions-in-most-advanced-economies/

Defender a QuIen deflende. (2020). *Protección de derechos durante el estado de alarma.* Accessed on 30 March 2022, from http://defenderaquiendefiende.org/wp-content/uploads/2020/08/Defender_a_quien_defiende-5-1.pdf

Defenseur des droits. (2017). *Enquête sur l'accès aux droits Volume 1: Relations police/population: le cas des contrôles d'identité.* Accessed on 30 March 2022, from https://defenseurdesdroits.fr/sites/default/files/atoms/files/enquete-relations-police-population-final2-11012017.pdf

Della Porta, D. (2020). *How social movements can save democracy: Democratic innovations from below.* Polity Press.

Emfiredia ton Syntakton. (2021). *Diki sto StE gia tis poreies.* Accessed on 12 December 2021, from https://www.efsyn.gr/ellada/dikaiosyni/288122_diki-sto-ste-gia-tis-poreies

Fittipaldi, R. (2021). The rise and struggle of presidents during the coronavirus emergency: National and sub-national evidence in Italy and Spain. *Partecipazione e Conflitto, 14*(1), 132–151. https://doi.org/10.1285/i20356609 14i1p132

García Bueno, J. (2021). *Justicia abordará la salud mental de los presos para prevenir suicidios.* El País. Accessed on 30 March 2021, from https://elpais.com/espana/catalunya/2021-07-05/justicia-abordara-la-salud-mental-de-los-presos-para-prevenir-suicidios.html

Graham, A. (1971). *Essence of decision: Explaining the Cuban missile crisis.* Little Brown.

Harari, Y. N. (2020). *El mundo después del coronavirus. La Vanguardia.* Accessed on 5th of April 2021, from https://www.lavanguardia.com/internacional/20200405/48285133216/yuval-harari-mundo-despues-coronavirus.html

Hellenic League for Human Rights. (2011a). *Katagelia gia ti stasi tis astynomias stin Igoumenitsa.* Accessed on 30 March 2022, from https://www.hlhr.gr/καταγγελία-για-τη-στάση-της-αστυνομία/

Hellenic League for Human Rights. (2011b). *Gia ta diakritika stis stoles ton astynomikon organon.* Accessed on 30 March 2022, from https://www.hlhr.gr/για-τα-διακριτικά-στις-στολές-των-αστυ/

Hellenic League for Human Rights. (2011c). *Anakoinosi tis EEDA gia ta nea peristatika astynomikis vias.* Accessed on 30 March 2022, from https://www.hlhr.gr/ανακοίνωση-της-εεδα-για-τα-νέα-περιστα/

Hellenic League for Human Rights. (2020). *O ios tis astynomikis afthairesias.* Accessed on 30 March 2022, from https://www.hlhr.gr/ο-ιός-της-αστυνομικής-αυθαιρεσίας/

Human Rights Watch. (2021). *World report: Greece events of 2020.* Accessed on 30 March 2022, from https://www.hrw.org/world-report/2021/country-chapters/greece

In.gr. (2021). *Nea Smyrni: Epeisodia stin poreia diamartyrias kata tis astynomikis vias.* Accessed on 12 December 2021, from https://www.in.gr/2021/03/09/greece/nea-smyrni-epeisodia-stin-poreia-diamartyrias-kata-tis-astynomikis-vias

International Press Institute. (2020). *The Covid-19 crisis highlights Greece's media problem.* Accessed on 25 September 2020, from https://ipi.media/the-COVID-19-crisis-highlights-greeces-media-problem/

Jaime Jiménez, Ó. (2001). *Policía, Terrorismo y Cambio político en España (1976–1996).* Universidad de Burgos.

Kitsantonis, N. (2020). Greek Orthodox Church faces criticism as virus hits its ranks. *The New York Times.* Accessed on 5 December 2021, from https://www.nytimes.com/2020/12/05/world/greece-orthodox-church-coronavirus.html

Kotronakis, S. (2020). *Sinechizontai ta aftoschedia party-ygeionomikes vomves.* ERT News. Acccessed on 12 December 2021, from https://www.ertnews.gr/featured/synechizontai-ta-aytoschedia-party-ygeionomikes-vomves-topika-metra-an-synechistoyn

Kouroundis, C. (2021). The new legal framework on assemblies and the constitution: Restrictions and bans in the shadow of the pandemic. *Journal of Administrative Law, 16*(2), 281–300.

Kritzinger, S., Foucault, M., Lachat, R., Partheymüller, J., Plescia, C., & Brouard, S. (2021). 'Rally round the flag': The COVID-19 crisis and trust in the national government. *West European Politics, 44*(5–6), 1205–1231. https://doi.org/10.1080/01402382.2021.1925017

La Vanguardia. (2021). *Suben los suicidios de presos en pandemia influidos por las medidas anticovid.* Accessed on 30 March 2021, from https://www.lavanguardia.com/vida/20210428/7414489/suben-suicidios-presos-pandemia-covid-coronavirus.html

Le Monde. (2020). *Vidéo : «Nous sommes en guerre», répète Macron dans son deuxième discours sur le coronavirus.* Accessed on 5 April 2021, from https://www.lemonde.fr/sante/video/2020/03/16/video-nous-sommes-en-guerre-repete-macron-dans-son-deuxieme-discours-sur-le-coronavirus_6033315_1651302.html

Lorino, P., & Mottis, N. (2020). Et l'organisation dans tout ça? Un oubli persistant, y compris en cas de crise.... *Revue française de gestion, 46*(288), 11–26. https://doi.org/10.3166/rfg.2020.00444

Mariette, A., & Pitti, L. (2020). *Covid-19 en Seine-Saint-Denis (1/2): quand l'épidémie aggrave les inégalités sociales de santé.* Métropolitiques. Accessed on 31 March 2022, from https://metropolitiques.eu/IMG/pdf/met_mariette-pitti_1.pdf

Mastor, W., & Saint-Bonnet, F. (2016). De l'inadaptation de l'état d'urgence face à la menace djihadiste. *Pouvoirs, 3*(158), 51–65. https://doi.org/10.3917/pouv.158.0051

MedicalXPress. (2020). *Spain virus deaths top 45,000 in March-May: Statistics institute.* Accessed on 30 March 2021, from https://medicalxpress.com/news/2020-12-spain-virus-deaths-march-may-statistics.html

Monjardet, D. (1995). *Ce que fait la police, sociologie de la force publique*. La Découverte.

Mouhanna, C. (2011). Rural policing in France: The end of genuine community policing. In R. I. Mawby & R. Yarwood (Eds.), *Rural policing and policing the rural: A constable countryside?* (pp. 45–57). Farnham, Surrey.

Mouhanna, C. (2020). *Les policiers, pris dans les paradoxes des politiques publiques*. The Conversation. Accessed on 30 March 2022, from https://theconversation.com/les-policiers-pris-dans-les-paradoxes-des-politiques-publiques-135498

Mouhanna, C. (2021). Reforms and unexpected events: The influence of terrorist attacks on policing strategies. Policing. *A Journal of Policy and Practice, 15*(1), 288–298. https://doi.org/10.1093/police/paab013

Newsbreak. (2020). *Kabanaki apo tous epistimones gia tis ygeionomikes vomves ton ypaithrion kokteil*. Accessed on 12 December 2021, from https://www.newsbreak.gr/ellada/97638/ygeionomikes-vomves-ypaithrion-kokteil-gemath-plateia/

Oldra, A. (2021). Être ou ne pas être à sa place, c'est là la question: à propos du sens de la place des militaires de l'operation Sentinelle dans l'espace public urbain. *Territoire en mouvement Revue de géographie et aménagement*, *48–49*, 1–49. https://doi.org/10.4000/tem.7343

Pressenza. (2020). *I iparxi orion apo to nomo einai anagkea pros kathe katefthynsi*. Accessed on 30 March 2022, from https://www.pressenza.com/el/2020/07/h-uparjh-oriwn-apo-to-nomo-einai-anagkaia/

Renaudie, O. (2020). La police sanitaire: un outil au service de la lutte contre le Coronavirus. *Civitas Europa, 45*(2), 43–55.

Reporters without borders. (n.d.a). *World Press Freedom Index*. RSF. Accessed on 25 September 2021, from https://rsf.org/en/ranking

Reporters without borders. (n.d.b). *Greece: dangerous cocktail for press freedom*. RSF. Accessed on 6 March 2022, from https://rsf.org/en/greece

Ridao, J. (2021). *Derecho de crisis y Estado autonómico. Del estado de alarma a la cogobernanza en la gestión de la COVID-19*. Marcial Pons.

Roché, S. (2005). *Police de proximité: Nos politiques de sécurité*. Seuil.

Rousseau, D. (2006). L'état d'urgence, un état vide de droit(s). *Revue Projet, 2*(291), 19–26. https://doi.org/10.3917/pro.291.0019

Safety of Journalists Platform. (2020). *Critical Greek media excluded or sidelined from state funding package during Covid-19*. Accessed on 25 September 2021, fromhttps://fom.coe.int/en/alerte/detail/69100052

Smith, H. (2021). Greek PM appeals for peace after police brutality ignites riots. *The Guardian*. Accessed on 30 March 2022, from https://www.theguardian.com/world/2021/mar/10/greek-pm-appeals-for-peace-after-police-brutality-ignites-riots

Stamouli, N. (2021). *Police brutality on the rise in locked-down Greece, activists warn*. POLITICO. Accessed on 30 March 2022, from https://www.politico.eu/article/police-brutality-on-the-rise-in-locked-down-greece-activists-warn/

Tartakowsky, D. (2020). *Le pouvoir est dans la rue*. Flammarion.

Thénault, S. (2007). L'état d'urgence (1955–2005). De l'Algérie coloniale à la France contemporaine: destin d'une loi. *Le mouvement social, 1*(218), 63–78. https://doi.org/10.3917/lms.218.0063

Tsoukala, A. (2021). Ou ausência de liberdade ou morte? Uma genealogia do discurso "liberdade ou sobrevivência". *Sociologia on Line, 26*, 97–109. https://doi.org/10.30553/sociologiaonline.2021.26.5

Ubasart-González, G. (2020). Ciudadanía virtual en tiempos de pandemia. Activismo, acción comunitaria e iniciativas culturales. In J. M. Reniu, & J. V. Messeguer (Eds.), ¿Política confinada? Nuevas tecnologías y toma de decisiones en un con texto de pandemia. Thomson-Reuters.

Wiseman, J. (2020). *Media freedom in Europe in the shadow of COVID-19 monitoring report*. International Press Institute. Accessed 12 October 2021, from https://ipi.media/wp-content/uploads/2020/12/IPI-FNF-Monitoring-Report-Media-Freedom-in-Europe-in-the-Shadow-of-Covid-19-Dec11.pdf

Zahariadis, N., Petridou, E., & Oztig, L. I. (2020). Claiming credit and avoiding blame: Political accountability in Greek and Turkish responses to the COVID-19 crisis. *European Policy Analysis, 6*(2), 159–169. https://doi.org/10.1002/epa2.1089

4

Police and Other Plural Policing Institutions in Central and Eastern Europe Facing COVID-19 Pandemic

Branko Lobnikar, László Christián, József Balla, Ádám Kalmár, Irena Cajner Mraović, Krunoslav Borovec, and Andrej Sotlar

1 Introduction

Central Europe is an area of Europe between Western Europe and Eastern Europe, based on a common historical, social and cultural identity (Jordan, 2005). Central and Eastern Europe have a variety of meanings. It denotes a political and geographical entity, but political definitions of Central and Eastern Europe are contradictory and ambiguous (Meško et al., 2013). Ponsaers (2013) discusses policing in Central and

B. Lobnikar (✉) · A. Sotlar
Faculty of Criminal Justice and Security, University of Maribor, Ljubljana, Slovenia
e-mail: branko.lobnikar@guest.um.si

A. Sotlar
e-mail: andrej.sotlar@um.si

L. Christián
Ludovika-University of Public Service, Budapest, Hungary
e-mail: christian.laszlo@uni-nke.hu

M. Den Boer et al. (eds.), *Plural Policing, Security and the COVID Crisis*, Palgrave's Critical Policing Studies, https://doi.org/10.1007/978-3-031-19177-0_4

Eastern Europe as an epiphenomenon of geopolitical events. An essential part of Central and Eastern Europe (CEE) consists of countries that emerged from the disintegration of the Austro-Hungarian monarchy. In this chapter, we will analyse the impact of the new COVID-19 coronavirus pandemic on the functioning of state and non-state police institutions in three countries originating from the former Austro-Hungarian monarchy: Hungary, Croatia and Slovenia. These former socialist countries, considering all the diversity of this geographical area, can be taken as an example to study the development of (plural) policing in Central and Eastern Europe.

Hungary is a landlocked country in Central Europe and covers 93,030 square kilometres with a population of 10 million. Since 1994, the police organisation has been regulated by a separate act that the Parliament accepted. In Hungary, law enforcement services are provided by two leading principal agencies: the National Police, which is under the command of the Ministry of Interior and includes the border police and the National Tax and Customs Office, which is under the command of the Ministry of National Economy (Leyrer, 2013). Slovenia, a country that covers 20,271 square kilometres and has a population of 2.1 million, gained independence in 1991. The Slovenian police service today is organised on state, regional and local levels. A landmark institutional reform of the police occurred in 1998 with the Police Act, which created

J. Balla
Baranya County Police Headquarters, Pécs, Hungary
e-mail: balla.jozsef@uni-nke.hu

I. C. Mraović
Faculty of Croatian Studies, University of Zagreb, Zagreb, Croatia
e-mail: icajner@hrstud.hr

K. Borovec
Police College, Police Academy Zagreb, Zagreb, Croatia
e-mail: Kborovec@mup.hr

Á. Kalmár
National University of Public Service, Budapest, Hungary
e-mail: kalmara@baranya.police.hu

a Police as an autonomous body within the Ministry of Interior. At the beginning of 2013, new police legislation was adopted, namely the Police tasks and powers act and the Organisation and work of the Police Act. The acts came into force in May 2013, substituting the former Act on Police, ensuring transparent and clear regulation in the area of policing. The Organization and Work of the Police Act has reinforced decentralisation and the strengthening of the independence and autonomy of police directorates (regional level), defining cooperation between the police and local community, emphasising the role and importance of community policing (Lobnikar & Modic, 2018). Croatia (which covers 56,594 square kilometres with a population of 3.8 million) gained independence simultaneously with Slovenia in 1991. Nowadays, Croatia has a national police force and is a centralised organisation headed by the Police Headquarters with 20 Police Administrations. The Croatian police force is a public service of the Ministry of the Interior (Kovčo Vukadin et al., 2013).

Policing in CEE has been subject to continuous change in several countries. One of such development trends is the pluralisation of policing in countries where police activity was previously traditionally linked to the state police. The public-private model of policing can be understood as a response to an overly narrow and traditional conception of police (and policing) and the overshadowing of new categories of policing. Fundamental notions that lie beneath the transformations of policing from traditional to this new model of policing include fragmentation, bifurcation, redistribution of police work, disintegration, interaction between police, consumerism, privatisation, (un)safety, accountability and the "new blue line" (Ponsaers, 2001). In former socialist countries of CEE, the political, economic and social systems enabled the emergence and expansion of the private security sector after the collapse of socialism in the late 1980s and at the beginning of the 1990s. The economic and financial crisis, starting in 2008, led to austerity measures in most of the countries in the region, which affected the funding of police and other state organisations. Consequently, state police organisations were forced to redefine their work priorities and leave fewer demanding tasks to private security firms (Meško et al., 2013). In the last two decades, state police organisations in the region have accepted that they have lost their monopolistic position in policing due to the development of plural policing. The pluralisation of social control institutions, which encompasses state police organisations, local community police organisations and private security organisations, has created a competition in the policing arena, with individual police (state) organisations being forced to constantly prove themselves and justify their existence (Meško et al., 2013).

The RAND Corporation identified the COVID-19 pandemic as the greatest threat of the twenty-first century. They are convinced that it is essential for the pandemic to be re-designated from an emergency public health situation to a national security crisis requiring the response of all available stakeholders. Therefore, action and control over an infectious disease need to be ensured on the national, regional and international levels, since in the event of ineffective action, a situation arises that can lead to economic, social and political instability in the world (Svicevic, 2020). Following the February 2020 outbreak of COVID-19, citizens in the European Union have faced health challenges not experienced for a long time. In the past, we have faced disease outbreaks and pandemics such as AIDS, Mexican flu, SARS and several veterinary diseases, but the extent and intensity of COVID-19 are the most extensive and have, compared to previous diseases, the most significant impact on modern societies. After the World Health Organization (WHO) declared the then widespread virus a pandemic on 11 March 2020, national governments across Europe began efforts to protect their populations from infection and maintain healthcare delivery. The most effective governmental measures were "lockdowns"—periods of several weeks during which all educational institutions, nearly all sports, entertainment and recreational facilities, and businesses other than grocery stores and petrol stations were closed. Citizens were asked to wear masks in public spaces, stay at home, work from home, minimise their social contacts and remain in local quarantine if they were out of town.

In the following, we will analyse how the COVID-19 pandemic affected police activities in Hungary, Croatia and Slovenia. In our analysis, we have determined the order of countries according to their size (in terms of territory and population)—we analyse the functioning of institutions in a large country (Hungary), a medium-sized country (Croatia) and a small country (Slovenia). We will first present the way of reacting to and reorganising the state police in individual countries, analyse the response of other institutions that can be classified as institutions of plural policing and conclude our analysis by showing residents' reactions to the activities of plural police institutions to the pandemic.

2 Policing Pandemic in Central and Eastern European Countries: The Case of Hungary, Croatia and Slovenia

In this section, we present the progress of the response of institutions to the COVID-19 pandemic in analysed countries in Central and Eastern Europe. We will describe the response of authorities to the appearance and spread of the pandemic, and as part of this, we will describe how various institutions of plural police activity, including the police, responded to the crisis.

2.1 New Legislation and Pandemic Response Organisation

Parliaments passed special legislation to respond to the pandemic in all three countries analysed. This legislation also included new powers and tasks for the police and other institutions of plural policing.

In Hungary, the government, under its power laid down in Article 53(1) of the Fundamental Law, declared a state of emergency (Government Decree 40/2020, 2020; Lánczos & Christián, 2021) in the entire territory of Hungary for the elimination of the consequences of the human epidemic endangering life and property and causing massive outbreaks of disease and for the protection of the health and lives of Hungarian citizens. The decree entered into force on 11 March 2020. According to Article 53(1) of the Fundamental Law of Hungary,[1] the

[1] On 18 April 2011, Parliament adopted Hungary's new Fundamental Law. The text of the new norm came into effect on 1 January 2012. The new Fundamental Law overruled the

Parliament enacted an extraordinary law that established specific rules for the first and second waves of the emergency declared by the government to avert the consequences of the SARS-CoV-2 coronavirus pandemic, which caused mass illnesses threatening the safety of life and property, and to protect the health and lives of Hungarian citizens. This means that the Parliament authorised the government to adopt the necessary government decrees for the protection and subsequent economic recovery during the declared epidemiological emergency and extend their validity until the end of the authorisation. This is the so-called Empowerment Act. Parliament has the mandate to revoke its authorisation prior to the expiry of an Empowerment Act. Besides the above-mentioned legal measures to combat the pandemic, the special legal order laws and government decrees and decisions were complemented by a novel regulatory solution, the so-called external domestic soft law. Until now, these non-binding measures hardly ever featured in the Hungarian regulatory toolbox, yet the unique challenges posed by the situation during the coronavirus and the ensuing lockdown meant that there was a need to guide businesses, bodies carrying out public services functions and schools on how to adjust their operation to deliver ongoing services both safely and effectively. These non-binding norms ensure flexibility in pressing situations (Lánczos & Christián, 2021). Following the declaration of a state of emergency for effective epidemiological control, a so-called Operative Corps was established in Hungary, going beyond ministries. The role of the Operative Corps was to organise the medical and epidemiological measures, to protect Hungarian citizens, coordinate the activities of other state bodies and provide up-to-date information to the population (Lánczos & Christián, 2021). The Operative Corps was led by the Interior Minister and the Minister of Human Capacities, composed of the Director-General of Public Security of the Ministry of the Interior, the chief of the National Police, the Director-General of the National Directorate General of Aliens Policing and

former Hungarian Constitution, which was adopted by Parliament in its original form on 18 August 1949; although the Constitution was amended several times between 1949 and 1989, with fundamental and radical changes included in 1989, Statute XX (1949) remained the Constitution of Hungary until January 2012 (https://2015-2019.kormany.hu/en/doc/the-hungarian-state/the-fundamental-law).

the Director-General of the Counter-Terrorism Information and Crime Analysis Centre (Government Decision 1012/2020, 2020).

On 20 February 2020, the Croatian Government activated the National Civil Protection Headquarters to coordinate all services in the event of the occurrence of the COVID-19 in Croatia. On 25 February 2020, the first coronavirus case was confirmed in Croatia. With the appearance of the infectious disease COVID-19, for the first time, the Republic of Croatia encountered a new legal situation, which was not explicitly prescribed in applicable laws at the time. Concerning COVID-19 disease, the situation manifested itself dually and cumulatively—the World Health Organization has been declared a global pandemic and, at the same time, an epidemic due to which the entire territory of the Republic of Croatia was considered an "endangered" area. Therefore, two valid laws: the Law on Protection of the Population from Infectious Diseases (2007, 2020) and the Civil Protection Act (2021), needed to be supplemented with provisions on the appropriate crisis management model in the event of a global pandemic. As a general legislative model of crisis management, appropriate to the severity of the pandemic, characterised by rapid and unpredictable changes and the constant danger of exponential growth of patients, an institutional model was proposed according to which the National Civil Protection Headquarters of the Republic of Croatia in cooperation with the Ministry of Health orders security measures and decides on their implementation (Civil Protection Headquarters of the Republic of Croatia, 2021). The proposed model was subject to Constitutional review because the measures that restrict human rights and freedoms are in the hands of the National Civil Protection Headquarters and under the direct supervision of the government but without any active role of the Croatian Parliament (Constitutional Court of the Republic of Croatia, 2020; Gardašević, 2020).

As a reaction to this threat and following the new legal regulations, the Croatian Government established the National Civil Protection Headquarters of the Republic of Croatia to coordinate all services in the event of the occurrence of the COVID-19 in Croatia. According to the Law on Civil Protection System, civil protection headquarters is an expert, operational and coordinating body established at state, regional and local levels that implement measures and activities of civil protection during big accidents and catastrophes. According to the Law on Civil Protection System (2021), large-scale accidents and catastrophes are unpredictable situations that endanger the life and health of citizens, assets of greater value, disrupt the environment, economic activity and cause significant economic damage. Deputy Prime Minister and Minister of the Interior were appointed Chief of the Headquarters, consisting of representatives of relevant sectors from public administration institutions, operational forces of the civil protection system and police, as well as representatives of other legal entities of special importance for the civil protection system of the Republic of Croatia (Civil Protection Headquarters of the Republic of Croatia, 2021). Parallel with the formation of the National Headquarters, a temporary National Corona Police Headquarters was established, responsible for coordinating and implementing police measures and activities at the state level.

The first case of infection with COVID-19 in Slovenia was confirmed on 4 March 2020. In March 2020, the following measures were decreed by the Slovenian Government (Meško & Urbas, 2021): a ban on public events in closed spaces, restrictions on sports and other events, a ban on gathering at public events in closed spaces and a ban on the arrival of aircraft from endangered areas, and control of the border with Italy, which is internal EU border, with crossing permitted only at six checkpoints. The Slovene national assembly adopted the Act Determining the Intervention Measures to Contain the COVID-19 Epidemic and Mitigate its Consequences for Citizens and the Economy on 2 April 2020, which entered into force on 11 April 2020. Before the Act mentioned above entered into force, a very vivid public debate took place since the government's initial draft proposal of the Act gave new powers to the police and even stipulated that the police could enter dwellings and other premises and can restrict the movement of persons without prior judicial authorisation. The draft proposal additionally provided that the police could obtain information on the location of an individual's means of communication if it were not otherwise possible to ensure compliance with the measures stemming from the decision or other act for the containment and control of the epidemic, without any court injunction whatsoever (Pirc Musar, 2021). A lively public debate was incited as one could not determine based on the proposed draft provisions, for instance, when the situation where the police could obtain the information on the location occurred. Furthermore, the draft did not specify how and especially in what order the police should exercise their new powers. The controversial proposal, which allowed for the tracking of citizens in quarantine through the locations of their mobile devices and entering the dwellings without a court order, was not accepted. The draft of the Act was modified after very adverse reactions from the public in this regard and following the opinion of the Information Commissioner and of the Ombudsman. Nevertheless, Article 103 of the Act in force still conferred (some) new powers to the police. The provision above stipulates that police officers may, for the time of the declared pandemic, for containment and control of the epidemic and to ensure compliance with special measures under the Communicable Diseases Act and orders or decrees adopted to contain and control the epidemic, use the powers already attributed under Police Tasks and Powers Act. Police could also have access to personal data, including special categories of personal data, which the National Institute of Public Health collects, e.g. information on the decision by which the sick person was ordered to be isolated or quarantined. Article 103 further provided that if a police officer finds that a person violates the measure ordered, he/she shall bring that person to the place specified in the decision on the isolation/quarantine and propose that a stricter measure be adopted (Pirc Musar, 2021). Police officers, together with other authorised inspection services, supervised the quarantine. About 13,000 inspections were carried out, about 2,000 violations were detected, for which fines were imposed, or misdemeanour proceedings were initiated (STA, 2021).[2] The second anti-corona law (the Act Amending the Act Determining Emergency Measures to Contain the COVID-19 Epidemic and Mitigate its Consequences for Citizens and the Economy [ZIUZEOP-A], 2020) was adopted in May 2020; by April 2022, the Slovenian Parliament had adopted as many as ten anti-corona laws. By September 2020, 66 ordinances and decrees had been adopted, in line with the pandemic

[2] STA (Slovene Press Agency). Almost 2,000 people were caught who did not comply with quarantine or self-insulation.

outlook and the recommendations of the National Institute of Public Health (NIJZ, 2020).

The above-described measures focused primarily on preventing disease transmission and ensuring health facility capacities. However, on the implementation level, it turned out that many things could not be achieved simply by raising awareness and trying to convince people. The effective implementation of measures also required the organisation of social controls (such as the police, municipal wardens, inspection services and private security). This was noted in particular when measures were enacted suspending the general right of inhabitants to free movement and pursuit of activities (e.g. the ban on travel outside one's municipality and/or region of permanent residence, gathering in groups in public areas, observing quarantine) or imposing rigorous enforcement of preventive measures (e.g. compulsory wearing of means of protection, number limits on entry to shops, banks and post offices, etc.).

2.2 Policing COVID-19 Pandemic in CEE

In Hungary, the protection of state and social order, obeying the law, preventing and eliminating infringements, and restoring the violated legal order is primarily carried out by public administration (state administration and local governmental bodies) organisations within the framework of law enforcement activities. As a state administration organisation, the police are responsible for protecting public safety, public order and ordered conditions of the state border. The local government law enforcement organisation supports the activities of the police and contributes to the maintenance of public safety locally. Private security enterprises and social crime prevention organisations (in Hungary, the unique Nationwide Civil Self-Defence Organization) also play a complementary role in providing security (Christián & Sotlar, 2018; Nalla & Christián, 2018). The measures introduced in response to the COVID-19 pandemic have transferred significant additional tasks to these organisations. The scope of their duties authorised by legislation was extended, and other organisations were also involved. The police (including the border policing branch) were primarily involved in managing the COVID-19 pandemic: they acted predominantly on the front line in public space. However, the National Tax and Customs Administration, the Nationwide Civil Self-Defence Organization and the Hungarian Defence Forces additionally played a significant role in relieving the police, which was ensured by legal mandate (Act CLXV of, 2011, 2011; Act CXXII of, 2010, 2010; Government Decree 410/2020, 2020). During the period of mass COVID-19 outbreaks, the government decree made it possible to assign "hospital commanders" in order to monitor the use of the supply of health purchased from budgetary resources for specialised in-patient care and specialised out-patient care linked to specialised in-patient care (Government Decree 72/2020, 2020). The foundations of the system of hospital commanders have also been laid—significantly—to the law enforcement administration by the government. The 109 hospital commanders assigned to this task in 108 health institutions started their activities on 30 March 2020. Of all the hospital commanders, 29 were police officers, 29 were from the disaster management agency, and 51 were from the Hungarian Armed Forces (Hornyik, 2020).

For the Hungarian police, a new task was to enforce stay-at-home orders between 28 March and 17 June in 2020 under the respective legislation (Government Decree 71/2020, 2020). The restrictive measures were similar to those in other European countries, i.e. to restrict social contact with other persons, to maintain a distance of at least 1.5 meters if possible, to stay in a catering facility except for those employed there and except for pick-up and delivery of takeaway food, a ban on leaving the residence with some exceptions (such as performance of work, personal obligations, economic, agricultural and forestry activities and shopping of technical goods, escort of minors in connection with day-care supervision, individual recreation of sports). Those who had attained the age of 65 were allowed to visit a grocery store, drugstore, market or pharmacy only in the morning between 9 and 12 a.m. These rules were sometimes enforced by the police and military police officers with the involvement of another law enforcement agency.

The pandemic of 2020 has shown that organisations that complement and support the activities of law enforcement agencies (e.g. complementary law enforcement; Christián, 2017a, 2017b) are essential in pandemic times: this demonstrated the presence of plural policing. Many municipalities introduced restrictive measures to prevent the spread of the epidemic. These measures mainly concerned the use of public spaces, but the introduction of night-time curfews was not unprecedented (e.g. in the city of Kecskemét). In addition to the state police, municipal law enforcement and civil volunteer security organisations played a key role in enforcing prevention rules, which varied from one municipality to another (Baranyai et al., 2020). Besides the police, local law enforcement forces and civil volunteer guards played a key role in enforcing the prevention rules and measures, which varied from one municipality to another. Local governmental law enforcement forces, typically operating in cities, managed the epidemiological situation in various ways, primarily in a supportive and assisting role. Among other tasks, this manifested itself in organisational tasks carried out at vaccination points, providing food and medicine to the quarantined people, to the population in need, and distribution and transporting of masks and other protective products. Private security also played its part in enforcing health and safety rules in enclosed spaces and facilities: monitoring wearing masks, compliance with social distancing regulations, checking body temperature, checking the shopping time slot of elderly people, etc. More than 60,000 civil volunteer guards performed many auxiliary logistical tasks, emphasising supplying the population and quarantining people. In addition, due to the police's wide-ranging tasks leading to a lack of officers present in the public spaces, their auxiliary presence next to police officers was valued by the public (Országos Polgárőr Szövetség, 2021). The National Public Health Centre had issued a vast number of epidemiological recommendations and measures in the form of administrative decisions. During the pandemic period, in many cases, these rules were enforced not by members of the state police forces but by employees of private civil security companies (e.g. personal and security guards), but also by trainee officers of the Faculty of Police Science of the National University of Public Service (Balla et al., 2021).

Due to the pandemic caused by the COVID-19 virus, there have been significant changes in the way of life and habits of the entire population and the crimes committed. Police and judicial authorities in Croatia face a double challenge: to respond to the new criminal threats (MUP, 2021) and adjust the operational methods to the new environment. Because of the instructions to police officers to perform only necessary and urgent tasks in direct contact with citizens, there was a necessary adjustment in the implementation of criminal investigations and the collection of data on crime and criminal offences. In this context, certain changes in criminal phenomenology have been noticed (Bagić & Šuljok, 2021; Ministry of the Interior RH, 2021). Perpetrators of property crime use new circumstances to commit criminal offences. Falsely presenting themselves as officials, they easily enter apartments. Wearing masks and gloves makes their identification difficult. However, due to citizens' changed economic flows and daily routine activities, a particular type of crime, primarily classic property crime, decreased. On the other hand, violent crimes such as murder, attempted murder and rape increased. These data should be taken with caution primarily because they are based on registered crimes reported to the police, which may have been affected by the reduced ability of citizens to make direct contact with police and report a crime. However, domestic violence cases increased due to the disrupted family dynamics and fewer social contacts (Ministry of the Interior RH Police Headquarters, 2021).

In Slovenia, analysis of the media portrayal of crime during the epidemic (Kokoravec & Meško, 2020) pointed to an increase in crime, while statistical data (Meško & Urbas, 2021) indicated that for the majority of criminal acts during this time, there had been a reduction in reporting activity. The results of the analysis in Slovenia are like those of a study which covers slightly different periods during the epidemic, as part of an international comparative study of the statistics of reported crime in large and major cities around the world, analyses crime in Ljubljana (Kokoravec & Meško, 2020). In the first eight months of 2020, the majority of crime dealt with in Ljubljana showed a numerical drop relative to the same period in the previous year. This analysis showed that in the first eight months and during the first wave of COVID-19 in the spring of 2020, compared to the same period of the previous year (2019), the police in Ljubljana dealt with fewer crimes. The analysis was based on a review of daily records of criminal acts and not on the communication of gathered criminal acts in a given period.

Regarding the classification of the minor offence and crime of domestic violence, there is at times a very fine and fuzzy boundary, so we add the findings of a review of statistical data on these offences pursuant to the Protection of Public Order Act (ZJRM-1, 2006), which points to a reduction in the number of reported domestic offences dealt with in the Ljubljana area in the two periods of 2020 (Spring during the first wave of COVID-19 and in the first eight months of 2020). A slightly different picture is painted by data from the analysis for the whole of Slovenia in the first nine months and during the COVID-19 epidemic in the spring of 2020. In the first nine months of 2020, an increase of 5% was observed (from 1,257 in 2019 to 1,324 in 2020). At the same time, during the first wave of the COVID-19 epidemic, we noted an increase of 34.1% relative to the same period in the previous year. These are the impact of COVID-19 on the quality and effectiveness of police activities, the exploitation of people's isolation for various abuses (ranging from online sexual abuse to the abuse of old people), the drugs markets, the changing and adaptation of organised crime, and COVID-19 as an opportunity for trading, online selling and online fraud, controlling disinformation about COVID-19 and the profitable activities of criminal groups, plus fake coronavirus medicines on the black market (Europol, 2020; Meško & Urbas, 2021).

The COVID-19 pandemic affected the organisation structure and operations of police agencies. On the one hand, the police had to protect themselves and limit their contact with the public. On the other hand, they had to provide the necessary police services and respond to the calls for service. The Croatian police, a centralised police agency, were no exception. Based on a June 2021 survey of 500 Croatian police officers, Borovec et al. (2022) analyse the police officer views about the operational and organisational changes, including proactive and reactive police practices. The respondents assessed whether things have changed and the extent of the changes.

The Croatian Guild of Security Guards in 2019 launched a national campaign, "*Together in prevention for a secure Croatia and the EU*". The campaign is carried out to affirm private security activities to give the general public an insight into the importance of the private security sector for the overall security of the Republic of Croatia. In the area of private security and corporate security, the pandemic had a significant impact. It should be noted that the basic law regulating the area of private security and powers of security guards, the Private Protection Act (2020), was not changed due to the circumstances arising from the pandemic. However, the outbreak of the pandemic has disrupted the activities of the economic sector to a large extent in the way that certain activities had been drastically reduced or completely suspended (such as tourism and the entertainment industry), and in other activities (primarily health and food sectors) the workload has increased significantly. Such changes required that all stakeholders in private security had to develop Sustainability and Business Continuity Plans in the first place and then reallocate resources following the new market requirements. It should be noted that there were no significant consequences in terms of staff leaving the service or the need for a large number of new employees (Vikić, 2019).

Due to the nature of the work of security guards and other employees in charge of security in the field of private and corporate security, they continued to be in first contact with employees and users of certain premises and facilities. In addition to that, they were assigned tasks of monitoring compliance with the epidemiological measures. In this sense, there was a public debate in Croatia, whether security guards should measure body temperature and control persons in terms of their health status. However, within their powers, security guards perform the tasks contracted by the employer, and the supervision of epidemiological measures has fallen under their jurisdiction.

Private security in Slovenia plays an important part in ensuring the internal security of the state (Resolution on the National Security Strategy of the Republic of Slovenia, 2019), although compared to national/public police activity, it is given less attention. This was seen immediately after the declaration of the epidemic in the Spring of 2020 when in addition to their classic security function, private security staff adopted the main role in implementing measures to prevent infection (e.g. in shops and other enterprises that were not closed). Nevertheless, the perception of the role of private security did not significantly change—the public communications of government representatives, where they involved the security aspect of the crisis, still emphasised the role of the police and partly that of municipal wardens, while practically no one mentioned private security. On the other hand, the response to the pandemic confirmed that the implementation of police activity was no longer limited just to the public police force but to all stakeholders with "police" powers. Security guards in Slovenia have often been the first to ensure and supervise the implementation of preventive measures such as social distancing, disinfecting facilities and hands and wearing protective masks, as recommended by the National Institute of Public Health (NIJZ, 2020). Security guards, therefore, took on an important and active role in ensuring preventive measures (Ministry of the Interior [MNZ], 2020), especially in ensuring safety in the most exposed activities, such as at healthcare institutions, shops, banks and at commercial undertakings that continued to operate. At the same time, a reorganisation was needed in the corporate security function in companies, especially where this involved the management of critical infrastructure since that must operate in all conditions. In practice, this meant that managers in charge of corporate security and security managers at private security firms had to coordinate to ensure the unimpeded functioning of commercial undertakings and the implementation of security functions within them (Sotlar & Dvojmoč, 2021).

The measures to contain the pandemic included municipal wardens, where we should note the operation of the biggest warden institution in Slovenia—the city wardens of Ljubljana, Slovenia's capital city. The method of managing and organising the warden service in Ljubljana is similar to the organisation and work of the state police and differs from warden services in other Slovenian municipalities in this respect. The warden service focused principally on controls related to a public gathering, preventive operations around pharmacies, schools, kindergartens, shops, petrol stations, playgrounds and playing fields, parks and other public areas intended for gathering and recreation,[3] ensuring public order and peace, and concern for public facilities and infrastructure, with the aim of reducing the risks of criminal acts (Sotlar et al.,

[3] Ljubljana city authorities closed all playgrounds at schools and kindergartens. Where this was possible, wardens sealed off playground equipment, benches and similar facilities with tape. Individuals persisted in using the playgrounds, so municipal wardens issued 1,946 warnings, which citizens heeded, thereby avoiding an escalation of measures (Fortuna, 2020).

2021). The organisation of mixed patrols involving municipal wardens and members of the Civil Protection, independent patrols of members of the Civil Protection, Fire Brigade, volunteer firefighting societies and the Mountain Rescue service was arranged. One important task was cooperation in the repatriation of citizens of countries of the former Yugoslavia (thirteen convoys—municipal warden patrols together with the police closed access roads to traffic; activities took place in cooperation with the Safety and Protection Centre and the Ljubljana Police Administration) and maintaining public order and keeping the peace in the accommodation centre. Municipal wardens in Ljubljana also controlled the operation of restaurants and bars and intervened due to threats to healthcare personnel in containers for taking. They also ensured unimpeded parking for vehicles at the Ljubljana Health Centre and access to critical areas (Fortuna, 2020).

Due to the COVID-19 pandemic, work was adapted at all offices of the Financial Administration of the Republic of Slovenia, and for a wide range of employees whose work allowed it, working from home was organised. The Financial Administration (2021) also participated in joint international actions to prevent the unlawful collection, transport and handling of sanitary waste originating from activities in the fight against the COVID-19 epidemic, coordinated by EUROPOL and the World Customs Organization. During the first wave of the COVID-19 epidemic, staff of the mobile units of financial offices performed critical tasks for the Financial Administration in the scope necessary for collaboration with other policing bodies (the Police and Civil Protection). As part of these activities, staff of individual mobile units worked together with the Police in escorting convoys of foreign-registered goods vehicles in transit through Slovenia using official vehicles with priority on the roads (Financial Administration, 2021). Mobile unit staff also offered assistance to the regional civil protection headquarters in the transport/distribution of protective equipment using official vehicles and vans, mainly within the territories of individual regional civil protection headquarters. From June to the end of October 2020, based on an agreement with the Health Inspectorate of Slovenia, mobile unit staff of financial offices identified irregularities in preventing COVID-19 infections in bars and restaurants. In performing regular controls,[4] they devoted additional attention to identifying irregularities related to the observance of government measures to restrict the offer and sale of goods and services to consumers in Slovenia and adherence to the prescribed recommendations of the National Institute of Public Health to prevent COVID-19 infections relating to bars and restaurants (Financial Administration, 2021).

In all three analysed countries, we found that the reorganisation of the state administration began with the change in legislation; there is a trend of centralisation and narrowing of operations in operational centres, where both the flow of information and the method of decision-making are concentrated. The experience should be an essential impetus to consider reorganising the crisis response, especially if the world is now in a period of instability and crises such as the new coronavirus pandemic will become more frequent. In all three countries analysed, we found that the police, besides health institutions, played an important role in responding to the pandemic. Less prominent, but no less important, was the role of the remaining institutions of the plural police family. The need for a rapid response dictated the need for coordinated cooperation, and the interdependence of these institutions was demonstrated. We will discuss this more at the end of this chapter.

One of the critical topics that will need to be analysed in the future in preparation for the next pandemic-like crisis is the relationship between the executive and the legislature. Due to the need for immediate action, it is understandable that governments have taken the initiative, but over time, governments (e.g. in Slovenia) have often been tempted to bypass the parliament. In Slovenia, the correctional factor was played by the Constitutional Court, which was approached by residents who believed that the government was excessively interfering with their rights and freedoms and that the rule of law was threatened. Thus, the Constitutional Court in Slovenia often referred the government to the legislative procedure in the Parliament and limited its management of pandemics by government decrees.

---

[4] Mainly illegal work and employment, and over the issuing and tax confirmation of invoices.

3 Assessment of the Functioning of (Plural) Police Institutions During a Pandemic in CEE Countries

In the following, we will present the findings of some studies of how residents in Hungary, Croatia and Slovenia assessed the quality and legitimacy of police and other institutions of plural policing measures in response to a pandemic.

Contrary to the United States and some Western European countries, Hungary did not experience street riots in the summer of 2020 protesting the measures of the police and law enforcement agencies.[5] A survey conducted in June 2020 examined attitudes towards certain Hungarian institutions and the level of trust in the police during the COVID-19 pandemic (Századvég, 2021). Of the institutions surveyed (e.g. police, courts, prosecution, parliament), the police were the most trusted, with 73% of respondents saying so. In consonance with this, 79% of the respondents were satisfied with the work of the Hungarian police, and not more than 17% of them expressed a different opinion. 80% of respondents said that the statement published in the Hungarian press that "*Police in Hungary would use unjustified violence in their measures*" was not true. Even more (82%) rejected the claim that Hungary would be a "*Police state with excessive law enforcement powers*". A significant proportion, 66% of the Hungarian population, would like to see more police officers on the streets and voted to increase the number of police officers and their presence in public places. The pollsters have concluded that Hungarian society obeys the law and follows the accepted rules in the present predicament. Furthermore, 88% of respondents disagreed with the idea of cutting public funding for the police, as has happened in some US cities (New York or Los Angeles). A similar proportion of respondents (87%) believed that such a measure would lead to the proliferation of more crime (Századvég, 2021).

[5] There was only one demonstration on 31 January 2021 in Heroes' Square in Budapest. Only a few hundred (approx. 200–300) people protested against the shop closures. It was organised on Facebook, it was peaceful without attacking any police officers. (https://www.theguardian.com/world/2021/jan/31/hundreds-arrested-at-anti-lockdown-protests-in-brussels-budapest-and-vienna, 24 April 2021).

From a CEE perspective, a survey (Republikon Intézet, 2020) conducted in late November 2020 in Hungary asked Slovenian and Hungarian citizens about human rights during the first epidemic wave. According to the study, people in Slovenia typically experienced the human rights situation worsening since the coronavirus outbreak, while Hungarian respondents were less pessimistic. During the virus situation, Hungarian respondents were more permissive about closing borders within the EU, while half of Slovenians insisted on the right to free movement within the EU. In terms of novel challenges of the protection measures, 66% of Hungarians considered the role of the police to be important, compared to 51% of Slovenians. Curfew restrictions were deemed more important by Hungarians, while Slovenians believed travel restrictions more important. Slovenians were generally more critical of the situation of fundamental freedoms; Slovene respondents perceived greater restrictions than Hungarian respondents for all the factors listed in the poll. In Slovenia, the population's dissatisfaction was shown by the fact that more than half of the respondents thought that there had been a negative trend for all but one human right.

One study measured citizens' satisfaction with the Hungarian Government's response to the COVID-19 coronavirus outbreak every week (Nézőpont, 2021) and found that by the end of the third wave, the proportion of those who had been more satisfied with the measures taken had risen to a high of 62% by the end of the third wave, the same high level at the beginning of 2021, and only 32% were somewhat more disillusioned. Although satisfaction slightly declined during the third wave of the pandemic, it never fell below 50 (Nézőpont, 2021).

The impact of stress caused by the COVID-19 pandemics on the work and conduct of police officers in an emergency stress situation in Croatia was explored by Borovec and colleagues (2022). Field research was conducted in May and June 2020 during the first pandemic wave. The obtained results suggest that the crisis caused by the pandemic has affected organisational changes in the police, changed the structure and scope of police tasks and had a significant impact on the professional health of police officers. On the one hand, the risk of infection has increased since police work continues to be carried out through direct contact with citizens, and on the other hand, it has increased exposure to stress. The COVID-19 pandemic affected the organisation structure and operations of police agencies.

On the one hand, the police had to protect themselves and limit their contact with the public, and at the same time, they had to provide the necessary police services and respond to the calls for service. The Croatian police were no exception. Based on a June 2021 survey, Borovec et al. (2022) analyse the police officers' views about the operational and organisational changes, including proactive and reactive police practices. The respondents assessed whether things have changed and the extent of the changes. The study explores the relationship between the effectiveness of police administration's COVID-19 instructions and the extent of police officers perceived stress. Receiving official instructions from the administration played a significant role in dealing with police officer stress. Other potential organisational stress alleviators—perceived effectiveness of dealing with the pandemic and availability of personal protective equipment—were not significant. Personal stress alleviators—spending time with family and getting sufficient sleep—are related to lower stress levels. Concern for family health and emotional exhaustion served as stress generators during the pandemic. Married officers expressed lower levels of stress during the pandemic peak.

In November 2021, a large rally in the Croatian capital Zagreb against mandatory COVID-19 passes and other epidemiological restrictions was followed by smaller protests (Grgurinovic, 2021). The protests against the mandatory pass and other epidemiological restrictions have been happening as Croatia records a spike in COVID-19 infections and virus-related deaths. In Zagreb, thousands marched to show their anger at mandatory vaccinations for public sector workers (BBC, 2021).

While demonstrations against pandemic containment measures were almost non-existent in Hungary (RFE/RL's Hungarian Service, 2021), this was not the case in Croatia, and the number of protests was high in Slovenia. As many as one hundred consecutive Fridays during the pandemic, protesters gathered in Ljubljana to oppose government action and police action (NN, 2022). In October 2021, there was also the most extensive use of police coercive means, including water cannon, extensive use of tear gas, police cavalry and the police helicopter. In the following days, there were outraged reactions from the population, and the police denied excessive use of force in a report on the use of coercive means, although they acknowledged the disproportionate and sometimes unprofessional use of coercive means (Policija, 2021).

The frequent use of the police in enforcing measures to prevent the spread of the new coronavirus in Slovenia was reflected in public opinion towards the police. Every two years, the Slovenian police force surveys assessments and views of the inhabitants of Slovenia regarding the work of the police. The latest survey from 2021 showed a decline in trust in the police among Slovenian inhabitants relative to previous years' surveys. In 2021, the police were trusted[6] by 30.5% of respondents, while in 2018, the proportion was 66.6% and 69.7% in 2016. In 2018, police were not trusted by 16.5% of respondents, while mistrust in 2021 had grown to as much as 49.9%, representing nearly half of the respondents. In 2018, a total of 17.8% of respondents were dissatisfied with the work of the police, while dissatisfaction grew in 2021 to as much as 52.2%, i.e. more than half of respondents (MNZ RS—Police, 2021; Rovan, 2021).

At the beginning of 2021, Lobnikar and Prislan (2021) conducted a survey on a sample of Slovenian police officers using a methodology devised to determine organisational changes to police work due to the response to the COVID-19 pandemic by Maskály et al. (2021). The authors merged the variables into three substantive sets. The first set comprised assertions through which we measured changes within the police organisation (impact on police morale, attitude to police leaders, sense of safety among police officers) and in the attitudes of police officers towards members of the communities where police officers performed police duties. Lobnikar and Prislan (2021) found that there had been a marked deterioration relative to the period before the pandemic regarding all dimensions included in the analysis. Police officers detected attitudes within the police organisation, and the relations of police officers with the community had deteriorated. 68% of police officers reported that police morale had dropped, and the same percentage reported that the sense of well-being and safety among police officers had deteriorated during the pandemic. 76% of surveyed police officers

[6] The sum of responses "I trust them" and "I completely trust them".

reported that people's trust in their work had deteriorated, and two-thirds of police officers reported that their trust in the police leadership had declined. As much as 78% of police officers reported that public respect for the police had declined (Lobnikar & Prislan, 2021). The same methodological approach to researching the impact of the pandemic on policing was also used in the public opinion study on the quality and acceptability of police work in Slovenia during the COVID-19 pandemic (Lobnikar et al., 2022). The authors conducted an online survey on the sample of 587 inhabitants of Slovenia on the implementation of police work during the pandemic. They found that the police pandemic-related performance seemed to impact the respect for the police negatively. About one-third of respondents reported that their willingness to cooperate with the police deteriorated and that their willingness to respect the laws worsened during the peak month of the pandemic. Furthermore, about one-half of the respondents stated that the COVID-19 police measures affected the police's success in dealing with crimes. In addition, about 60% of the respondents stated that they neither trust the police nor the government. The results also demonstrate that most of the respondents—about two-thirds—evaluated that the police had not successfully tackled the challenges of the pandemic (Lobnikar et al., 2022).

In their survey among managers of security firms and the heads of corporate security at critical infrastructure companies in Slovenia, Sotlar and Dvojmoč (2021) determined that conditions in 2020 were genuinely unique and adjustments in the area of corporate security and private security firms were essential for fulfilling the demands of the state and clients requiring security services. The study results indicate that the actual operation of security organisations and companies operating during the declared epidemic did not significantly change. The most significant number of changes in the working of companies took place in HR management, where employers had to ensure safe and effective work from home for at least a part of their workforce. This was followed by numerous restrictive and protective measures to reduce the possibility of transmitting COVID-19 to a minimum. Since each imposition or amendment of the measures set out in Slovenian Government ordinances encroached on the ordinary lives of inhabitants, many of them responded by disagreeing with the measure, and many did not even know them, which often led to verbal conflict with private security officers trying to impose upon them the compulsory adherence to the measures. This was exacerbated by differing interpretations of the measures by government representatives and the media. This led to conflicts that in the past had not been observed in private security firms, so their complaints departments were swamped with complaints about "unprofessional, uninformed and inhuman" security guards. With the increased scope of work, some guards quit since they no longer wished to perform their work under new COVID-19-related circumstances (Sotlar & Dvojmoč, 2021). Security guards took action against offenders by restraining them until the arrival of the police, who took direct action and issued fines against the offenders. The stringent imposition of fines due to non-compliance with the measures taken by security guards kept the situation within acceptable frameworks, such that the cooperation between private security staff and police officers can be assessed as right and proper (Sotlar & Dvojmoč, 2021).

4 Discussion and Conclusion

At the beginning of the pandemic, the analysed countries responded in a very similar way. As a rule, the governments first strengthened healthcare capacities, but almost at the same time also their national security institutions, first and foremost the police (Sotlar & Dvojmoč, 2021). Police duties were associated with enforcing and supervising policies, laws and rules through which governments rearranged the rules of public life (e.g. maintaining social distance, restricting movement, control of state border crossings, ordering and monitoring quarantine). In this way, the police assumed the supervision and implementation of operational tasks that would supposedly most effectively limit the spread of the virus (Laufs & Waseem, 2020). While the police carried out their duties in public spaces, these activities in semi-public and private spaces of those economic undertakings that could not transfer to "working remotely" (such as retail centres) were left to the operatives of private security firms.

An analysis of the response to the pandemic in Hungary, Croatia and Slovenia showed that countries relied heavily on police measures in implementing pandemic containment measures. This affected both the reorganisation of the work of the police and the expansion of the tasks and police powers. However, in our analysis, we found that the state police was by no means the only institution that was intensively involved in enforcing government decisions in connection with the pandemic. The police enforced the rules on the closure of the state and the rules banning associations in public places. All this, however, overshadowed other institutions from the family of plural policing, such as municipal wardens, security guards or customs officers. The findings of our analysis are in line with the findings of the Confederation of European Security Services (CoESS) (2020a), that security staff have been a hidden workforce in Europe, ensuring and drawing attention at all levels to the observance of measures to contain the pandemic. We have seen that Hungary, Croatia and Slovenia are no exception. Catherine Piana, Director General of CoESS, noted that companies were having difficulty retaining employees (CoESS, 2020a), which we saw was the case in Slovenia as well.

In all the countries analysed, we saw that the operation and cooperation of various institutions from plural policing had a significant impact on the effectiveness of the pandemic response and on ensuring the security and other needs of the population. Experience from Hungary, Slovenia and Croatia indicates the correctness of the proposal of CoESS (2020b) to establish a security continuum, which needs to be created between state and local enforcement authorities and private security operators. This is important mainly because security guards, as well as municipal wardens and other members of institutions of plural policing, are in the "front line" in ensuring protection for critical infrastructure, warehouses and supply chains, shops and hospitals, for which they also deserve appropriate recognition and status in national security systems. In the new, unstable reality, a family of non-state plural police institutions support state authorities and (could) play a vital part in ensuring security in modern societies.

The findings of our analysis agree with Gambhir (2020) that the global pandemic brought additional dimensions to security issues, including growing social unrest and the growth in police brutality and criminality. Public responses to the implementation of pandemic-related rules set by the state have varied. If we barely noticed opposition to these measures in Hungary, their resistance in Slovenia was intense. The fact that the analysed countries are not monolithic is shown by the differences in public opinion on the measures taken. In the period of responding to the health crisis, security institutions have been striving to consolidate their operation and the prominence of their role within national security systems, where they highlight the important role of the shared public-private model of police activity as we know it through the prism of plural police activity (Prislan & Lobnikar, 2019). The mobilisation of various frameworks and institutions to respond to the pandemic brings dangers, especially in protecting human rights, the importance of public health, limits on migration and protection of individual rights.

The tendency to understand the outbreak of the COVID-19 pandemic as an international security issue could lead to a new form of structural violence. This is especially important if the measures and powers we have described in response to the pandemic remain in place after the end of the pandemic. We do not find this only for the analysed countries of Central and Eastern Europe; in this publication, we have observed similar findings elsewhere. Responding to the pandemic increases the probability of rising social unrest and violence, which can impact the resilience of modern societies (Sotlar & Dvojmoč, 2021). Multi-institutional responses to the pandemic associated with various restrictions can lead to various forms of violence stemming from inequality of power, resources and life possibilities. The phenomenon of strengthening the supervisory function was pointed out by MacLeod (2020) since, from the beginning of the pandemic, we witnessed an increased demand for certain non-state security services on the part of states and companies in Europe. In order to manage pandemics, numerous governments have resorted to "emergency" legislation (an example of such a response is, for example, in Slovenia, where the government enforced rules through governmental decrees and thus turned the role of Parliament into a passive one; see Pirc Musar, 2021) and, consequently, other than-state providers of security to fill the gaps in public safety. Pandemic reinforces the need to rethink our attitudes toward plural policing institutions and their position in the national security structure (Sotlar & Dvojmoč, 2021), primarily through the prism of legitimacy (Flander, 2021).

References

Act CLXV of 2011 on the Nationwide Civil Self-Defence Organization and the rules governing its activities. (2011). https://njt.hu/jogszabaly/2011-165-00-00

Act CXXII of 2010 on the National Tax and Customs Administration. (2010). https://njt.hu/jogszabaly/2010-122-00-00

Bagić, D., & Šuljok, A. (2021). „Stavi masku i odmakni se "–istraživanje determinanti protektivnog ponašanja od bolesti COVID-19 u Hrvatskoj. *Sociologija i prostor: časopis za istraživanje prostornoga i sociokulturnog razvoja, 59*(219), 119–147. https://doi.org/10.5673/sip.59.0.5

Balla, J., Christián, L., & Hautzinger, Z. (2021). Rendészet a járványügyi veszélyhelyzet idején. In A. Koltay & B. Török (Eds.), *Járvány sújtotta társadalom: A koronavírus a társadalomtudományok szemüvegén keresztül* (pp. 67–86). Magyarország Ludovika Egyetemi Kiadó.

Baranyai, N., Barsi, B., & Nárai, M. (2020). Önkormányzati kommunikáció járványhelyzetben: hol, mit és hogyan? *Tér és Társadalom, 34*(3), 282–294. https://doi.org/10.17649/TET.34.3.3294

BBC. (2021). Covid: Huge protests across Europe over new restrictions. *BBC News*. https://www.bbc.com/news/world-europe-59363256

Borovec, K., Delač Fabris, S., & Rosić – Jakupović, A. (2022). Impact of stress caused by the Covid-19 Pandemic on the work and conduct of police officers in stressful emergency situations. *European Law Enforcement Research Bulletin*, (SCE 5), 99–110. https://doi.org/10.7725/eulerb.v0iSCE%205.490

Christián, L. (2017a). The role of complementary law enforcement institutions in Hungary: Efficient synergy in the field of complementary law enforcement—A new approach. In N. Visminienė & P. Lesko (Eds.),

Public security and public order: Scientific Articles (pp. 132–139). Mykolo Romerio-Universitetas.

Christián, L. (2017b). Overview of law enforcement in Hungary, with special respect to local level law enforcement. *Magyar Rendészet, 17*(4), 143–155.

Christián, L., & Sotlar, A. (2018). Private security regulation in Hungary and Slovenia: A comparative study based on legislation and societal foundations. *Varstvoslovje, 20*(2), 143–162.

Civil Protection Headquarters of the Republic of Croatia. (2021). *Odluke Stožera civilne zaštite RH za sprečavanje širenja zaraze koronavirusom.* https://civilna-zastita.gov.hr/odluke-stozera-civilne-zastite-rh-za-sprecavanje-sirenja-zaraze-koronavirusom/2304

Confederation of European Security Services (CoESS). (2020a). *Beyond COVID-19: Private security services call for political action.* Accessed on 17 April 2022, from https://www.coess.org/newsroom.php?news=Beyond-COVID-19-Private-Security-Services-call-for-Political-Action

Confederation of European Security Services (CoESS). (2020b). *Private security between public recognition and neglection.* CoESS. https://www.coess.org/newsroom.php?news=COVID-19-Private-Security-between-public-recognition-and-neglection

Constitutional Court of the Republic of Croatia. (2020). *Rješenje Ustavnog suda Republike Hrvatske broj: U-I-1372/2020 i dr. od 14. rujna 2020. i pet izdvojenih mišljenja sudaca.* https://narodne-novine.nn.hr/clanci/sluzbeni/full/2020_09_105_1971.html

Europol. (2020). *How COVID-19-related crime infected Europe during 2020.* https://www.europol.europa.eu/sites/default/files/documents/how_covid-19-related_crime_infected_europe_during_2020.pdf

Financial Administration. (2021). *Republic of Slovenia.* https://www.fu.gov.si/en/

Flander, B. (2021). Epidemija in ukrepi za njeno zajezitev: Omejitev gibanja na občine in »policijska ura«. *Revija za kriminalistiko in kriminologijo, 72*(1), 51–64.

Fortuna, R. (2020). *Delo Mestnega redarstva ob razglasitvi epidemije COVID-19 – dileme in izzivi.* Varensvet.si. http://www.varensvet.si/delo-mestnega-redarstva-ob-razglasitvi-epidemije-covid-19-dileme-in-izzivi/

Gambhir, B. (2020). *Handling complex security challenges during the Covid-19 pandemic.* International SOS. https://www.internationalsos.com/insights/handling-complex-security-challenges-during-the-covid-19-pandemic

Gardašević, Đ. (2020). Pandemija i Ustav Republike Hrvatske. *Informator, 6623*, 1–4.

Government Decision 1012/2020. (I. 31.) on the establishment of the Task Force responsible for the Protection against the Corona Virus Epidemic. https://njt.hu/jogszabaly/2020-1012-30-22

Government Decree 40/2020. (III.11) on the declaration of the state of danger. (2020). https://njt.hu/translation/J2020R0040K_20200326_FIN.pdf

Government Decree 410/2020. (VIII.30.) on the contribution of the Hungarian Defence Forces in tasks related to epidemiological preparedness. (2020). https://njt.hu/jogszabaly/2020-410-20-22

Government Decree 71/2020. (III.27) on restricting movement. (2020). https://njt.hu/translation/J2020R0071K_20200410_FIN.pdf

Government Decree 72/2020 (III.28.) on the Hospital Commander and the protection of the health stocks. (2020). http://jogszabalykereso.mhk.hu/translated/doc/J2020R0072K_20200430_FIN.pdf

Grgurinovic, M. (2021). *Mandatory COVID-19 passes cause discontent in Croatia.* BalkanInsight. https://balkaninsight.com/2021/11/23/mandatory-covid-19-passes-cause-discontent-in-croatia/

Hornyik, Z. (2020). A kórház-főparancsnokságtól a tranzithálózatig. *Belügyi Szemle, 68*(6), 157–160. https://doi.org/10.38146/BSZ.2020.6.9

Jordan, P. (2005). Großgliederung Europas nach kulturräumlichen Kriterien. *Europa Regional, 13*(4), 162–173.

Kokoravec, I., & Meško, G. (2020). Kriminaliteta v Ljubljani v času pandemije covida-19. In G. Meško, R. Hacin, & K. Eman (Eds.), *6. nacionalna konferenca o varnosti v lokalnih skupnostih: varnost v ruralnih in urbanih okoljih* (pp. 141–150). Univerzitetna založba Univerze v Mariboru. https://doi.org/10.18690/978-961-286-404-0.14

Kovčo Vukadin, I., Borovec, K., & Ljubin Golub, T. (2013). Policing in Croatia: The main challenges on the path to democratic policing. In G. Meško, C. B. Fields, B. Lobnikar, & A. Sotlar (Eds.), *Handbook on policing in Central and Eastern Europe* (pp. 31–55). Springer.

Lánczos, P. L., & Christián, L. (2021). Domestic Soft Law Regulation during the COVID-19 lockdown in Hungary: A Novel Regulatory approach to a unique global challenge. *European Journal of Risk Regulation, 12*(1), 77–92. https://doi.org/10.1017/err.2020.115

Laufs, J., & Waseem, Z. (2020). Policing in pandemics: A systematic review and best practices for police response to COVID-19. *International Journal of Disaster Risk Reduction, 51*, 1–17. https://doi.org/10.1016/j.ijdrr.2020.101812

Leyrer, R. (2013). Finding the right path of policing in Hungary. In G. Meško, C. B. Fields, B. Lobnikar, & A. Sotlar (Eds.), *Handbook on policing in Central and Eastern Europe* (pp. 115–128). Springer.

Lobnikar, B., & Modic, M. (2018). Profesionalizacija slovenske policije. [Professionalization of the Slovenian police]. *Revija Varstvoslovje, 20*(4), 286–308.

Lobnikar, B., & Prislan, K. (2021). Vpliv pandemije covida-19 na izvajanje policijske dejavnosti v Sloveniji: pogled slovenskih policistov. In G. Meško & I. Kokoravec (Eds.), *7. Nacionalna konferenca o varnosti v lokalnih skupnostih: Policijsko delo v skupnosti in zagotavljanje varnosti v lokalnih skupnostih: konferenčni zbornik* (pp. 5–23). Univerza v Mariboru/Univerzitetna založba.

Lobnikar, B., Prislan, K., Kutnjak Ivkovic, S., Maskaly, J., & Neyroud, P. (2022). Mnenje prebivalcev Slovenije o načinih in uspešnosti policijskega dela v času epidemije COVIDA-19. In M. Modic, B. Flander, B. Lobnikar, & T. Pavvsic Mrevlje (Eds.), *23. dnevi varstvoslovja, Laško, 8. in 9. junij 2022: zbornik povzetkov.* Univerzitetna založba Maribor.

MacLeod, S. (2020). *Private security, human rights and Covid-19.* EJIL:Talk! https://www.ejiltalk.org/private-security-human-rights-and-covid-19/

Maskály, J., Ivković, S. K., & Neyroud, P. (2021). Policing the COVID-19 pandemic: Exploratory study of the types of organizational changes and police activities across the globe. *International Criminal Justice Review, 31*(3), 266–285.

Meško, G., Lobnikar, B., Jere, M., & Sotlar, A. (2013). Recent developments of policing in Slovenia. In G. Meško, C. B. Fields, B. Lobnikar, & A. Sotlar (Eds.), *Handbook on policing in Central and Eastern Europe* (pp. 263–286). Springer.

Meško, G., & Urbas, V. (2021). Delo policije na področju preiskovanja kriminalitete v Sloveniji v času covida-19s poudarkom na prvem valu epidemije covida-19 spomladi 2020. *Revija za kriminalistiko in kriminologijo, 72*(1), 21–35.

Ministrstvo za notranje zadeve. (2020). *Inšpektorji IRSNZ z izrednimi nadzori v zagotavljanje spoštovanja ukrepov za obvladovanje epidemije COVID-19* [IRSNZ inspectors with extraordinary controls to ensure compliance with COVID-19 epidemic control measures]. https://www.gov.si/novice/2020-04-03-inspektorji-irsnz-z-izrednimi-nadzori-v-zagotavljanje-spostovanja-ukrepov-za-obvladovanje-epidemije-covid-19/

Ministrstvo za notranje zadeve RS – Policija. (2021). *Ocene in stališča prebivalcev Slovenije o delu policije 2021* [Estimates and attitudes of the population of Slovenia on the work of the police in 2021]. Generalna policijska uprava, Policijska akademija. https://www.policija.si/images/stories/NovinarskoSredisce/SporocilaZaJavnost/2021/05_maj/25_nk_letno_porocilo_jm_anketa_predstavitev/Porocilo_Javno_mnenje_o_delu_policije_2021.pdf

MUP [Ministarstvo unutarnjih poslova Kabinet ministra]. (2021). *COVID i kriminalitet u 2020: Komentar pokazatelja sigurnosti u Republici Hrvatskoj.* https://mup.gov.hr/UserDocsImages/2021/04/Covid%20i%20kriminalitet%20u%202020%20-%20Komentar%20pokazatelja%20sigurnosti%20u%20Republici%20Hrvatskoj.pdfBranko

Nalla, M. K., & Christián, L. (2018). Citizens' views of Private Security Guards in Hungary: A preliminary analysis. *Magyar Rendészet, 18*(4), 147–156.

Nézőpont. (2021). *Kétharmados elégedettség a járványkezeléssel.* https://nezopont.hu/ketharmados-elegedettseg/

NIJZ - Nacionalni inštitut za javno zdravje. (2020). *Navodila za delovne organizacije v zvezi z novim koronavirusom SARS-CoV-2.* https://www.nijz.si/sl/navodila-za-delovne-organizacije-v-zvezi-z-novim-koronavirusom-sars-cov-2

NN. (2022). *Danes 100. petkov protest: »Zoper nedemokratični, protiustavni in koruptivni vladi«* Ljubljana info. https://ljubljanainfo.com/novica/lokalno/danes-100-petkov-protest-zoper-nedemokraticni-protiustavni-koruptivni-vladi/189972

Országos Polgárőr Szövetség. (2021). *Köszöntő.* https://opsz.hu/koszonto/

Pirc Musar, N. (2021). *New powers accorded to the police due to covid-19 in Slovenia.* Law Firc Pirc Musar & Lemut Strle. https://pirc-musar.si/en/

Policija. (2021). *Varovanje javnega shoda, ki je potekal 5. oktobra v Ljubljani - poročilo komisije.* https://www.policija.si/medijsko-sredisce/sporocila-za-javnost/sporocila-za-javnost-gpue/111641-varovanje-javnega-shoda-ki-je-potekal-5-oktobra-v-ljubljani-porocilo-komisije

Ponsaers, P. (2001). Reading about "community (oriented) policing" and police models. *Policing: An International Journal of Police Strategies & Management, 24*(4), 470–496. https://doi.org/10.1108/EUM0000000006496

Ponsaers, P. (2013). Policing in Central and Eastern Europe as an epiphenomenon of geopolitical events. In G. Meško, C. B. Fields, B. Lobnikar, & A. Sotlar (Eds.), *Handbook on policing in Central and Eastern Europe* (pp. 5–13). Springer.

Prislan, K., & Lobnikar, B. (2019). Modern trends in policing: Public perception of the preferred policing models in Slovenia. *Revija za kriminalistiko in kriminologijo, 70*(5), 483–500.

Republikon Intézet. (2020). *Az emberi jogok helyzete Szlovéniába és Magyarországon a járvány első hulláma alatt.* http://republikon.hu/media/88696/20-11-27-republikon-szloven-magyar-kutatas.pdf

Resolution on the National Security Strategy of the Republic of Slovenia. (2019). *Official gazette of the republic of Slovenia [Uradni list RS], No. 59/19.* Accessed at http://www.pisrs.si/Pis.web/pregledPredpisa?id=RESO124

RFE/RL's Hungarian Service. (2021). *Hungarians protest against lockdown measures, despite ban on gatherings.* RFERL. https://www.rferl.org/a/hungarians-protest-covid-lockdown-measures-despite-ban-gatherings/31078966.html

Rovan, L. (2021). *Implementacija policijskega dela v skupnosti na območju Policijske postaje Ribnica* [Master Thesis, University of Maribor]. Digitalna knjižnica Univerze v Mariboru. https://dk.um.si/IzpisGradiva.php?id=80728&lang=eng

Sotlar, A., & Dvojmoč, M. (2021). Zasebno varovanje in korporativna varnost v času epidemije covida-19 v Sloveniji. *Revija Za Kriminalistiko in Kriminologijo, 72*(1), 79–90.

Sotlar, A., Modic, M., & Lobnikar, B. (2021). *Preoblikovanje mestnega redarstva mestne uprave Mestne občine Ljubljana na podlagi posodobitve občinskega programa varnosti Mestne občine Ljubljana.* Univerza v Mariboru.

STA. (2021). *Ujeli skoraj 2.000 oseb, ki niso upoštevale karantene oz. samoizolacije.* N1. Accessed on 14 April 2022, from https://n1info.si/koronavirus/ujeli-skoraj-2-000-oseb-ki-niso-upostevale-karantene-oz-samoizolacije/

Svicevic, M. (2020). Re-assessing the (continued) need for UN Security Council Authorisation of Regional Enforcement Action: The African Union twenty years on. *South African Yearbook of International Law, 45*(1), 1–32.

Századvég. (2021). *Magyarország a rend és a rendőrség pártján áll.* https://szazadveg.hu/hu/2020/06/24/magyarorszag-a-rend-es-a-rendorseg-partjan-all-n310

Vikić, D. (2019). Konferencija Hrvatskog ceha zaštitara "Hrvatska 2020 – 1#EU". *a&S Adria.* https://www.asadria.com/konferencija-hrvatskog-ceha-zastitara-hrvatska-2020-1eu/

5

Policing the COVID-19 Pandemic in Germany: Challenges and Learnings for Future Crises

Hartmut Aden

1 Introduction

Natural disasters, terrorist attacks or a pandemic may lead to major crises which can often have a high impact upon the political agenda for internal security. Political reactions in such situations often lead to enhanced powers for public administration, particularly for police agencies, including far-reaching restrictions upon the citizens' fundamental rights (Fährmann et al., 2022 on the impact in Germany). This usually occurs in a situation in which many citizens expect quick and effective reactions to a crisis and therefore may be prepared to accept more restrictions upon their fundamental rights than in "normal" times. Thus, a pandemic such as COVID-19 is a major challenge for democratic rule of law systems. Governments, parliaments and public administrations must meet high expectations with respect to effective crisis management and

H. Aden (✉)
Berlin, Germany
e-mail: hartmut.aden@hwr-berlin.de

M. Den Boer et al. (eds.), *Plural Policing, Security and the COVID Crisis*, Palgrave's Critical Policing Studies, https://doi.org/10.1007/978-3-031-19177-0_5

the containment of the pandemic, while ensuring that these measures do not weaken democracy and the rule of law after the crisis.

This chapter looks at the impact of the COVID-19 crisis on policing in the specific German context of a federal system with decentralised police forces at a state (*Länder*) level. Starting from analysing the growing executive powers during the pandemic in the German federal system, the chapter asks how far policing differs during a pandemic crisis compared to "normal", and how public policing was interconnected with public health administration and private security in this specific situation. Based on the answers to these questions, the paper looks at lessons that may be drawn from the pandemic experiences since early 2020 in order to be better prepared for responding to future risks and crises. The chapter seeks answers to these questions from a transdisciplinary legal and public policy perspective.

2 Extended Executive Powers: The German Federal Multilevel Setting During the COVID-19 Pandemic

The German political system is characterised by a federal structure with a central government (*Bund*) and sixteen state *(Länder)* governments. Together with one or several levels of partly autonomous local authorities and the European Union, policy-making and the reactions to crises are, therefore, distributed among at least these four geographical levels of government: local, regional, national and supranational. This multilevel setting may be perceived as (over-)complex, but it may also facilitate flexible reactions where problems differ between regions. For example, during a pandemic, infections may spread at a different pace in different regions (Behnke, 2020, 12; Kingreen, 2021, 2767; Lanfer, 2022; Münch, 2020, 217).

In the German context, policing a pandemic such as COVID-19 is characterised by a specific combination of federal and state authority. Regarding policing, the sixteen *Länder* exercise legislative power. Each state has its own police agency and a police law for the prevention of dangers, while local authorities only have limited police powers and mostly do not have any general police forces. Additionally, the federal state (*Bund)* has its own police forces for specific purposes: the Federal Criminal Investigation Office (*Bundeskriminalamt)*, the Federal Police (*Bundespolizei*) for airport and railway security and the Customs Administration *(Zoll)*. Each has its own specific and limited authority. Thus, compared to other countries, the German police system can be perceived as semi-centralised or semi-decentralised, as it is much more centralised, compared for example with the US system, but much less centralised compared to, for example, the French police system with nation-wide police forces (Aden & Frevel, 2017, 242; Frevel, 2018, 77–85). In the range of federal political systems, German federalism is a cooperative variation characterised by close horizontal and vertical cooperation. For policing and internal security, the sixteen state ministers cooperate closely with the federal minister of the interior in the Permanent Conference of Interior Ministers (*Ständige Konferenz der Innenminister und -senatoren der Länder/Innenministerkonferenz* [IMK]). This conference has a number of permanent working groups that play a key role in the coordination of internal security in Germany (Aden & Fährmann, 2021; Aden & Frevel, 2017, 230; Frevel, 2018). The health ministers have their own permanent coordination structure (*Gesundheitsministerkonferenz*) that has gained importance during the COVID-19 pandemic.

2.1 Rule-Making Under the Pressure of Crises and Uncertainty

During crises, governments and public administration are usually able to react faster compared to parliaments and courts, which may need time for deliberation before they make decisions. Crises usually require swift responses in order to mitigate further damage. In the case of COVID-19, preventing a collapse of the hospital system was a major issue. In such situations, governments will usually be the first and main actors to manage the reaction to a crisis. This often leads to a shift of powers from parliaments toward governments and public administration (Papier, 2020, 6; Schäfer, 2021). This is what occurred during the first phase of the COVID-19 pandemic in Germany (Fährmann et al., 2022; Merkel, 2020; Münch, 2020)—as in many other countries (see the other contributions to this book, den Boer et al., 2022 in a comparative perspective and Dantan et al., 2020 for France).

However, in contrast to several other countries, the German constitution (*Grundgesetz*) does not permit the option to declare a state of emergency during a pandemic. The constitution only opens this option for a situation of defence against a military attack.[1] These emergency rules were introduced by an amendment of the constitution in 1968, but they have never been used thus far. For natural disasters or cases of major threats to the democratic system, the constitution includes enhanced obligations for cooperation between the sixteen states and the federal government.[2] Thus, even if the crisis caused by the COVID-19 pandemic and the political reactions to it had some characteristics of a state emergency (Ramadani, 2020, 73), legislative powers had to be adapted according to the usual parliamentary procedures. Already before COVID-19, the federal law on the protection against infections (*Infektionsschutzgesetz)* had established legal bases for executive powers to prevent dangerous infections from spreading, including far-reaching restrictions upon the fundamental rights of those infected with certain diseases (e.g. malaria). However, these options primarily focused on individual cases rather than quickly spreading infections which may affect the national population and beyond. Therefore, this law has been amended several times since the spring of 2020 to adapt it to the quickly evolving pandemic situation (see Rixen, 2020 for an overview of the first round of amendments related to the COVID-19 pandemic in 2020).

While policing, in general, is mostly a task of the sixteen German *Länder*, the federal constitution attributes the right to legislate on criminal law, criminal procedural law and health law to the federation (Articles 70 to 74). Thus, federal law-making and coordination of rules played a central role throughout the pandemic, while the sixteen state police forces and de-centralised health administrations, which are mostly

[1] Articles 115 a to 115 l, 80a *Verteidigungsfall.*

[2] Article 35 and 91.

attached to regional authorities (*Landkreise*), had to make sure that citizens respected these rules. In such situations, both police agencies and health authorities depend upon clear and proportionate federal rules in order to convince citizens to comply.

A health crisis like a pandemic, which is caused by a newly emerging virus, is typically characterised by a high degree of uncertainty until the virus' transmissibility is fully understood. In such a situation, rule-making and enforcement (under the pressures of uncertainty and a lack of adequate time) is an obvious challenge for public administration and specifically for policing. Reactions to a crisis usually cannot wait for the results of scientific studies or lengthy and controversial parliamentary debates. However, decision-making under uncertainty challenges established democratic standards (Aden et al., 2020a; Papier, 2020). Knowledge about the way in which the virus spreads was limited in the initial phase of the COVID-19 pandemic in early 2020. Variations of the virus and sometimes quickly rising infection numbers triggered frequent modifications of the legal rules including far-reaching restrictions to fundamental rights such as the obligation to stay at home, to close shops, schools and universities, to force people to work from home and the prohibitions on travel or staying in hotels for leisure. Quickly evolving rules hardly allowed citizens to adapt their everyday lives to these changes (Fährmann et al., 2022, 96; den Boer et al., 2022 in a comparative perspective). Police agencies were assigned the task of enforcing rules that were sometimes unclear and disproportionate, especially during the first phase of the pandemic in the Spring of 2020 (see Aden et al., 2020a, 99; Bosch et al, 2020).

2.2 Coordination and Conflicts Between Central and De-centralised Levels of Decision-Making in a Multilevel Setting

As the German political system is based on a cooperative version of federalism, state and federal governments, as well as their subordinated administrations, cooperate intensively horizontally and vertically. The close cooperation within the Permanent Conference of Interior Ministers leads to similarities between the 16 state police forces with respect to police tactics and the legal rules governing them, despite the *Länder* authority to legislate general policing (Aden & Fährmann, 2021).

During the COVID-19 pandemic, the conference of the heads of governments (*Konferenz der Ministerpräsidentinnen und Ministerpräsidenten*) played a central role as a coordinating body that met every few weeks with the Federal Chancellor and the Federal Minister of Health. At the beginning of the pandemic, in early 2020, the *Infektionsschutzgesetz* did not include any specific rules on a pandemic which would affect all citizens, such as COVID-19. Applying rules on quarantining and other measures required for highly infectious diseases such as malaria were quickly revealed to be insufficient. During the COVID-19 pandemic, the federal legislator established basic federal rules for anti-pandemic measures that restricted citizens' rights, and subsequently delegated the establishment of more detailed rules to the sixteen *Länder* governments. In several temporary and permanent amendments to the *Infektionsschutzgesetz*, the federal legislator opted for general rules to be adapted to specific regional situations by the sixteen *Länder* governments. The law authorised the sixteen state governments to issue binding rules by state decrees (*Rechtsverordnungen*). The coordination of these rules was the core topic of frequent conferences between the heads of the *Länder* governments.

Naturally, this mode of governance during the pandemic crisis did not remain uncontested (Behnke, 2020). Political conflicts arose on the degree to which rules should be uniform throughout the country, as well as the obligations placed on populaces (such as the duration of lockdowns or the obligation to carry medical masks in public).

2.3 Lack of Preparedness and Other Shortcomings in the Administration of the COVID-19 Pandemic

As is typical for a newly emerging crisis, German governments and public administration turned out to be rather poorly prepared for the COVID-19 pandemic. Since the 1980s, attempts to reduce the cost of public health had led to a significant reduction in the public health infrastructure. Numerous hospitals were closed or privatised. After privatisation, these hospitals were often managed with the aim to increase efficiency and profit rather than effective preparedness for a major incident such as a pandemic (see also Schreyögg, 2020 on structural deficits of the German hospital system). Stocks of medical products such as medical masks or vaccines were replaced by "just in time" supply chains and production in low-wage countries with long-distance shipping. All of this was revealed to be problematic during the COVID-19 pandemic. For several months this led to serious disruptions of supply chains and a lack of medical equipment.

While advanced digitalisation helped to resolve problems during the pandemic, for example with improved tools for online communication, public administration turned out to be under-digitalised in many respects. At the beginning of the COVID-19 pandemic, most branches of public administration, including the police, were not sufficiently digitalised to enable civil servants to work from home when their presence in the office was not strictly necessary. In some cases, this led to the interruption of basic public services such as issuing passports to citizens or visas to students from abroad wishing to study in Germany. At several stages of the pandemic, the decentralised health administration system could not collect and communicate information on infections correctly and efficiently (Fährmann et al., 2022, 106). The lack of reliable and up-to-date information made coordination among different branches of administration difficult.

3 Plural Policing in a Federal Multilevel Setting During the COVID-19 Pandemic

This section looks at plural policing—in the sense of the "co-production" of security by several public and private actors—in the context of the COVID-19 pandemic. It discusses how tasks were distributed between police agencies and other actors such as health administration and private security companies, how they cooperated during the pandemic and what kind of problems occurred with respect to their cooperation.

3.1 Policing the "Normal" Versus Policing a Pandemic Crisis?

Many police tasks are related to emergency intervention in crisis cases of individual citizens or small groups. Domestic violence, traffic accidents or burglaries may be perceived as "everyday crises" from the perspective of professional responders, such as police and rescue services. These situations vary considerably. Therefore, beyond everyday bureaucratic routine and the training of police tactics, there is hardly a "normal" situation that police agencies can prepare for. Coping with these kinds of "everyday crises" is part of policing "the normal".

Nonetheless, a pandemic crisis differs from everyday emergencies due to its scope. During the COVID-19 crisis, new and frequently changing rules had to be respected by all citizens. Policing unfamiliar rules was combined with a high number of potential breaches of those rules. Therefore, police officers could perceive citizens who would usually never get in contact with the police as potential lawbreakers of rules such as not leaving home, refraining from travelling or wearing protective masks (Fährmann et al., 2022, 107). This led to specific challenges for police agencies, as well as stressful situations for officers (see Kyprianides et al., 2022for the UK). These challenges were heightened during periods when many officers were on sick leave, which limited the police agencies' and private security companies' capacity to act (see Olschok & Wiegand, 2022, 438 for German private security companies).

3.2 Public Health and Public Order: Distribution of Tasks and Authority Between Police Agencies and Health Administration

When analysing the containment of a quickly spreading virus and the general prevention of risk, some structural similarities arise from a legal perspective. Political systems in Western countries usually rely upon a differentiated administrative system based on specialisation and distribution of labour. In such a system, police agencies have their own specialised tasks—the most prominent one is the investigation of crimes and the preparation of criminal proceedings under the supervision of criminal justice institutions (courts, public prosecutors). In addition to this specialised role, German police agencies are tasked with serving a general, emergency function for other administrations responsible for specific areas related to the prevention of dangers (such as health or environmental protection) when the administrative staff are unavailable, mostly due to restricted office hours. The police must carry out this function when the specific situation cannot wait until the specialised administrations are operational again. During the COVID-19 pandemic, this subsidiary function became even more relevant than usual, as many specialised agencies were submitted to lockdown measures, and public administrators were forced to work from home. Additionally, health administrations were quickly stuck with a very high workload with respect to the local containment of the pandemic.

From the perspective of police agencies, this led to an increased margin of discretion with respect to who was targeted by police, as well as the prioritisation of which rules were more stringently enforced. Due to the sometimes quickly changing rules, police agencies usually did not develop policies on how to prioritise the enforcement of containment rules for the pandemic. The lack of such enforcement policies at the agency level meant that street-level officers had broad discretion concerning whom to stop, which rules to enforce and whom to sanction for administrative contraventions. The use of such broad discretion is usually influenced by the individual patrol officer's professional and personal experiences (see Aden et al., 2022 for police stops).

3.3 Public Policing of Far-Reaching Restrictions to Fundamental rights—Just Another Variation of Police Discretion?

Many of the COVID-19 lockdown measures led to far-reaching restrictions of fundamental rights—to an extent that had been unknown in democratic West Germany since the 1950s. Restrictions were created around, for example, leaving one's own house (see Schmitt, 2020 on the legal limits of this far-reaching measure); using public transport; travelling to other parts of the country or abroad; opening shops to customers; and holidaying in a hotel. These are only some of the far-reaching measures that were temporally utilised to contain the pandemic, legally embedded in the frequently amended state rules implementing the margin of manoeuvre opened by the federal law (see Fährmann et al., 2022 for further examples).

From a legal standpoint, due to the potential consequences of mass infection, overcrowded hospitals and a significant mortality rate, the states were required to balance the task of protecting human life and health (Article 2 (2) of the German constitution) with their restriction of fundamental rights to aid the virus' containment. Restrictions concerned several fundamental rights guaranteed by the German constitution, including personal freedoms (Article 2), the right to undisturbed practice of religion (Article 4), the freedom of assembly (Article 8), the freedom of movement (Article 11) and occupational freedom (Article 12) (Aden et al., 2020a, 101; Papier, 2020, 5; Thiel, 2022, 54).

Observation of policing during the first phase of the pandemic (in the spring of 2020) revealed that the principle of proportionality did not always fulfil its function of limiting the restrictive powers to only be used if strictly necessary for the protection of human health against COVID-19 (examples Bosch et al., 2020). The margin of discretion for policing grew with additional rules applicable to all citizens. Policing all rules equally became even less possible than in "normal" times (for Brazil, see: Alcadipani et al., 2020, 400, and for Germany: Fährmann et al., 2022, 94).

3.4 Data Collected for Combating the Pandemic—to Be Used for Policing Purposes?

Data played a crucial role in public policy related to the COVID-19 pandemic. Personal data is protected by the fundamental right to privacy and data protection[3] (Aden, 2022). Data related to the health of a natural person is classified as sensitive.[4] Thus, the processing of data on a COVID-19 infection of an individual is only allowed for very limited purposes and submitted to enhanced proportionality requirements.

When public spaces were temporarily allowed to reopen in the summer of 2020 after the first phase of shutdowns, contact tracing became a major tool for containing the virus. Restaurants or venues for cultural events had to register their lists of guests and retain them for two weeks, before handing them over to the health authorities for infection tracing purposes. However, in some cases, health administrations transferred lists of infected people to the police, or the police seized guest lists directly from restaurants or cultural venues in order to find criminals (Fährmann & Arzt, 2020, 802). Obviously, this was not in line with the fundamental right to privacy and data protection. The transfer of such sensitive data to the police would only have been allowed for very limited and highly important purposes, for example, in the context of protecting other people against infections. Seizing guest lists for criminal investigation purposes would have required a clear legal basis implementing the principle of proportionality and excluding the seizure of such data for petty crime (Fährmann et al., 2020).

At a later stage of the pandemic, specific smartphone apps were developed in order to trace contacts and to issue electronic vaccination certificates. Again, the data collected by such apps was highly sensitive in nature, and therefore, the use for policing purposes was subject to strict limitations with respect to the fundamental right to privacy and data protection.

---

[3] Articles 7 and 8 of the EU Charter of Fundamental Rights; Article 2(1) combined with Article 1(1) of the German constitution.

[4] Article 9 (2) of the EU General Data Protection Regulation (GDPR) 2016/679.

3.5 Problems of Protest Policing During the Pandemic

Protest policing was particularly problematic during the pandemic. According to Article 8 of the German constitution, peaceful assemblies can be held in Germany without any prior authorisation. The legislation only requires prior notification to the public authorities for outdoor assemblies. In the first phase of the pandemic, some of the *Länder* governmental regulations simply prohibited any kind of assembly without taking into account the specific risks for public health, which were dependent upon the number of expected participants and the available space. The Federal Constitutional Court (*Bundesverfassungsgericht*) stopped this practice and underlined that a case-by-case decision-making framework remains necessary in order to balance the protection of human health, on the one hand, with the protection of the freedom of assembly and the freedom of expression, on the other; both are highly relevant for a democratic society (Aden et al., 2020b; Frankewitsch, 2022; Martini et al., 2020, 250; Thiel, 2022, 58–60).

At later stages of the pandemic, protest policing became even more complex due to assemblies organised by groups contesting COVID-19 containment measures, some of whom simply denied the risk of the virus, while others were opposed to vaccination. Empirical data on this protest reveals that, compared to other kinds of public protest, protesters were on average older, predominantly male and more than 30% of the protestors were made up of supporters of far-right parties, such as the *Alternative für Deutschland* in Germany or the *Schweizer Volkspartei* (SVP) in Switzerland (Nachtwey et al., 2020, 8; Van Ham et al., 2021 and Vieten, 2020 for international perspectives). In a situation of crisis, the right to peaceful protest against containment measures is clearly protected by the freedom of assembly. With that said, the refusal to observe protective public health measures such as wearing masks or keeping social distancing (as was common at such protests), these assemblies constituted risks for public health. Even if courts mostly confirmed restrictive measures against such kinds of protests for public health reasons, police agencies initially had some difficulties enforcing restrictive measures and using force against these groups. The audiences present at these assemblies included far-right protesters, but they were also made up of other middle-class protesters with a habitus that police officers may be more familiar with among their own family and friends—this may make it more difficult for them to use force against such kinds of protests.

From a more long-term perspective, there is a risk that the acceptance of restrictive measures against political protest during the COVID-19 pandemic may harm the freedom of assembly by establishing examples for restrictive measures in a situation of crisis.

3.6 Plural Policing in a Pandemic: New Tasks for Private Security Forces

While some areas of private security faced heavy financial losses due to the COVID-19 pandemic, others were booming due to the newly emerging opportunities presented by the pandemic. During the initial lockdown phase in the Spring of 2020, private security companies were affected by a decrease in their turnover, due to restrictions and lockdowns in sectors such as events and airport security (Olschok & Wiegand, 2022, 424). Similar developments emerged in other European countries (Confederation of European Security Services, CoESS, 2020). In some respect, the COVID-19 crisis is even likely to lead to permanent changes in private security. This is particularly the case for cash transport, which had already been in decline before the pandemic—this was a trend that was accelerated by the pandemic when card payments grew in importance, in parallel to the increasing trend towards online shopping (Olschok & Wiegand, 2022, 432).

While many businesses had to close during numerous lockdowns and send their employees home, private security continued to work in some areas. In low-wage professions (like hospitality), some of the people who lost their jobs due to the pandemic found new jobs in security. At later stages of the pandemic, public vaccination centres, hospitals and shopkeepers who had to implement restrictive social distancing measures, for example, with respect to the maximum number of customers allowed in their shop, hired additional private security guards. This opened new areas of business for private security companies, but it also presented a challenge for recruitment capacities (Olschok & Wiegand, 2022, 434).

Thus, plural policing, established in Germany for decades already (Aden, 2021; Hirschmann, 2016), could be observed in a new variation during the pandemic, where both public police agencies and private security companies continued to conduct their security tasks, while major parts of public administration and private companies were subject to lockdown rules. The associations of private security providers used this situation to promote improved recognition of private security's role within the system of internal security, specifically with respect to the protection of critical infrastructure (Confederation of European Security Services, CoESS, 2020, 17; Olschok & Wiegand, 2022, 439).

4 Learning for Future Crises

Among experts from various scholarly disciplines, there is a broad consensus that the measures taken against the COVID-19 pandemic need to be evaluated in order to learn for future crises. The German government established an expert group to evaluate the policy measures used during the pandemic. Their evaluation report, published in June 2022, looks at the range of restrictive measures taken during the pandemic, such as lockdowns and travel restrictions, as well as risk communication and data management (Allmendinger et al., 2022). Nonetheless, the policing of the pandemic is not systematically covered by this report. Consequently, regarding policing, the learning process has not yet been systematically initiated.

4.1 Uncertainty, Risks and Policing

Over the past decades, various types of risks have characterised public life and policy-making in many countries, some of them to a global extent. For the European Union, Mark Rhinard has suggested, prior to the COVID-19 pandemic, using the term "*crisisification*" for "changes to collective policy-making processes in the EU which emphasise: finding the next urgent event, prioritizing speed in decision-making, ushering in new constellations of concerned actors and emphasizing new narratives of what matters in European governance" (Rhinard, 2019, 617). For most of the crises concerned this can also be perceived as a new variation of the concept of *securitisation* (going back to Buzan et al., 1998). In this variation of securitisation, "crisis-oriented modes of thinking, typically articulated in terms of preventing, preparing for, responding to and recovering from critical events" (Rhinard, 2019, 617) have become the predominant pattern of policy-making. This also occurred during the COVID-19 pandemic when safety and security purposes largely dominated crisis management (den Boer et al., 2022).

In the 1980s, the sociologist *Ulrich Beck* established the term *risk society* (*Risikogesellschaft)* to draw attention to risks deriving from technological developments, industrial production and the human domination of nature (Beck, 1986, 300 et passim). Since then, globalisation and new technologies have contributed to significantly increasing the mobility of people and goods. As a side effect, diseases caused by infections spread more easily and much faster than before. Obviously, the risks deriving from this development can hardly be contained by policing. Policing will usually intervene when a risk has already materialised into a crisis, where police agencies will aid the enforcement of containment measures.

Risks are closely related to uncertainty about whether, how and when they may cause damage. Each risk is different. The COVID-19 pandemic has demonstrated that even different variations of the same virus cause different problems at different points in time, depending upon multiple factors (including the availability of vaccines). Thus, it is not possible to be perfectly prepared for any and all kinds of risks. However, it is possible to improve preparedness and establish structures that can help societies to react quickly to new risks, to evaluate the probability of damage and to prepare for effective containment measures (Mezes & Opitz, 2020). Most countries, including Germany, have established professional structures for that purpose (Hustedt, 2019). Policing is an important factor on the reactive side, but it needs to be integrated into a system of professional responses to crises. Due to the far-reaching authority of policing with respect to the restriction of fundamental rights, potentially negative side effects of crisis policing on democracy and the rule of law must be taken into account.

4.2 Towards a Culture of Learning from Errors

Due to the high degree of uncertainty that characterises the early stage of a crisis, when risks materialise into tangible danger and cause damage, reactions necessarily incorporate decisions that may later reveal to be wrong or disproportionate. Thus, being well prepared for future crises requires a culture of learning from previous errors. In Germany, as in numerous other countries, this tends to be underdeveloped within policing. Policing is risk-prone and tends to rely on well-established ideas about what is right or wrong. By contrast, a police culture that is ready to learn from errors would require openness to admit that "things may go wrong" without necessarily sanctioning the individual officers who commit errors (Behrendes, 2013, 46).

After a major crisis, reflection processes need to be established inside police agencies and in cooperation with external oversight bodies such as parliamentary committees to enable a learning process. This process would show what worked well during the pandemic, as well as what went wrong. This could help police agencies to be better prepared for future crises. However, this cannot be detached from a clear normative orientation of policing towards democracy and the rule of law.

5 Conclusion and Outlook

This chapter has shown that German police agencies and private security companies—together with other actors, notably health administrators—had to deal with numerous unexpected tasks throughout the COVID-19 pandemic. Due to the extent of the crisis and the far-reaching containment measures restricting the fundamental rights of practically the whole population, the policing tasks clearly went beyond policing in "normal" times. Public administration tends to prepare for risks and incidents that have already occurred, while overlooking new kinds of risks.

The German policing system, characterised by its semi-(de-)centralised structure with the sixteen state police forces, had to cope with challenging tasks in a quickly evolving multilevel regulatory environment during the pandemic. In a crisis (be it a pandemic or otherwise), a de-centralised setting allows flexible reactions concerning the extent of the crisis in a specific region. It also allows taking into account regional particularities. However, decentralised structures make coordination a challenge, particularly when police agencies need to coordinate their work with other specialised administrations (such as health authorities). Thus, the necessity to be better prepared for effective coordination in a situation of crisis is one of the main lessons from the COVID-19 pandemic. This also includes the respect of fundamental rights and strict proportionality regarding the restriction of citizens' rights. The dominance of executive actors during a crisis, combined with citizens' expectations of effective crisis management, favours authoritarian law and order solutions that may damage democracy and the rule of law beyond the actual crisis (Fährmann et al., 2022; Klement, 2020). After the conclusion of a crisis, police agencies and other branches of public administration may perceive extended powers as useful and therefore push governments and parliaments to transfer extraordinary powers attributed to them during the crisis into permanent powers. Such a trend toward the "normalisation" of a state of emergency has been observed during the past decade in several countries, including France (after the 2015 terrorist attacks, see Jobard, 2017), Hungary (Halmai et al., 2020) and Turkey (Göztepe, 2018).

Despite that, with respect to the rule of law and the citizens' fundamental rights, it is of particular importance that executive powers and restrictions of fundamental rights will be terminated as soon as they are not needed anymore—or if their use is no longer proportionate (Thiel, 2022, 75). The preparation for future crises cannot justify maintaining restrictions upon fundamental rights beyond what is strictly necessary (Fährmann et al., 2022, 113).

The chapter has also shown that German police agencies are not well prepared to openly evaluate the quality of policing in order to learn for future crises. Politics will have to establish new structures to transform police agencies into learning organisations with a culture that is open to learning from errors.

References

Aden, H. (2021). Problemfelder an den Schnittstellen zwischen Polizei und privaten Sicherheitsdiensten. In A. Ruch, & T. Singelnstein (Eds.), *Auf neuen Wegen. Kriminologie, Kriminalpolitik und Polizeiwissenschaft aus interdisziplinärer Perspektive: Festschrift für Thomas Feltes zum 70* (pp. 303–318). Duncker & Humblot.

Aden, H. (2022). Privacy and Security: German perspectives, European trends and ethical implications. In R. Iphofen & D. O'Mathuna (Eds.), *Ethical Issues in Covert Research and Surveillance* (pp. 119–129). Emerald Publishing.

Aden, H., Arzt, C., & Fährmann, J. (2020a.) Gefährdete Freiheitsrechte in Krisenzeiten—Lehren aus der COVID-19-Pandemie, *vorgänge. Zeitschrift für Bürgerrechte und Gesellschaftspolitik Nr.* 230, *59*(2), 99–111.

Aden, H., Arzt, C., & Fährmann, J. (2020b). Gefährdung der Versammlungsfreiheit in Krisenzeiten—Lehren aus der COVID-19-Pandemie. *Die Polizei, 111*(12), 474–484.

Aden, H., & Fährmann, J. (2021). Argumente für einen besseren Musterentwurf für einheitlichere Polizeigesetze. Kritische Analyse von Entwicklungen im Polizeirecht aus rechtsstaatlicher und bürgerrechtlicher Perspektive. In M. H. W. Möllers, & R.C van Ooyen (Eds.), *Jahrbuch Öffentliche Sicherheit 2020/2021* (pp. 580–615). Verlag für Polizeiwissenschaft.

Aden, H., Fährmann, J., Bosch, A., & Thurn, R. (2022). Police stops in Germany—between legal rules and informal practices. *Journal of Organizational Ethnography, 11*(2), 116–131.

Aden, H., & Frevel, B. (2017). Policing metropolises in a system of cooperative federalism: Berlin as the German capital and a city-state compared to Cologne as the biggest city in North Rhine-Westphalia. In E. Devroe, A. Edwards, & P. Ponsaers (Eds.), *Policing European Metropolises* (pp. 229–248). Routledge.

Alcadipani, R., Cabral, S., Fernandes, A., & Lotta, G. (2020). Street-level bureaucrats under COVID-19: Police officers' responses in constrained settings. *Administrative Theory & Praxis, 42*(3), 394–403.

Allmendinger, J., Bergholz, W., Brenner M., Bunte, A., Domschke, K., Dreier, H., Drosten, C., Huster, S., Kießling, A., Kingreen, T., Kroemer, H. K., Rosenbrock, R., Rübsamen-Schaeff, H., Schmidt, C. M., Siegmund, B., Stöhr, K., Streeck, H., Taupitz, J., & Teichert, U. (2022). *Evaluation der Rechtsgrundlagen und Maßnahmen der Pandemiepolitik: Bericht des Sachverständigenausschusses nach § 5 Abs. 9 IfSG,* Berlin: Sachverständigenausschuss. Accessed on 15 July 2022, from https://www.bundesgesundheitsministerium.de/fileadmin/Dateien/3_Downloads/S/Sachverstaendigenausschuss/220630_Evaluationsbericht_IFSG_NEU.pdf

Beck, U. (1986). *Risikogesellschaft: Auf dem Weg in eine andere Moderne.* Suhrkamp.

Behnke, N. (2020). Föderalismus in der (Corona-)Krise. *Aus Politik Und Zeitgeschichte, 70*(35–37), 9–15.

Behrendes, U. (2013). Wechselwirkungen zwischen externer Kontrolle und interner Fehlerkultur der Polizei. *vorgänge. Zeitschrift für Bürgerrechte und Gesellschaftspolitik Nr. 204*, *52*(4), 41–49.

Boer, M. den, Bervoets, E., & Hak, L. (2022). Preparing for future pandemic policing. *European law enforcement research bulletin* (SCE 5), 261–271.

Bosch, A., Fährmann, J., & Aden, H. (2020). Polizei im Ausnahmezustand: Beobachtungen während der Pandemie. *Bürgerrechte & Polizei/CILIP Nr. 123, 42* (3), 20–27.

Buzan, B., Wæver, O., & de Wilde, J. (1998). *Security : A new framework for analysis*. Lynne Rienner Publishers.

Confederation of European Security Services (CoESS). (2020). *The new normal 2.0: private security and COVID-19 in Europe. A strategic review and foresight.* CoESS.

Dantan, E., Lange, F., Boulestreau, M., Casse, S., Fernandez, Y., & Louis, V. (2020). Les pratiques policières pendant l'état d'urgence sanitaire. *La Revue des droits de l'homme.* Accessed on 15 July 2022, from https://journals.openedition.org/revdh/10623

Fährmann, J., Aden, H., & Bosch, A. (2022). Exekutive in der Pandemie: Machtzuwächse, Sachzwänge und Gefahren für Demokratie und Rechtsstaat. In H. J. Lange (Ed.), *Politik zwischen Macht und Ohnmacht. Zum politischen Umgang mit der Corona-Pandemie in Deutschland* (pp. 93–122). Springer VS.

Fährmann, J., & Arzt, C. (2020). Polizeilicher Umgang mit personenbezogenen Daten in der Corona-Pandemie. *Datenschutz und Datensicherheit—DuD, 44*(12), 801–805.

Fährmann, J., Arzt, C., & Aden, H. (2020). *Corona-Gästelisten—maßlose polizeiliche Datennutzung.* Verfassungsblog *(VerfBlog).* Accessed on 15 July 2022, from, https://verfassungsblog.de/corona-gaestelisten-masslose-polizeiliche-datennutzung/

Frankewitsch, A. (2022). Die Demokratie im Spannungsfeld zwischen dem Demonstrationsrecht und der Schutzpflicht des Staates. In H. J. Lange (Ed.), *Politik zwischen Macht und Ohnmacht. Zum politischen Umgang mit der Corona-Pandemie in Deutschland* (pp. 241–282). Springer VS.

Frevel, B. (2018). *Innere Sicherheit.* Springer VS.

Göztepe, E. (2018). The permanency of the state of emergency in Turkey. The rise of a constituent power or only a new quality of the state? *Zeitschrift für Politikwissenschaft, 28*, 521–534.

Halmai, G., Mészáros, G., & Scheppele, K. L. (2020). *From emergency to disaster: How Hungary's second pandemic emergency will further destroy the rule of law.* Verfassungsblog (VerfBlog*).* Accessed on 15 July 2022, from https://verfassungsblog.de/from-emergency-to-disaster/

van Ham, T., Rovers, M., & den Boer, M. (2021). 'Wisdom of the crowds': Crowd control and intelligence gaps during the COVID-19 pandemic. *Journal of European and American Intelligence Studies, 4*(1), 11–30.

Hirschmann, N. (2016). *Sicherheit als professionelle Dienstleistung und Mythos. Eine soziologische Analyse der gewerblichen Sicherheit.* Springer VS.

Hustedt, T. (2019). Verwaltung und der Umgang mit Krisen und Katastrophen. In S. Veit, C. Reichard, & G. Wewer (Eds.), *Handbuch zur Verwaltungsreform* (5th ed., pp. 181–190). Springer VS.

Jobard, F. (2017). Ausnahmezustand und Anti-Terror-Recht in Frankreich. *Bürgerrechte & Polizei/CILIP Nr. 112, 56*(1), 42–49.

Kingreen, T. (2021). Der demokratische Rechtsstaat in der Corona-Pandemie. *Neue Juristische Wochenschrift, 74*(21), 2766–2771.

Klement, K. (2020). Angst Macht Vernunft. Zur politischen Rationalität der Coronakrise. In C. Arnold, O. Flügel-Martinsen, S. Mohammed, & A. Vasilache (Eds.), *Kritik in der Krise: Perspektiven politischer Theorie auf die Corona-Pandemie* (pp. 103–116), Nomos.

Kyprianides, A., Bradford, B., Beale, M., Savigar-Shaw, L., Stott, C., & Radburn, M. (2022). Policing the COVID-19 pandemic: Police officer well-being and commitment to democratic modes of policing. *Policing and Society, 32*(4), 504–521.

Lanfer, J. (2022). Föderalismus in der Corona-Krise: Kapazitäten, Legitimation und Krisenmanagement. In H. J. Lange (Ed.), *Politik zwischen Macht und*

Ohnmacht. Zum politischen Umgang mit der Corona-Pandemie in Deutschland (pp. 125–155). Springer VS.

Martini, M., Thiessen, B., & Ganter, J. (2020). Zwischen Vermummungsverbot und Maskengebot: Die Versammlungsfreiheit in Zeiten der Corona-Pandemie. *Neue Juristische Online-Zeitschrift, 20*(31), 929–935.

Merkel, W. (2020). Wer regiert in der Krise? Demokratie in Zeiten der Pandemie. *WSI-Mitteilungen, 73*(6), 445–453.

Mezes, C., & Opitz, S. (2020). Die (un)vorbereitete Pandemie und die Grenzen der Preparedness. Zur Biopolitik um COVID-19. *Leviathan, 48*(3), 381–406.

Münch, U. (2020). Wenn dem Bundesstaat die Stunde der Exekutive schlägt: der deutsche (Exekutiv-) Föderalismus in Zeiten der Coronakrise. In Europäischen Zentrum für Föderalismus-Forschung Tübingen (Ed), *Jahrbuch des Föderalismus 2020: Föderalismus, Subsidiarität und Regionen in Europa* (pp. 209–225). Nomos Verlag.

Nachtwey, O., Schäfer, R., & Frei, N. (2020). *Politische Soziologie der Corona Proteste: Grundauswertung*. Universität Basel. Accessed on 15 July 2022, from https://osf.io/preprints/socarxiv/zyp3f/

Olschok, H., & Wiegand, K. (2022). Private Sicherheitsdienste in Zeiten von Corona. In H. J. Lange (Ed.), *Politik zwischen Macht und Ohnmacht. Zum politischen Umgang mit der Corona-Pandemie in Deutschland* (pp. 421–447). Springer VS.

Papier, H. J. (2020). Umgang mit der Corona-Pandemie: Verfassungsrechtliche Perspektiven. *Aus Politik Und Zeitgeschichte, 70*(35–37), 4–8.

Ramadani, D. (2020). Mundschutz oder mundtot? Corona-Krise als Ausnahmezustand für und durch die Demokratie. In C. Arnold, O. Flügel-Martinsen, S. Mohammed, & A. Vasilache (Eds.), *Kritik in der Krise: Perspektiven politischer Theorie auf die Corona-Pandemie* (pp. 73–85). Nomos.

Rhinard, M. (2019). The crisisification of policy-making in the European Union. *Journal of Common Market Studies, 57*(3), 616–633.

Rixen, S. (2020). Gesundheitsschutz in der Coronavirus-Krise – Die (Neu-)Regelungen des Infektionsschutzgesetzes. *Neue Juristische Wochenschrift, 72*(16), 1097–1103.

Schäfer, K. (2021). Welche Rolle sollten Parlamente in der Corona-Krise spielen? *Gesellschaft, Wirtschaft, Politik, 70*(1), 31–37.

Schmitt, F. (2020). Die Verfassungswidrigkeit der landesweiten Ausgangsverbote. *Neue Juristische Wochenschrift, 72*(23), 1626–1631.

Schreyögg, J. (2020). Corona-Krise trifft auf Strukturprobleme im Gesundheitswesen. *Wirtschaftsdienst, 100*(4), 226–227.

Thiel, M. (2022). Freiheit vs. Sicherheit? Grundrechtliche Aspekte der Pandemiebekämpfung. In H. J. Lange (Ed.), *Politik zwischen Macht und Ohnmacht. Zum politischen Umgang mit der Corona-Pandemie in Deutschland* (pp. 49–90). Springer VS.

Vieten, U. (2020). The "new normal" and "pandemic populism": The COVID-19 crisis and anti-hygienic mobilisation of the far-right. Social sciences. *MDPI, Open Access Journal, 9*(9), 1–14.

6

Policing by Consent in a Pandemic: Security Governance and Policing of COVID-19 in the United Kingdom

Saskia Hufnagel, Rudi Fortson, Clive Walker, and Megan O'Neill

1 Introduction

The policing of COVID-19 regulations in the UK has been repeatedly criticised for its lack of legal clarity, its bias and its uneven application which has slewed between heavy-handedness and abeyance. While

S. Hufnagel (✉)
London, UK
e-mail: s.m.hufnagel@qmul.ac.uk

R. Fortson
London, UK
e-mail: rudi4law@gmail.com

C. Walker
Leeds, UK
e-mail: C.P.Walker@leeds.ac.uk

M. O'Neill
Dundee, UK
e-mail: m.oneill@dundee.ac.uk

M. Den Boer et al. (eds.), *Plural Policing, Security and the COVID Crisis*, Palgrave's Critical Policing Studies, https://doi.org/10.1007/978-3-031-19177-0_6

the UK avoided the assertion that COVID-19 amounted to an 'emergency' for legislative purposes,[1] and the emergency legislation in the Civil Contingencies Act 2004, Pt.II, was not invoked, a vast amount of legislation was introduced that infringed civil rights and was susceptible to a wide range of interpretations and uncertainties. Between 27 January 2020 and 6 February 2022, it is reckoned that 570 pandemic-related regulations had been laid before Parliament (Hansard Society, 2020). Most were made under the Public Health Act 1984, Part 2A; 27 of them fell under the Coronavirus Act 2020. The latter legislation had been passed in a panic when consultations with the general public and expert authorities were bypassed or extremely brief, and discussions within Parliament were cursory. Hence, it comes as no surprise that both the regulation and its enforcement have been subject to legal challenges.[2]

In the sphere of policing, an inadequate legislative framework may increase the risk of arbitrary and inconsistent application of the law and consequent legal challenge.[3] If, for example, definitions included in the law are unclear, it is more difficult for law enforcement officers to enforce prohibitions with consistency.[4] The policing of the COVID-19 restrictions in the UK have been a prime example. Norms were created that lacked certainty, predictability and determinacy, and their implementation in practice was consequently inconsistent and led to the infringement of human rights. Enforcement, furthermore, varied geographically between regions, cities and even districts. Courts across the country were called upon to examine this patchwork of enforcement in order to discern legality and the impact on fundamental rights. Furthermore, many challenges to prosecutions brought under the coronavirus legislation were frequently successful. Completed prosecutions between March 2020 and August 2021 revealed that for Public Health Regulations, 2098 prosecutions were finalised (eight were found not

[1] Hansard (House of Commons) vol.673 col.1188 19 March 2020. As a result, the emergency legislation in the Civil Contingencies Act 2004, Pt.II, was not invoked.

[2] Amongst the broadest challenges were: *R (Dolan) v Secretary of State for Health & Social Care* [2020] EWCA Civ 1605; *R (Hussein) v Secretary of State for Health & Social Care* [2020] EWHC 1392; *Re Philip* [2021] CSOH 32.

[3] The low quality of regulations is explained in the House of Lords and House of Commons Joint Committee on Statutory Instruments (2020).

[4] Consider, for example, *R v. Rimmington* [2005] UKHL 63.

guilty) but 445 were incorrectly charged and 349 withdrawn; under the Coronavirus Act 2020, 295 prosecutions were finalised (zero not guilty), but 295 were incorrectly charged and 240 withdrawn (Crown Prosecution Service, 2021a).

This chapter focuses on the policing of COVID-19-related restrictions since the start of the pandemic. Various regulations and policies applied throughout the UK, including England which is by far the largest jurisdiction. There were significant variants for Wales, Scotland and Northern Ireland under the Government of Wales Act 1998, the Scotland Act 1998 and the Northern Ireland Act 1998. These variants are touched upon to some extent, but our main focus is England where most policing occurred and where most trends were set. Apart from the COVID-19 specific law enforcement, which is at the centre of this chapter, many policing tasks resulting from emergency situations could have been considered. During the COVID-19 pandemic, officers had to adapt to different and diverse, former and new responsibilities such as enforcing lockdown restrictions, harm reduction activities to prevent the spread of infection, crime control and response, and public order maintenance (Aitkenhead et al., 2022). In addition to this great variety of responsibilities, policing styles and strategies were altered at various stages of the pandemic to accommodate different priorities, behaviours and expectations. Such adaptation of policing to disaster situations has previously been observed and is not unique to COVID-19 (Adams & Stewart, 2015; Bonkiewicz & Ruback, 2010, 2012). However, public responses to public health emergency exigencies brought with them alterations to police practices and to community stances in response to policing.

Guidelines developed by the UK College of Policing at the start of the pandemic are crucial in understanding the police perspective and response. From the outset, the College of Policing announced the '4 Es' framework, which specified a staged and restrained response to policing of the regulations, including lockdown restrictions. Thus, Engagement, Explanation and Encouragement to comply with the law should be the main responses, with Enforcement by applying coercive powers and charges as a last resort (Brown, 2020; National Police Chiefs' Council & College of Policing, 2020b). The approach may have reflected the traditional ('Peelian') principle of policing with consent (Emsley, 2020;

Grieve, 2015; Loader, 2016), as well as taking heed of a sense of public solidarity in a crisis, and the practical constraints of policing resources.

The focus of this edited collection is on 'plural policing', which views policing as a function within a social system that is not uniquely performed by the uniformed police force and other state security actors, but also by private actors, communities and institutions (Loader, 2000). This chapter, therefore, explores the various levels of policing that were exercised beyond the police and involved institutions, private companies and individuals. What could frequently be observed during the pandemic in the UK is that the invocation and application of policing often did not result from the police investigating and detecting breaches of COVID-19 regulation in the private sphere, but concerned neighbours and citizens more generally drawing attention to behaviour they deemed to be unacceptable (Den Boer et al., 2022). One might go so far to say that, without such a public information flow, breaches of COVID-19 regulation in the private environment would have rarely been detected (Sheldon, 2021). Furthermore, throughout the UK, the differentiated enforcement of the COVID-19 regulation became apparent. For example, mask-wearing in public spaces, such as trains, tubes, busses and stations, was rarely enforced even though the wearing of masks on public transport was mandatory (Zhang et al., 2021). The situation was different at airports, probably due to the higher density of security personnel and mandatory channelling of passengers (Pan & Liu, 2022). As for professional policing, approaches have differed both geographically and between types of regulation. While the Chief Constable of Northamptonshire threatened to set up roadblocks and search shopping trollies for 'non-essentials' in the first phase of the pandemic, no similar enforcement of lockdown restrictions was visible in London (Simpson, 2022). Under the overall tactical approach of restraint promoted by the College of Policing (as explained earlier), just 106,451 notices were issued between 27 March and 18 July 2021 despite the reporting of 'hundreds of thousands of COVID-19 related incidents' (National Police Chiefs' Council, 2020, 2021). However, the £10,000 Fixed Penalty Notice for large gatherings proved controversial and was frequently and successfully challenged (Brown, 2020). A further perspective on this relatively low rate of formal enforcement may be gained from the comparison of English with overseas practices up to around the mid-2020s: the police in England and Wales issued two fines per 10,000 people; in Spain, the rate peaked at 133 per 10,000; in France, 136 fines per 10,000; and in Italy, 51 fines per 10,000 people (Aitkenhead et al., 2022). In contrast, the Dutch authorities issued seven per 10,000 people, though that figure may have risen considerably in the 2022 stages of lockdown when protests became widespread and severe (Henley, 2021).

It follows that the policing of COVID-19 regulations in the UK, as anywhere else in the world, has been complex and involved a plurality of state and non-state actors. Some restrictions were not enforced at all, while others were enforced unevenly depending on socio-economic or ethnic profiles, young black males and poorer households being the more likely targets (Currenti & Flatley, 2020; Scott et al., n.d.), emphasising the wide possibilities to exercise policing discretion for good or ill in this sphere as in others.

Furthermore, this chapter addresses the legitimacy of COVID-19 policing in the UK in the light of legal frameworks. Mismatches of police and community expectations and priorities, inadequate styles of policing before, during and after disasters, can lead to diminution in support of policing by citizens and communities in emergency situations. However, only a few systematic assessments of public responses are available which highlight such inadequacies and the way they were encountered in the UK (Caluori & Clements, 2020). The focus of this chapter is, therefore, more prominently on legal implementation and legitimacy rather than community perceptions.

The thesis of the book is that 'security organisations such as police and border management organisations were not only confronted [by] but also created the normative gap that transpired throughout the COVID-epidemic'. On that basis, the thesis of this chapter is to make the same assertion in regard to the UK and then to test the assertion according to six steps which are outlined here. After this introduction, the plurality of security actors in the area of COVID-19 policing is discussed and concentrates on local policing (by law enforcement agencies, state and non-state institutions, private companies and members of the community) rather than border control and movement between external or UK internal (England, Wales, Northern Ireland and Scotland) jurisdictions. The third part of the chapter discusses crisis management structures in the UK generally as well as various types of measures that were introduced to limit the spread of the pandemic. This part of the chapter evaluates mechanisms and police performance throughout the COVID-19 pandemic response in the UK. Legislation, regulations and guidance are outlined in depth with a view to implementation and enforcement. In the fourth part, surveillance mechanisms are discussed with a view to mobile technology employed to support policing the pandemic. Finally, the chapter concludes by outlining the way plural policing has unfolded throughout the pandemic and addresses the interaction between police, private security providers and the community in light of the pandemic and possible lessons learned for the future.

2 Security Actors Influencing UK COVID-19 Policing

COVID-19 policing in the UK may be attributed to three main security actors. First, professional police bodies were involved in enforcing regulation geared at limiting the spread of the virus. Second, local authorities were given wide powers to curtail public activities. For example, the Health Protection (Coronavirus, Restrictions) (England) (No. 3) Regulations 2020, issued in July 2020, authorised every local authority to impose prohibitions, requirements or restrictions in relation to specified premises, the holding of an event or outdoor places (such as parks or squares).[5] Third, policing was carried out by individuals and businesses in their locality either as part of the government response (by implementing regulations such as social distancing) and/or to protect their own safety as a matter of 'house rules' such as remote ordering and delivery of goods and services (UK Government, 2021), which can be associated with 'self-policing'.

While this chapter mainly concentrates on local policing by public professional bodies, it acknowledges that there has been self-policing

[5] SI 2020/750.

from below by the public (and by private operators such as businesses, for example, by providing testing or enforcing COVID-19 regulation on their own premises). The context for public professional policing in the UK will be briefly outlined first. Policing in the UK is decentralised and so is the governance of COVID-19 regulation. This means that not only the policing styles differed until the so-called 'Freedom Day' on 19 July 2021 (Prime Minister's Office & The Rt Hon Boris Johnson MP, 2021a)—when most restrictions in relation to the pandemic in the UK were lifted, but also which regulations were enforced and how so. Enforcement not only differed locally, but also varied over time as the pandemic waxed and waned over two years.

As of 2021, there are 48 civilian police forces in the UK. 43 of them are the territorial (geographically constituted) police forces in England and Wales. Scotland and Northern Ireland each have a single police force (Brown, 2021; Fyfe & Scott, 2013). There are furthermore various specialised police forces in the UK, the prime bodies being the British Transport Police, the Civil Nuclear Constabulary and the Ministry of Defence Police.[6] UK territorial police forces differ significantly in size, ranging from 33,128 police officers in the London-based Metropolitan Police Service (Metropolitan Police, n.d.) and 17,283 in Scotland (the second largest force in the UK) (Justice Directorate, 2021) to 1043 officers in Warwickshire, which is the smallest (Philip Seccombe Police and Crime Commissioner for Warwickshire, 2020). Despite any variation in size or locality, uniformity in standards and organisation is achieved to a large extent by way of funding and oversight imposed by the central government's Home Office, acting under powers in the Police Act 1996. Detailed work is also undertaken by the National Police Chiefs' Council and the College of Policing (both funded by the Home Office) acting under Section 22A of the Police Act 1996 and Sections 123 to 130 of the Anti-Social Behaviour, Crime and Policing Act 2014, respectively. Under the 'PEEL programme' Her Majesty's Chief Inspector of Constabulary and Fire & Rescue Services inspects forces in relation to effectiveness, efficiency and legitimacy. Each force can be rated: outstanding, good, adequate, requires improvement or inadequate. PEEL inspections were suspended in March 2020 until 2022, so no data are yet available from this crucial source on police performance in relation to the pandemic (Her Majesty's Inspectorate of Constabulary and Fire & Rescue Services, 2022).

In addition to enforcement through police services, English local authorities, as well as devolved administrations in Northern Ireland, Scotland and Wales, are empowered to implement a range of regulations. As mentioned, above, the broad legislative instrument, the Health Protection (Coronavirus, Restrictions) (England) (No. 3) Regulations 2020, offers a sound illustration of the powers afforded to a local administration to direct public access and behaviour[7] (see also National Police Chief's Council, & College of Policing, 2020a). The affected premises and outside locations can be privately owned and therefore not secured by police, but overseen by private actors, such as security companies, owners and managers (Moeckli, 2016). According to the Regulation, a local authority may issue a direction in response to a serious and imminent threat to public health, if the direction is necessary for the purpose of preventing, protecting against, controlling or providing a public health response in the local authority's area and if the requirements of the direction are a proportionate way of achieving this purpose. The local authority issuing the direction must review the decision every seven days.

The enforcement of directions imposing prohibitions was delegated to the private and/or public parties owning, managing or working in the private or public premises. This applied to the enforcement of requirements or restrictions in relation to the entry into, departure from, or location of persons in, specified premises in the local authority's area. The local authority was required to give advance notice to the persons involved in running the premises and owners/occupiers. In relation to outdoor spaces, access could be limited at specific times or generally. A local authority, or any other person who owns, occupies or is responsible for land in a public outdoor place to which a direction relates, must take reasonable steps to prevent or restrict public access to the public outdoor

[6] House of Commons Library (n.25), 4.

[7] SI 2020/750.

place or places, or the land, to which the direction relates. The local authority had to restrict access to anyone without a reasonable excuse. A limited list of reasonable excuses was provided in the Regulations but was not exhaustive of the term, availing authorities a large margin of discretion.[8]

As outlined above, a regulatory landscape was created whereby vague rules could be interpreted in variable/divergent ways in different locations. To give some examples of the vagaries and inconsistencies of enforcement, the London Metropolitan Police Service considered the overarching aim of their response to the COVID-19 pandemic 'to encourage people to follow the regulations for the safety of themselves and others' (London Metropolitan Police, n.d.). However, that edict did not seem to be followed in the policing of public demonstrations at Clapham Common in March 2021 following the murder of Sarah Everard by a serving Metropolitan Police Officer (Wayne Couzens) when the police sought to disperse a vigil without taking due account of the right to peaceful and safe protest or the possibility of reasonable excuse (All Party Parliamentary Group on Democracy and the Constitution, 2021; Crown Prosecution Service, 2021b; Home Office & The Rt Hon Priti Patel MP, 2021).[9] The policing of other public demonstrations was equally problematic for several police services (Mead, 2021). Aggressive stances were also adopted by some other police forces, like the Thames Valley Police, which set up special reporting websites for citizens to report breaches of COVID-19 regulations (Thames Valley Police, n.d.) expanded on the trend by issuing weekly reports on enforcement.[10] Some police forces went so far as to use drones to monitor outside gatherings. The Derbyshire Police became notorious for drone surveillance and 'lockdown shaming' of individuals gathering in public outdoor areas who were filmed by the drones. This form of lockdown surveillance was heavily criticised for breaching privacy rights (BBC News, 2020).

---

[8] SI 2020/750, para.7.

[9] See *Leigh v Commissioner of the Metropolis* [2021] EWHC 661 (Admin); *Leigh and oths v Commissioner of the Metropolis* [2022] EWHC 527 (Admin).

[10] See, for example, the 'Enforcement and Response Data' website for Police Scotland (n.d.), which shows the weekly numbers of reports for COVID-19 breaches, and the number of those which were followed up.

3 Implementing COVID-19 Regulations

Meeting the multiple and severe challenges posed by COVID-19 has generated a wide array of legal and other regulatory responses which affect policing throughout the UK. The normative outcomes have comprised varied instruments, shades of persuasion and coercion, overlapping jurisdictions, and public and private actors. The result is a complex regulatory assemblage, in other words, a heterogeneous formation that is 'mobile, emergent and dispersed' (De Goede, 2018). Discretion was here not just for the police but for the citizen and again reflects the idea of policing by consent, which means that policing rests on social acceptance. One further notable point is that most of the leading cases were brought in the High Court in the form of judicial review under the Civil Procedure Rules Part 54. This process is complex and expensive. As stated at the outset, our explanations of this complex landscape will primarily relate to England, which is by far the largest jurisdiction and tended to set the initiative.

In some respects, it is surprising to encounter such a regulatory melange in the UK legal response to COVID-19. The UK state has garnered formidable prowess in handling emergencies, reflected most prominently in its encyclopaedic counterterrorism laws (Walker, 2014). Less widely appreciated are the extensive codes available to the UK government which deal with other real or imagined risks, ranging from floods to meteor strikes and including public health risks. Here too, extensive and detailed legislation has been installed, including the all-encompassing Civil Contingencies Act 2004 ('CCA2004'), which responded to animal health and transportation crises, and adds broadly to the sectoral Public Health (Control of Disease) Act 1984 ('PHA1984') (Walker, 2015; Walker & Broderick, 2006). Despite these available 'all hazards' models, the COVID-19 pandemic induced legislative panic. Rather than utilising the carefully designed laws already in place, the Coronavirus Act 2020 ('CA2020') was passed in response to the outbreak within seven days (19–25 March 2020),[11] having been

[11] See https://services.parliament.uk/Bills/2019-21/coronavirus/stages.html. Some additions followed for Scotland: Coronavirus (Scotland) Act 2020 (Asp.7); Coronavirus (Scotland) (No. 2)

subjected to brief and poorly attended debates, after which Parliament vanished into recess for four weeks. However, the UK government also installed, with even less scrutiny in any format, extensive regulations under the PHA1984 which became the chief legal instruments of policy. These competing legislative sources will now be explained further.[12]

Given the timing and bulk of the CA2020, one might suppose that it would offer the chief legislative platform for a response to COVID-19. But the CA2020 has been relatively shadowy and has mainly impacted through, not so much public policing but various schemes of aid to businesses (Browning et al., 2022) and the furloughing of employees (HM Revenue & Customs, 2020).[13] Proposals to impinge on policing and criminal justice have generally been rebuffed, including severe curtailments (or even abolition) of the right to jury trial (House of Commons Justice Committee, 2019; Quirk, 2020), though the greater use of live video and audio court hearings in the criminal courts are set to persist beyond any emergency (as explained further below).[14] Nevertheless, the CA2020 was not used as much as the PHA1984 to curtail public freedoms. Many of the restrictions affecting individuals (such as the wearing of face masks and limits on gatherings and travel) were lifted in Summer 2021, and the CA2020 was further curtailed by allowing the expiration

---

Act 2020 (asp.10); Coronavirus (Extension and Expiry) (Scotland) Act 2021 (Asp.9). Scotland, Northern Ireland and Wales administrations also relied upon adaptations under the PHA1984; for details, see below.

12 The CA2020 is very extensive (342 pages). Its stated purpose was to implement the UK government's *Coronavirus: Action Plan* of 3 March 2020 (Department of Health and Social Care, 2020b), which sought to 'Contain, Delay, Research, and Mitigate'. That *Plan* was replaced by others, including *Our Plan to Rebuild*, Command Paper 239, 2020; the *Winter Plan* of 2020, Command Paper 324, 2020;a stepped roadmap in Spring 2021 (Cabinet Office, 2021); Health Protection (Coronavirus, Restrictions) (Steps) (England) Regulations 2021, SI 2021/364. and then the *Autumn and Winter Plan* 2021 (HM Government, 2021). While the most contentious legislative measures concerned containing and delaying the spread of coronavirus via varying degrees of lockdown of populations and businesses, the bulk of the legislation is technical and specialised in nature. However, with respect to policing, it allowed for grave impacts on personal liberties. Regulatory powers allowed the enforcement of quarantining under Sect. 51 (Department of Health and Social Care, 2020c), and, under Sect. 52, banning events, gatherings and the use of communal premises. Rights of due process might also be affected under Sects. 53 to 57, by which various pre-trial hearings may take place by live video links.

13 The schemes rely on the CA2020, ss.71, 76.

14 See Police, Crime, Sentencing and Courts Bill 2021–22 HL no.40, cl.169 and Schedule 19 https://bills.parliament.uk/bills/2839.

of around 20 measures in Autumn 2021 (Department of Health & Social Care, 2022).[15]

Accountability could be secured in two main ways. By Section 97, the Secretary of State must prepare and publish a report every two months on the status of the provisions in the Act and that the status of those provisions is 'appropriate' (Department of Health & Social Care, 2020a). Second, by Section 98, the House of Commons (but not the House of Lords) is enabled to debate and vote on the continuation of the Coronavirus Act 2020 every six months.[16] However, after some 18 months of limited use, Parliament seemed to have lost interest in the CA2020. At the renewal debate on 19 October 2021, the Deputy Speaker even refused to allow a vote to take place because of the strong sentiment in favour of renewal.[17] It was deemed to be passed without a vote because the Speaker can determine the will of the House.

Some of these experiences were replicated in the regional jurisdictions of the UK. For instance, the Coronavirus (Scotland) Act 2020 was quickly passed,[18] and the Coronavirus (Extension and Expiry) (Scotland) Act 2021[19] has extended the legislation (with some omissions) at least until 31 March 2022. In Scotland, more concerted (and perhaps opportunistic) efforts were made to suspend trial by jury and to add exceptions to hearsay rules of evidence (Scottish Government, 2020), but they were rebuffed by the vocal opposition of Scottish legal professions.

The CA2020 received Royal Assent on 25 March 2020. Yet the very next day, far more significant policing measures were introduced via the PHA1984, Part 2A which had been inserted by the Health and Social Care Act 2008 following the UK's experience of SARS in 2003 and to give effect to international standards (World Health Organization, 2016). It provides powers under Sections 45C(1), (3)(c), (4)(d), 45F(2) and 45P which authorise the executive authorities to issue regulations to

[15] Coronavirus Act 2020 (Early Expiry) Regulations 2020, SI 202/856.

[16] The initial draft set two years which was a point of criticism: House of Lords Select Committee on the Constitution, *Coronavirus Bill* (2019–21 HL 44) para.8.

[17] Hansard (House of Commons) vol. 649 col.673 19 October 2021, Rosie Winterton.

[18] Asp.7 (devolved legislation applicable to Scotland only).

[19] Asp.19 (devolved legislation applicable to Scotland only).

protect against infectious disease. Under these powers, the Health Protection (Coronavirus, Restrictions) (England) Regulations 2020[20] were issued. Corresponding instruments were issued for Wales,[21] Scotland (Scott, 2020; Shiels, 2020)[22] and Northern Ireland[23] (Holder, 2020) albeit with many inexplicable variations. These regulations expanded upon an earlier regulatory order issued in February 2020[24] which had been, as might be expected for public health legislation, confined to the detention for screening or treatment of potentially infected individuals. In stark contrast, the subsequent powers were directed against the general population. Many later amendments, variants and editions followed and were largely replicated throughout the UK in impact.[25]

The PHA1984 regulations have gone far beyond dealing with the sick. One major aspect of policy was to minimise social interactions, including by 'lockdowns', which prevailed in various forms and levels, including by potential policing enforcement, at least until 19 July 2021 when, in England, most restrictions were lifted (Prime Minister's Office & The Rt Hon Boris Johnson MP, 2021b),[26] though some restrictions resumed because of the emergence of the Omicron variant in November 2021 (Pocklington, 2021).[27] The PHA1984 regulations entailed the enforced closure of some businesses and severe restrictions on others (regulations 4

---

20 SI 2020/350.

21 Health Protection (Coronavirus Restrictions) (Wales) Regulations 2020, SI 2020/353 (W80).

22 Health Protection (Coronavirus) (Restrictions) (Scotland) Regulations 2020, SSI 2020/103.

23 Health Protection (Coronavirus, Restrictions) Regulations (Northern Ireland) 2020, NISR 2020/55.

24 Health Protection (Coronavirus) Regulations 2020, SI 2020/129.

25 See especially (No. 2) SI 2020/684; (No. 3) SI 2020/750; (No. 4) SI 2020/1200; SI 2021/364.

26 Health Protection (Coronavirus, Restrictions) (Steps etc.) (England) (Revocation and Amendment) Regulations 2021, SI 2021/848; Health Protection (Coronavirus, Restrictions) (Self-Isolation) (England) (Amendment) Regulations 2021, SI 2021/851.

27 See Health Protection (Coronavirus, International Travel and Operator Liability) (England) (Amendment) Regulations 2021, (No. 19) SI 2021/1323, (No. 20), SI 2021/1331, (No. 21), SI 2021/1339; Health Protection (Coronavirus, Restrictions) (Self-Isolation) (England) (Amendment) (No. 4) Regulations 2021, SI 2021/1338; Health Protection (Coronavirus, Wearing of Face Coverings) (England) Regulations 2021, SI 2021/1340.

and 5).[28] Most draconian of all, the initial lockdown under regulation 6 stated that, 'no person may leave the place where they are living without reasonable excuse'. Under regulation 7, public gatherings of more than a specified number of people (which varied over time and jurisdiction) were forbidden. A person who contravened these requirements committed an offence, punishable by a fine, and the police were given powers to disperse gatherings and to issue fixed penalty notices to individual transgressors (regulations 8 to 10). Large gatherings (of more than 30 people) in breach of the regulations became subject to a Fixed Penalty Notice of £10,000 just before the August Bank (Public) Holiday 2020.[29] These key regulations grew through hundreds of amendments (Moosavian et al., 2021) and embodied multiple problems: divergences between the CA2020 and the regulations; obscurities in the meaning of the regulations; confusing government and guidance, especially the status and enforceability of police guidance (House of Lords Delegated Powers & Regulatory Reform Committee, 2021; House of Lords Select Committee on the Constitution, 2021a; Sorabji & Vaughan, 2021); excessive or inconsistent police enforcement; and arguments that some elements have been *ultra vires* (most of which failed because of a strong dose of judicial deference to the travails of the government).[30] As well as judicial deference, legislative quiescence prevailed since most regulations under the PHA 1984 were not required to be approved in advance of issuance and, even if they were, the scrutiny often did not happen or was perfunctory (House of Lords Delegated Powers & Regulatory Reform Committee, 2021; House of Lords Secondary Legislation Scrutiny Committee, 2020; House of Lords Select Committee on the Constitution, 2021a; Scottish Parliament Delegated Powers & Law Reform Committee, 2022).

[28] Further enforcement powers were added by the Health Protection (Coronavirus, Restrictions) (Local Authority Enforcement Powers and Amendment) (England) Regulations 2020, SI 2020/1375.

[29] Health Protection (Coronavirus) (Restrictions on Holding of Gatherings and Amendment) (England) Regulations 2020, SI 2020/907, r.2.

[30] See especially *R (Francis) v Secretary of State for Health & Social Care* [2020] EWHC 3287 (Admin); *R (Dolan) v Secretary of State for Health & Social Care* [2020] EWHC 1786 and [2020] EWCA Civ 1605; *R (Hussein) v Secretary of State for Health & Social Care* [2020] EWHC 1392; *Philip for Judicial Review of the Closure of Places of Worship in Scotland* [2021] CSOH 32.

A more appropriate set of powers, designed exactly with major emergencies in mind, is the CCA2004. This legislation consolidated and expanded legal duties and powers to ensure that public authorities prepare for contingencies (Part 1) (Davies, 2021a),[31] and can respond even in an emergency (Part II) to, the wide variety of risks as set out in the *National Risk Register* (in which pandemic influenza is high on the list) (HM Government, 2020). While the CCA2004 was impelled by domestic and global crises, it was not enacted in haste but benefited from a prolonged consultation period led by a special parliamentary joint select committee (House of Lords & House of Commons, 2002), and it ensures vital legal and parliamentary oversight to avert improper responses. The widest range of risks is addressed: terrorist attacks, protests, environmental events, plus human and animal disease pandemics. Consequently, the CCA2004 was expressly designed to tackle circumstances such as COVID-19. Indeed, the Speaker's Counsel, Daniel Greenberg, confirmed 'unequivocally that the powers under the Civil Contingencies Act (…) are absolutely appropriate for the current emergency'.[32] Yet, the UK government resorted to alternative legislation. This failure may relate to a lack of capacity or prioritisation in the relevant branch of state, the Cabinet Office's Civil Contingencies Secretariat, which should provide the core of emergency management, but has been missing in action in terms of clear coordination and messaging (Cabinet Office, 2018; Telegraph Reporters, 2020; Shilson-Thomas et al., 2021). Perhaps there has been some hollowing out of its authority both downwards through devolution and sideways by the growth of the powerful Environment Agency which has 10,000 staff compared to less than 100 within the Cabinet Office's Civil Contingencies Secretariat (Davies, 2021c).[33] Reliance on the CCA2004 could have avoided three major failings which beset the handling of the COVID-19 pandemic in the UK (House of Commons Health and Social Care and Science and Technology Committees, 2021).

---

[31] Part I already requires what the National Audit Office has called for in terms of coordination and the development of 'playbooks': *Initial Learning from the Government's Response to COVID-19* (2021–22 HC 66).

[32] Hansard (House of Commons) vol.674 cols.118–119 23 March 2020 David Davis.

[33] Hansard (House of Commons) UIN 207,215, 17 January 2019.

First, the levels of accountability and oversight were inadequate. The judicial and especially the legislative failures are perhaps reflected in the executive's choice of legislative instruments. Thus, the emphasis on the PHA1984 and the CA2020 conveniently avoided much more stringent oversight and accountability in the CCA2004 (which includes approval by Parliament every 28 days and lists limits on the exercise of powers, including in relation to criminal justice, in Part II). By contrast the PHA1984 and CA2020 pay less heed to the protection of rights, with widespread and often inconsistent impacts on the rights such as to run businesses or to travel abroad.[34]

Second, reliance on the CCA2004 alone could have unified the legislative process and so reduced the proliferation of instruments, each source bearing different processes and consequences and sometimes interactions between them. Thus, a single source could have more readily avoided some of the confusion between guidance, especially police guidance, as compared to the primary regulatory texts (House of Lords Select Committee on the Constitution, 2021a; Sorabji & Vaughan, 2021). The inability of Ministers to answer 'basic questions' about the choice and meaning of measures was condemned as 'lamentable and unacceptable' by the House of Commons Public Administration and Constitutional Affairs Committee.[35] As suggested by the Hansard Society problems ensuing from an inadequate legislative superstructure include: rapid amendment, repeat amendment and revocation arising from poor quality of drafting and misconceptions, technical errors and omissions (Cormacain & Bar-Siman-Tov, 2020; Hansard Society, 2020). Unclear powers also increase the risk of arbitrary or inconsistent application and are more susceptible to legal challenge. One illustration of the confusion relates to the powers relating to lockdowns. The extent of these legal powers, and their variance from accompanying guidance (Home Affairs Committee, 2019), has caused confusion, the vacating of convictions (as

[34] The restrictions on travel abroad emerged in June 2020, when track and trace systems were considered more effective to monitor the restrictions. See Health Protection (Coronavirus, International Travel) (England) Regulations 2020, SI 2020/568, and 2021, SI 2021/582; House of Lords Secondary Legislation Scrutiny Committee, *37th Report* (2019–21 HL 189).

[35] See *Government Transparency and Accountability during COVID 19* (2019–21 HC 803) para.143.

already described), the need to revise and reissue regulations, and huge backlogs in court business (Davies, 2021b; Justice Committee, 2021). Resulting problems for the police have been mitigated by the sensible compliance of the public and the calming down of police approaches, including by reference to the College of Policing's mantra, 'Engage, Explain, Encourage, Enforce'.

A third potential benefit of the CCA2004 is its national coverage, and so it can better ensure unity of purpose and action, whereas the PHA1984 and the CA2020 are subject to more possibilities of regional variations, which have nothing to do with Scottish, Welsh or Irish mutations in the virus or even distinct legal features in those jurisdictions but are attributable to variant policy choices without clear rational basis and without much regard for public confusion.[36] For example, Scottish legislation was passed in Autumn 2020 to add restrictions on leaving or entering Scotland, and these were then imposed to restrict travel to areas of north-west England, even though they were largely unenforceable and even though parts of Scotland had worse infection rates (Massie & Elliot, 2021).[37] In addition, localised inputs and controls can tempt local politicians into decisions or behaviour which appears to show partiality, such as the attendance by Northern Ireland Ministers at the funeral of Bobby Storey on 30 June 2020 in potential breach of regulations about large gatherings (Her Majesty's Inspectorate of Constabulary and Fire & Rescue Services, 2020; Public Prosecution Service, 2021), though allegations of favouritism have also arisen in England in connection with the non-prosecution of government adviser Dominic Cummings.[38] The assertion of the primacy of devolved administrations in public health

---

[36] Compare: Health Protection (Coronavirus, Restrictions) (All Tiers) (England) Regulations 2020, SI 2020/1374; Health Protection (Coronavirus) (Restrictions and Requirements) (Local Levels) (Scotland) Regulations 2020, SSI 2020/344. Wales and Northern Ireland operated unitary restrictions across their entire jurisdiction: Health Protection (Coronavirus Restrictions and Functions of Local Authorities) (Amendment) (Wales) Regulations 2020, SI 2020/1409; Health Protection (Coronavirus, Restrictions) (No. 2) Regulations (Northern Ireland) 2020 and Amendment Nos. 15 and 17, NISR 2020/150, 256 and 287. See House of Lords Select Committee on the Constitution (2021a).

[37] See Health Protection (Coronavirus) (Restrictions and Requirements) (Local Levels) (Scotland) Regulations 2020, SSI 2020/344, Sch.7A, as amended by SSI 2020/389, SSI 2021/193, 211, 242 and 262.

[38] *Redston v DPP* [2020] EWHC 2962 (Admin).

affairs only makes sense if one views the COVID-19 pandemic as a localised emergency. In reality, a national and comprehensive response is usually required due to its global reach. Arising out of the jurisdictional confusion created by a sectoral public health approach, which then is amplified by devolved administrations, many of the first 200 convictions under the PHA1984 had to be set aside: 'Errors usually involved Welsh regulations being applied in England or vice versa' (Chief Crown Prosecution, 2020). Likewise, the House of Commons Scottish Affairs Committee expressed concern about jurisdictional divergence when dealing with exactly the same problems and wondered how Scottish interests might fit alongside institutions including the Cabinet Office structures such as the Cabinet Office Briefing Rooms (COBR) and the Joint Biosecurity Centre (Evans, 2021; McEwen et al., 2019). Internal to Scotland, enhanced monitoring has been accorded to policing activities (Scott et al., n.d.), but such efforts are of limited utility if standard-setting and policy also happens elsewhere and if local variant policing efforts cause further public uncertainty when they receive mixed messages from national media.

The foregoing regulatory excursus was terminated by official plans issued on 21 February 2022, *COVID-19 Response: Living with COVID-19* (Cabinet Office, 2022a). The official explanation was that the protection of vaccines had transformed the risk calculation, along with the milder Omicron form of COVID-19. Thus, it was time to remove almost all of the remaining restrictions (including most of the 20 out of 40 measures under the CA2020 which remained after 2021 and even vaccination compulsion for care workers),[39] subject to the permanent retention of four CA2020 measures (including live links in courts).[40] The CCA2004 and PHA1984 remain available, and the former has been given an almost entirely clean bill of health following a review by the Cabinet Office (2022c). This treatment of COVID as another endemic winter illness is viewed by some as unwise, but its faith in medical science and the prioritisation of individual freedom starkly contrasts

[39] Health and Social Care Act 2008 (Regulated Activities) (Amendment) Coronavirus) Regulations 2021, SI 2021/891.

[40] Compare the plans in Scotland to retain more powers: Coronavirus (Recovery and Reform) (Scotland) Bill 2022 SP Bill 9.

with contemporary turmoil elsewhere such as the 2022 declaration of an emergency in Canada against Truck Convoy protests.[41]

4 COVID-19 Police Surveillance

This part of the chapter outlines key forms of surveillance that have been employed during the COVID-19 pandemic in the UK, in particular the use of mobile technologies, to gain insight on compliance with legislation and guidance to control its spread. First the English 'Test and Trace' and equivalent Scottish 'Test and Protect' strategies are outlined as instances of surveillance targeted at virus detection through a mobile phone app. In the English context, this development took a long time and much money to develop, and experienced frequent flaws (Pagliari, 2020). After discussing the app, this section turns to an analysis of both self-reporting, needed for testing, tracing and protecting, and the reporting of other contacts, which was part of the surveillance system that helped enforce COVID-19 regulations. Were it not for this participation of citizens as agents of surveillance, regulations would have remained unenforced to a large extent.

When the Test and Trace system was first introduced in England in 2020 (UK Health Security Agency, 2020), it worked on the basis that people experiencing COVID-19 symptoms had to self-isolate for at least a week and undertake a test, either at home or at a testing centre. When testing positive, they would be notified by the Test and Trace service with instructions on how to share details of possible infected contacts. Contact tracers then informed contacts by email, text or phone that they had to self-isolate for fourteen days. The information on test results and contacts is held in the database of Public Health England's Contact Tracing and Advisory Service (Vize, 2020). The UK Government's Scientific Advisory Group for Emergencies monitored Test and Trace from its introduction in May 2020 but in September 2020 described the system as 'having a marginal impact on transmission' (Scientific Advisory Group

[41] PC 2022–0106, https://orders-in-council.canada.ca/attachment.php?attach=41560&lang=en, 14 February 2022.

for Emergencies, 2020). Problems included ongoing testing delays and low levels of public acceptance that the restriction of freedoms inherent in this system was justified by its public health benefits, with consequent detriment for rates of observance of self-isolation requirements (Cheng et al., 2021; O'Hagan & Westerman, 2021; Smith et al., 2021).

A corresponding system of 'Test and Protect' was adopted in Scotland (NHS Inform, n.d.). Like the situation in England, positive COVID-19 cases would be contacted by the National Contact Tracing Centre and asked for details of people with whom they have been in contact. These individuals are then also contacted and asked to take a test. The Test and Protect system in Scotland did not receive the same level of criticism as did the Test and Trace service in England, though much of the variant perceptions related to controversy surrounding the immense costs (Public Accounts Committee, 2019) and the allocation of lucrative appointments and contracts[42] rather than the intrinsic value of, or support for, the respective systems (gender, age and ethnicity were more important variables [Smith et al., 2021]).

Test and Trace was then included in a more user-friendly NHS App, in September 2020 (National Health Service, n.d.). Between its launch on 24 September 2020 and the end of 2020, the app was downloaded on 21 million separate devices and, between 1 November and 11 December 2020, it was regularly used by an average of about 16.5 million users, which is about 49% of the eligible population, or 28% of the total population of England and Wales. Moreover, 72% of app-using individuals who tested positive for COVID-19 consented to an app-based exposure notification being sent after testing positive (Wang, 2021; Wymant et al., 2021). In Scotland, the Test and Protect service was supported by the 'Protect Scotland' app, also launched at the end of 2020 (The Scottish Government, n.d.). It was downloaded more than 2 million times but shows only about 900,000 'active' users (BBC, 2021). The NHS App and associated structures withstood most court challenges on grounds of infringement of privacy[43] but remained controversial on those grounds

[42] See *R (Good Law Project and Runnymede Trust) v Prime Minister and Secretary of State for Health and Social Care* [2022] EWHC 298 (Admin).

[43] *R (Francis) v Secretary of State for Health & Social Care* [2020] EWHC 3287 (Admin); *Williams v Minister of Health for Northern Ireland and Department of Health for Northern*

(Guinchard, 2021; Joint Committee on Human Rights, 2019; Oswald & Grace, 2020).[44]

5 Conclusion

A full and considered verdict on policing during the COVID-19 pandemic and indeed the performance of other state apparatus, including the health service and government departments, must await the inquiry chaired by Baroness Heather Hallett that began work in Spring 2022, and has been furnished with the powers under the Inquiries Act 2005 (Cabinet Office et al., 2021). On 12 May 2022, the Chair asked the UK Prime Minister to extend the terms of reference of the Inquiry to consider (1) children and young people, including the impact on health, well-being and social care education and early years provision; (2) impacts on mental health and well-being of the UK population; and (3) collaboration between central government, Devolved Administrations, local authorities and the voluntary and community sector (UK COVID-19 Inquiry, 2022).[45] A separate inquiry has also been commissioned in Scotland under Lady Poole (Scottish Government, 2021).

In the meantime, some very helpful findings on overall policing performance were made available in early 2022 by the Police Foundation and Crest Advisory report, *Policing the Pandemic* (Aitkenhead et al., 2022), which chime with the findings in this chapter. It reported that support for the police approach to enforcing the COVID-19 regulations, as conditioned by the College of Policing mantra (Engage, Explain, Encourage and Enforce), was relatively well-received as welcome adaptation of traditional 'policing by consent' even in the tribulation of a pandemic. The public seemed to recognise the difficulties faced by the police in terms of uncertain legal expectations, the absence of extra

Ireland [2022] NIQB 12; *In the matter of an application by Risteard O'Murchu* [2022] NIQB 13.

[44] At the time of writing, the systems were due to be terminated following the latest policy statement, *COVID-19 Response: Living with COVID-19* (Cabinet Office, 2022a).

[45] https://bit.ly/39fdS6S.

resources and the intrusions invited into so many aspects of private lives. Of course, public consent was not aided by policing actions which were viewed as either too interventionist (such as the policing or protests) or too lackadaisical (the non-prosecution of government adviser, Dominic Cummings[46] and the revelation of the 'Partygate' alleged gatherings in government offices, often with police officers in attendance (Cabinet Office, 2022b; Metropolitan Police, 2022) might be cited here). As for the latter, by 12 May 2022, the London Metropolitan Police issued some 100 'fixed penalty notices' for breaches of COVID-19 rules through primarily social gatherings in Downing Street and other government buildings (Parkinson, 2022). The Prime Minister, his wife and the Chancellor of the Exchequer had each received such a penalty for breach (Scott, 2022), which they have decided not to challenge (the prospects for which are not great, as illustrated by the case of *Kozubikova and oths* [2022] NIQB 22). Assuming that the breaches were not wilful, a generous inference is that the defaulters had been ensnared by the lack of legal clarity inherent in the rules that they enacted. An alternative explanation is that it was never the Government's intention that (in England) the legislation would be strictly policed, but it was promulgated to engender a sense of individual and social responsibility to observe public health precautions. One abiding concern seemed to be that the National Health Service should not be overwhelmed,[47] nor indeed should the police and criminal courts collapse under the weight of regulatory enforcement.

Overall, the police's response displayed a high level of organisational resilience, and core policing services were maintained. However, the avoidance of external shortcomings, such as the shoddy design of the regulatory frameworks and the, sometimes chaotic, roll-out of policies and projects, would have greatly aided policing to be more effective and fair. The controversy that arose in respect of a particular event at No. 10 Downing Street in respect of which at least one attendee had received

---

[46] See *Redston v DPP* [2020] EWHC 2962 (Admin).

[47] Dominic Cummings, a former chief adviser to the Prime Minister and widely discredited himself for breach of the regulations (Cummings, 2020), has asserted that the Prime Minister doubted that the National Health Service would be overwhelmed and said (allegedly) that he was not prepared to lock down the country to save people in their 80 s (Elgot, 2021).

a Fixed Penalty Notice (FPN), but not the Prime Minister (BBC News, 2022), exposed the Metropolitan Police to some scrutiny of its decision-making process when issuing such Notices. Strictly speaking, a FPN is an administrative penalty and a creature of statute. It is an alternative to prosecution. It does not constitute a conviction, and it is not a fine (properly so-called). The FPN is an exception to the sharp distinction that is drawn in English law between criminal and civil law processes. But the controversy highlights the fact that the police are not required to give written reasons for decisions taken with respect to the issuance of FPNs notwithstanding that the police perform a quasi-judicial role when interpreting words and phrases in the legislation, deciding whether or not there has been a breach of the rules, and whether to issue a FPN.[48]

The House of Commons Public Administration and Constitutional Affairs Committee has indicated that pre-legislative scrutiny of statutory measures, which are designed to meet a given emergency, might help to avoid errors made in respect of the COVID-19 regime.[49] However, 'on the shelf' legislation might not be wholly practicable given the difficulty of predicting, accurately, the nature of the next emergency or pandemic. As for England, it seems likely that, with the benefit of hindsight, the government would have imposed lockdowns with greater circumscription and would have relied more on other harm-minimisation policies. But the emergency circumstances are known for their tendency to encourage state authorities to grab powers, ignore principles, rules and procedures, and demand compliance in the national interest. Even with carefully designed powers already available (such as the CCA2004), one cannot be confident that the same mistakes would not be made again, even after Baroness Heather Hallett has delivered her wisest words.

When taking the management of the pandemic as a whole, the UK did, however, get many things right. It mostly avoided the over-enforcement of vague rules and started the vaccination roll-out early. It thereby put more emphasis on the protection of its citizens and public health than on the policing of wrongdoers. More importantly, unlike

[48] In relation to unfair jeopardy, especially when the penalty for some breaches is fixed at £10000, see House of Commons et al. (2021).

[49] House of Commons Public Administration and Constitutional Affairs Committee, *Coronavirus Act 2020 Two Years On* (2021–22 HC 978).

in many other countries, the vaccine was made available to everyone in the UK, without discrimination in relation to, in particular, immigration status. This could be considered a voluntary suspension of the policing of immigration offences for the benefit of public health. Furthermore, vaccination mandates, for example for students and teaching staff, were never put in place. The UK avoided longer restrictions and lockdowns as well as achieving a 75% vaccination rate without significant legal enforcement. It thereby prevented (at least a COVID-19 related) large-scale deterioration of trust in the government and its executive.

References

Adams, T. M., & Stewart, L. D. (2015). Chaos theory and organizational crisis: A theoretical analysis of the challenges faced by the New Orleans Police Department during Hurricane Katrina. *Public Organization Review, 15*(3), 415–431. https://doi.org/10.1007/s11115-014-0284-9

Aitkenhead, E., Clements, J., Lumley, J., Muir, R., Redgrave, H., & Skidmore, M. (2022). *Policing the pandemic*. The Police Foundation. https://www.police-foundation.org.uk/2017/wpcontent/uploads/2010/10/policing_the_pandemic_final.pdf

All Party Parliamentary Group on Democracy and the Constitution. (2021). *Police Power and the Right to Peaceful Protest: An Inquiry into police conduct at the Clapham Vigil and Bristol Protests and the implications for the Police Crime Sentencing and Courts Bill by the All- Party Parliamentary Group on Democracy and the Constitution. Funded by the Joseph Rowntree Reform Trust.* Institute for Constitutional and Democratic Research. Accessed on 24 February 2022, from https://netpol.org/wpcontent/uploads/2021/06/Clapham-and-Bristol-Inquiry-Report-APPROVED.pdf

BBC News. (2020). *Coronavirus: Peak District drone police criticised for "lockdown shaming"*. Accessed on 24 February 2022, from https://www.bbc.com/news/uk-england-derbyshire-52055201

BBC News. (2021). *Covid in Scotland: Thousands turn off tracking app.* Accessed on 24 February 2022, from https://www.bbc.com/news/uk-scotland-57941343

BBC News. (2022). *Partygate: Boris Johnson facing questions after photos emerge.* Accessed on 24 May 2022, from https://www.bbc.com/news/uk-politics-61560535

Boer, M., Bervoets, E., & Hak, L. (2022). Preparing for future pandemic policing. *European Law Enforcement Research Bulletin, (SCE 5)*, 261–271. https://doi.org/10.7725/eulerb.v0iSCE%205.491

Bonkiewicz, L., & Ruback, R. B. (2010). Policing Iowa's Katrina: Law enforcement response in flood disasters. *Policing: A Journal of Policy and Practice, 4*(4), 373–383. https://doi.org/10.1093/police/paq034

Bonkiewicz, L., & Ruback, R. B. (2012). The role of the police in evacuations: Responding to the social impact of a disaster. *Police Quarterly, 15*(2), 137–156. https://doi.org/10.1177/1098611112442808

Brown, J. (2020). *Coronavirus: Enforcing restrictions* (No. 9024). House of Commons Library. Accessed on 24 February 2022, from https://researchbriefings.files.parliament.uk/documents/CBP-9024/CBP-9024.pdf

Brown, J. (2021). *Policing in the UK* (No. 8582). House of Commons Library. Accessed on 24 February 2022, from https://researchbriefings.files.parliament.uk/documents/CBP-8582/CBP-8582.pdf

Browning, S., Seely, A., Sandford, M., Shalchi, A., & Powell, A. (2022). *Coronavirus: Support for businesses.* House of Commons Library. Accessed on 24 February 2022, from https://commonslibrary.parliament.uk/research-briefings/cbp-8847/

Cabinet Office. (2018). *Preparation and planning for emergencies.* GOV.UK. Accessed on 24 February 2022, from https://www.gov.uk/guidance/preparation-and-planning-for-emergencies-the-capabilities-programme

Cabinet Office. (2021). *COVID-19 Response—Spring 2021.* GOV.UK. Accessed on 24 February 2022, from https://www.gov.uk/government/publications/covid-19-response-spring-2021/covid-19-response-spring-2021

Cabinet Office. (2022a). *COVID-19 Response: Living with COVID-19.* GOV.UK. Accessed on 24 February 2022a, from https://www.gov.uk/government/publications/covid-19-response-living-with-covid-19

Cabinet Office. (2022b). *Investigation into Alleged Gatherings on Government Premises during Covid Restrictions—Update.* GOV.UK. Accessed on 24 February 2022b, from https://assets.publishing.service.gov.uk/government/uploads/system/uploads/attachment_data/file/1051374/Investigation_into_alleged_gatherings_on_government_premises_during_Covid_restrictions_-_Update.pdf

Cabinet Office. (2022c). *The Civil Contingencies Act 2004–2022c Post-Implementation Review.* GOV.UK. Accessed on 24 February 2022, from https://assets.publishing.service.gov.uk/government/uploads/system/uploads/attachment_data/file/1076209/cca-pir-2022.pdf

Cabinet Office. Prime Minister's Office, 10 Downing Street., & The Rt Hon Boris Johnson MP. (2021). *Prime Minister announces COVID-19 Inquiry Chair.* GOV.UK. Accessed on 24 February 2022, from https://www.gov.uk/government/news/prime-minister-announces-covid-19-inquiry-chair

Caluori, J., & Clements, J. (2020). *Policing the COVID-19 lockdown—What the public thinks.* Crest. Accessed on 24 February 2022, from https://www.crestadvisory.com/post/policing-the-covid-19-lockdown-what-the-public-thinks

Carrera, S., Mitsilegas, V., & Stefan, M. (2021). *Criminal justice, fundamental rights and the rule of law in the digital age.* Centre for European Policy Studies. Accessed on 24 February 2022, from https://www.ceps.eu/ceps-publications/criminal-justice-fundamental-rights-and-the-rule-of-law-in-the-digital-age/

Cheng, H., Cohen, T., & Lin, H. (2021). Test, trace, and isolate in the UK: Gaps in adherence undermine effectiveness at every stage. *British Medical Journal, 372*(822), 1–2. https://doi.org/10.1136/bmj.n822

Chief Crown Prosecution. (2020). *CPS announces review findings for first 200 cases under coronavirus laws.* Accessed on 24 February 2022, from https://www.cps.gov.uk/cps/news/cps-announces-review-findings-first-200-cases-under-coronavirus-laws

Committee of Public Accounts. (2019). *Transforming Courts and Tribunals: progress review.* House of Commons. Accessed on 24 February 2022, from https://publications.parliament.uk/pa/cm201919/cmselect/cmpubacc/27/27.pdf

Cormacain, R., & Bar-Siman-Tov, I. (2020). Legislatures in the Time of Covid-19. *The Theory and Practice of Legislation, 8*(1–2), 3–9. https://doi.org/10.1080/20508840.2020.1816017

Courts and Tribunals Judiciary. (2022). *Lord Chief Justice—Remote attendance by advocates in the Crown Court.* Accessed on 24 February 2022, from https://www.judiciary.uk/announcements/message-from-the-lord-chief-justice-remote-attendance-by-advocates-in-the-crown-court

Criminal Justice Joint Inspection. (2022). *The impact of the Covid-19 pandemic on the criminal justice system—A progress report.* Accessed on 24 February 2022, from https://www.justiceinspectorates.gov.uk/cjji/wp-content/uploads/sites/2/2022/05/CJ-Covid-19-recovery-progress-report-web-2022.pdf

Crown Prosecution Service. (2021a). *Coronavirus review findings, March-August 2021a|The Crown Prosecution Service.* Accessed on 24 February

2022, from https://www.cps.gov.uk/cps/news/coronavirus-review-findings-march-august-2021

Crown Prosecution Service. (2021b). *Wayne Couzens sentenced to whole life term for the kidnap, rape and murder of Sarah Everard*. Accessed on 24 February 2022, from https://www.cps.gov.uk/cps/news/wayne-couzens-sentenced-whole-life-term-kidnap-rape-and-murder-sarah-everard

Cummings, D. (2020). *Read in full: Durham police statement on Dominic Cummings.* Politics Home. Accessed on 24 May 2022, from https://www.politicshome.com/news/article/read-in-full-durham-police-statement-on-dominic-cummings

Currenti, R., & Flatley, J. (2020). *Policing the pandemic: Detailed analysis on police enforcement of the Public Health Regulations and an assessment on disproportionality across ethnic groups (No. 15).* National Police Chiefs' Council. Accessed on 24 February 2022, from https://cdn.prgloo.com/media/download/608327f7e62a4432a59ce05c5c1554bc

Davies, G. (2021a). *Initial Learning from the Government's Response to COVID 19.* National Audit Office. Accessed on 24 February 2022, from https://www.nao.org.uk/wp-content/uploads/2021a/05/Initial-learning-from-the-governments-response-to-the-COVID-19-pandemic.pdf

Davies, G. (2021b). *Reducing the backlog in criminal courts.* National Audit Office. Accessed on 24 February 2022, from https://www.nao.org.uk/wp-content/uploads/2021b/10/Reducing-the-backlog-in-criminal-courts.pdf

Davies, G. (2021c). *The government's preparedness for the COVID-19 pandemic: lessons for government on risk management.* National Audit Office. Accessed on 24 February 2022, from https://www.nao.org.uk/wp-content/uploads/2021c/11/The-governments-preparedness-for-the-COVID-19-pandemic-lessons-for-government-on-risk-management.pdf

Demir, M., & Park, S. (2021). The Effect of COVID-19 on domestic violence and assaults. *Criminal Justice Review,* 1–19. https://doi.org/10.1177/07340168211061160

Department of Health and Social Care. (2020a). *Coronavirus Act reports.* GOV.UK. Accessed on 24 February 2022, from https://www.gov.uk/government/collections/coronavirus-act-two-monthly-reports

Department of Health and Social Care. (2020b). *Coronavirus: Action Plan. A guide to what you can expect across the UK.* Department of Health & Social Care, Scottish Government, Department of Health, Welsh Government. Accessed on 24 February 2022, from https://www.gov.uk/government/publications/coronavirus-action-plan

Department of Health and Social Care. (2020c). *Memorandum to the Joint Committee on Human Rights: The Coronavirus Bill* 2020c. Accessed on 24 February 2022, from https://publications.parliament.uk/pa/bills/cbill/58-01/0122/Memorandum%20to%20the%20Joint%20Committee%20on%20Human%20Rights%20-%20The%20Coronavirus%20Bill%202020.pdf

Department of Health & Social Care. (2022). *Two Monthly Report on the status on the non- devolved provisions of the Coronavirus Act 2020: January 2022.* Accessed on 24 February 2022, from https://assets.publishing.service.gov.uk/government/uploads/system/uploads/attachment_data/file/1050693/coronavirus-act-2020-eleventh-two-monthly-report-web-accessible.pdf

Elgot, J. (2021). *Dominic Cummings tells BBC Johnson denied Covid would overwhelm NHS.* The Guardian. Accessed on 24 May 2022, from https://www.theguardian.com/politics/2021/jul/19/dominic-cummings-tells-bbc-that-pm-denied-covid-would-overwhelm-nhs

Emsley, C. (2013). Peel's principles, police principles. In J. M. Brown (Ed.), *The future of policing* (pp. 11–22). Routledge.

Evans, G. P. (2021). Devolution and COVID-19: Towards a "new normal" in the territorial constitution? *Public Law, 1*, 19–27.

Fyfe, N. R., & Scott, K. (2013). In search of sustainable policing? Creating a national police force in Scotland. In N. R. Fyfe, J. Terpstra, & P. Tops (Eds.), *Centralizing forces? Comparative perspectives on contemporary police reform in Northern and Western Europe* (pp. 119–135). Eleven.

Goede, M. de (2018). Counter-Terrorism Financing Assemblages after 9/11. In C. King, C Walker, & J. Gurulé (Eds.), *The Palgrave handbook of criminal and terrorism financing law* (pp. 761). Palgrave MacMillan.

Gray, A. (2015). The right to confrontation in common law systems: A critical comparison. *New Criminal Law Review, 18*(1), 129–165. https://doi.org/10.1525/nclr.2015.18.1.129

Grieve, J. G. D. (2015). Historical perspective: British policing and the democratic ideal. In P. Wankhade & D. Weir (Eds.), *Police Services* (pp. 427–444). Springer.

Guinchard, A. (2021). Our digital footprint under Covid-19: Should we fear the UK digital contact tracing app? *International Review of Law, Computers and Technology, 35*(1), 84–97. https://doi.org/10.1080/13600869.2020.1794569

Hansard Society. (2020). *Coronavirus Statutory Instruments Dashboard, 2020–2022.* Accessed on 24 February 2022, from https://www.hansardsociety.org.uk/publications/data/coronavirus-statutory-instruments-dashboard

Henley, J. (2021). *Netherlands shaken by third night of riots over Covid curfew*. The Guardian. Accessed on 24 February 2022, from https://www.theguardian.com/world/2021/jan/26/netherlands-third-night-riots-covid-curfew-lockdown-protesters

Her Majesty's Inspectorate of Constabulary and Fire & Rescue Services (HMICFRS). (2020). *The Police Service of Northern Ireland: An inspection into the Police Service of Northern Ireland's handling of the Bobby Storey funeral on 30 June 2020*. Accessed on 24 February 2022, from https://www.justiceinspectorates.gov.uk/hmicfrs/wp-content/uploads/inspection-into-psni-handling-of-the-bobby-storey-funeral-30-june-2020.pdf

Her Majesty's Inspectorate of Constabulary and Fire & Rescue Services (HMICFRS). (2022). *PEEL assessments 2021/22*. Accessed on 24 February 2022, from https://www.justiceinspectorates.gov.uk/hmicfrs/peel-assessments/what-is-peel/peel-assessments-2021-22/

HM Government. (2020). *National Risk Register 2020 edition*. Accessed on 24 February 2022, from https://assets.publishing.service.gov.uk/government/uploads/system/uploads/attachment_data/file/952959/6.6920_CO_CCS_s_National_Risk_Register_2020_11-1-21-FINAL.pdf

HM Government. (2021). *COVID-19 Response: Autumn and Winter Plan 2021*. Accessed on 24 February 2022, from https://assets.publishing.service.gov.uk/government/uploads/system/uploads/attachment_data/file/1017404/COVID-19-response-autumn-and-winter-plan-2021.pdf

HM Revenue & Customs. (2020). *Coronavirus Job Retention Scheme*. GOV.UK. Accessed on 24 February 2022, from https://www.gov.uk/government/collections/coronavirus-job-retention-scheme

Holder, D. (2020). From special powers to legislating the lockdown: The Health Protection (Coronavirus, Restrictions) Regulations (Northern Ireland) 2020. *Northern Ireland Legal Quarterly*, *71*(4), 537–555. https://doi.org/10.53386/nilq.v71i4.915

Home Affairs Committee. (2019). *Home Office Preparedness for COVID 19 (Coronavirus): Policing*. House of Commons. Accessed on 24 February 2022, from https://committees.parliament.uk/publications/686/documents/3298/default/

Home Office & The Rt Hon Priti Patel MP. (2021). *Home Secretary appoints chair to Sarah Everard inquiry*. GOV.UK. Accessed on 24 February 2022, from https://www.gov.uk/government/news/home-secretary-appoints-chair-to-sarah-everard-inquiry

House of Commons Health and Social Care and Science and Technology Committees. (2021). *Coronavirus: Lessons Learned to Date*. House of

Commons. Accessed on 24 February 2022, from https://committees.parliament.uk/publications/7496/documents/78687/default/

House of Commons Justice Committee. (2019). *Coronavirus (COVID-19): The impact on courts*. UK Parliament. Accessed on 24 February 2022, from https://publications.parliament.uk/pa/cm5801/cmselect/cmjust/519/51908.htm

House of Commons. (2022). *Courts: Coronavirus. Question for Ministry of Justice* UIN 120753. UK Parliament. Accessed on 24 February 2022, from https://questions-statements.parliament.uk/written-questions/detail/2022-02-08/120753

House of Commons., House of Lords., & Joint Committee on Human Rights. (2021). *The Government response to covid-19: Fixed penalty notices: Fourteenth Report of Session 2019–21*. Accessed on 24 February 2022, from https://publications.parliament.uk/pa/jt5801/jtselect/jtrights/1364/1364.pdf

House of Lords & House of Commons. (2002). *Draft Civil Contingencies Bill Session 2002–03 Report and evidence*. The Stationary Office Limited. Accessed on 24 February 2022, from https://publications.parliament.uk/pa/jt200203/jtselect/jtdcc/184/184.pdf

House of Lords Delegated Powers and Regulatory Reform Committee. (2021). *Democracy Denied? The urgent need to rebalance power between Parliament and the Executive*. House of Lords. Accessed on 24 February 2022, from https://committees.parliament.uk/publications/7960/documents/82286/default/

House of Lords House and of Commons Joint Committee on Statutory Instruments. (2021). *Rule of Law Themes from COVID-19 Regulations*. House of Lords House of Commons. Accessed on 24 February 2022, from https://committees.parliament.uk/publications/6952/documents/72746/default/

House of Lords Secondary Legislation Scrutiny Committee. (2020). *Government by Diktat: A call to return power to Parliament*. The House of Lords. Accessed on 24 February 2022, from https://committees.parliament.uk/publications/7941/documents/82225/default/

House of Lords Select Committee on the Constitution. (2021a). *COVID-19 and the use and scrutiny of emergency powers*. House of Lords. Accessed on 24 February 2022, from https://committees.parliament.uk/publications/6212/documents/69015/default/

House of Lords Select Committee on the Constitution. (2021b). *Select Committee on the Constitution COVID-19 and the Courts*. UK Parliament. Accessed on 24 February 2022, from https://publications.parliament.uk/pa/ld5801/ldselect/ldconst/257/25702.htm

Joint Committee on Human Rights. (2019). *Human Rights and the Government's Response to Covid-19: Digital Contact Tracing*. House of Commons House of Lords. Accessed on 24 February 2022, from https://publications.parliament.uk/pa/jt5801/jtselect/jtrights/343/343.pdf

Judiciary of Scotland. (2020). *First jury trial since lockdown*. Accessed on 24 February 2022, from https://www.judiciary.scot/home/media-information/media-hub-news/2020/07/22/first-jury-trial-since-lockdown

Justice Committee. (2021). *Covid-19 and the criminal law*. House of Commons. Accessed on 24 February 2022, from https://committees.parliament.uk/publications/7439/documents/77794/default/

Justice Directorate. (2021). *Police officer quarterly strength statistics: 31 March 2021*. Scottish Government. Accessed on 24 February 2022, from https://www.gov.scot/publications/police-officer-quarterly-strength-statistics-31-march-2021/

Loader, I. (2000). Plural policing and democratic governance. *Social & Legal Studies, 9*(3), 323–345. https://doi.org/10.1177/096466390000900301

Loader, I. (2016). In search of civic policing: Recasting the 'Peelian' principles. *Criminal Law and Philosophy, 10*(3), 427–440. https://doi.org/10.1007/s11572-014-9318-1

London Metropolitan Police (n.d.) *Our approach*. Accessed on 24 February 2022, from https://www.met.police.uk/advice/advice-and-information/c19/coronavirus-covid-19/met/our-approach/?__cf_chl_tk=V41HRUczuhgdvNoMxrbRMKw1%20ExIfxSBrOJWEHyOKeOM-1645019218-0-gaNycGzNCRE

Magistrates Association. (2022). *Magistrates' courts and Covid-19: Magistrates' experiences in criminal courts during the pandemic*. Accessed on 24 February 2022, from https://www.transformjustice.org.uk/wp-content/uploads/2022/04/TJ003_MagCourt_Report_SCREEN.pdf

Massie, A., & Elliot, C. (2021). *Scots' maladies laid bare in Dundee, the Covid capital of Europe*. The Sunday Times. Accessed on 24 February 2022, from https://www.thetimes.co.uk/article/scots-maladies-laid-bare-in-dundee-the-covid-capital-of-europe-23nl57zdv

McCallum, F. (2020). *Coronavirus (Covid-19): trial by jury*. The Scottish Parliament. Accessed on 24 February 2022, from https://spice-spotlight.scot/2020/05/14/coronavirus-covid-19-trial-by-jury/

McConville, M., & Marsh, L. (2022). Resuscitating criminal courts after Covid-19: Trialling a cure worse than the disease. *International Journal of Evidence & Proof, 26*(2), 103–120.

McEwen, N., Bell, D., & Paun, A. (2019). *Coronavirus and Scotland: Interim Report on Intergovernmental Working*. House of Commons. Accessed on 24 February 2022, from https://www.centreonconstitutionalchange.ac.uk/sites/default/files/2020-07/Coronavirus%20and%20Scotland.pdf

Mead, D. (2021). Policing protest in a pandemic. *King's Law Journal, 32*(1), 96–108. https://doi.org/10.1080/09615768.2021.1885323

Metropolitan Police. (n.d.). *Structure: The structure of the MET*. Accessed on 24 February 2022, from https://www.met.police.uk/cy-GB/heddluoedd/metropolitan-police/areas/about-us/about-the-met/structure

Metropolitan Police. (2022). *Update—Investigation into alleged Covid breaches in Downing Street and Whitehall.* Accessed on 24 February 2022, from https://news.met.police.uk/news/update-investigation-into-alleged-covid-breaches-in-downing-street-and-whitehall-441571

Ministry of Justice., HM Courts., & Tribunals Service, & James Cartlidge MP. (2022). *Press release: Nightingale Courts extended to support justice recovery.* GOV.UK. Accessed on 24 February 2022, from https://www.gov.uk/government/news/nightingale-courts-extended-to-support-justice-recovery

Ministry of Justice. (2016). *Transforming our Justice System: By the Lord Chancellor, the Lord Chief Justice and the Senior President of Tribunals.* Accessed on 24 February 2022, from https://assets.publishing.service.gov.uk/government/uploads/system/uploads/attachment_data/file/553261/joint-vision-statement.pdf

Moeckli, D. (2016) *Exclusion from Public Space: A Comparative Constitutional Analysis*. Cambridge University Press

Moosavian, R., Walker, C., & Blick, A. (2021). Coronavirus legislative responses in the UK: regression to panic and disdain of constitutionalism. *Northern Ireland Legal Quarterly, 72*(S1), 1–36. https://doi.org/10.53386/nilq.v72S1

Morse, A. (2018). *HM Courts and Tribunals Service: Early progress in transforming courts and tribunals.* National Audit Office. Accessed on 24 February 2022, from https://www.nao.org.uk/report/early-progressin-transforming-courts-and-tribunals

Mulcahy, L. (2010). *Legal architecture: Justice*. Routledge.

National Health Service. (n.d.). *COVID-19 response*. Accessed on 24 February 2022, from https://www.nhsx.nhs.uk/covid-19-response/

National Police Chief's Council & College of Policing. (2020a). *COVID-19 Policing Brief in Response to Health Protection (Coronavirus, Restrictions)*

(England) (No. 3) Regulation. Accessed on 24 February 2022, from https://assets.college.police.uk/s3fs-public/2021-01/COVID-19-Briefing-English-No3-080121.pdf

National Police Chiefs' Council & College of Policing. (2020b). *Engage, explain, encourage, enforce—Applying the four 'E's.* Accessed on 24 February 2022, from https://web.archive.org/web/20200522004245/https://www.college.police.uk/What-we-do/COVID-19/Documents/Engage-Explain-Encourage-Enforce-guidance.pdf

National Police Chiefs' Council. (2020). *Fixed penalty notices issued under COVID-19 emergency health regulations by police forces in England and Wales.* Accessed on 24 February 2022, from https://cdn.prgloo.com/media/c1d4c067cf244a50a6cb2cc6749b96dd.pdf

National Police Chiefs' Council. (2021). *Update on Coronavirus FPNs issued by police—October 2021.* Accessed on 24 February 2022, from https://news.npcc.police.uk/releases/update-on-coronavirus-fpns-issued-by-police-october-2021

NHS Inform. (n.d.). *Test and Protect: Help stop the spread of coronavirus (COVID-19).* Accessed on 24 February 2022, from https://www.nhsinform.scot/campaigns/test-and-protect

O'Hagan, A., & Westerman, B. L. (2021). An investigation into the effectiveness of the test and trace system for the SARS-CoV-2 pandemic within the UK. *Forensic Research and Criminology International Journal, 9*(2), 74–82.

Oswald, M., & Grace, J. (2020). The COVID-19 Contact Tracing App in England and 'Experimental Proportionality'. *Forthcoming: Public Law*, 27–37.

Pagliari, C. (2020). The ethics and value of contact tracing apps: International insights and implications for Scotland's COVID-19 response. *Journal of Global Health, 10*(2), 1–18. https://doi.org/10.7189/jogh.10.020103

Pan, J. Y., & Liu, D. (2022). Mask-wearing intentions on airplanes during COVID-19– Application of theory of planned behavior model. *Transport Policy, 119*, 32–44. https://doi.org/10.1016/j.tranpol.2022.01.023

Parkinson, J. (2022). *Police issue 50 more fines over Covid-rule breaking in Downing Street.* BBC.com. Accessed on 24 May 2022, from https://www.bbc.co.uk/news/uk-politics-61422144

Philip Seccombe Police and Crime Commissioner for Warwickshire. (2020). *Warwickshire Police tops the national tables for officer recruitment.* Accessed on 24 February 2022, from https://www.warwickshire-pcc.gov.uk/warwickshire-police-tops-the-national-tables-for-officer-recruitment/

Phillimore, S. (2020). Credibility versus demeanour—The impact of remote court hearings. *Family Law, 50*, 971–972.

Pocklington, D. (2021). *COVID-19: Omicron variant*. Law & Religion UK. Accessed on 24 May 2022, from https://lawandreligionuk.com/2021/11/30/covid-19-omicron-variant/

Police Scotland. (n.d.). *Enforcement and response data—Police Scotland*. Accessed on 24 February 2022, from https://www.scotland.police.uk/about-us/covid-19-police-scotland-response/enforcement-and-response-data/

Prime Minister's Office & The Rt Hon Boris Johnson MP. (2021a). *PM statement at coronavirus press conference: 19 July 2021a*. GOV.UK. Accessed on 24 February 2022, from https://www.gov.uk/government/speeches/pm-statement-at-coronavirus-press-conference-19-july-2021

Prime Minister's Office & The Rt Hon Boris Johnson MP. (2021b). *PM statement at coronavirus press conference: 14 June 2021b*. GOV.UK. Accessed on 24 February 2022, from https://www.gov.uk/government/speeches/pm-statement-at-coronavirus-press-conference-14-june-2021

Public Accounts Committee. (2019). *COVID-19: Test, Track and Trace (Part 1)*. House of Commons. Accessed on 24 February 2022, from https://committees.parliament.uk/publications/4976/documents/50058/default/

Public Prosecution Service. (2021). PPS upholds decisions not to prosecute any individual in connection with Storey funeral. Accessed on 24 February 2022, from https://www.ppsni.gov.uk/news-centre/pps-upholds-decisions-not-prosecute-any-individual-connection-storey-funeral

Quirk, H. (2020). Covid-19 and juryless trials? *Criminal Law Review, 2020*(7), 569–571.

Qureshi, A. (2014). Relying on demeanour evidence to assess credibility during trial—A critical examination. *Criminal Law Quarterly, 61*, 235–267.

Scientific Advisory Group for Emergencies. (2020). *Summary of the effectiveness and harms of different non-pharmaceutical interventions*. Accessed on 24 February 2022, from https://assets.publishing.service.gov.uk/government/uploads/system/uploads/attachment_data/file/925854/S0769_Summary_of_effectiveness_and_harms_of_NPIs.pdf

Scott, J. (2022). *Boris Johnson and Rishi Sunak reject calls to resign over lockdown fines*. BBC.com. Accessed on 24 May 2022, from https://www.bbc.co.uk/news/uk-politics-61083402

Scott, J., Quiroz, D., McVie, S., Pringle, A., Borowski, E., McAuliffe, N., Adamson, B., Logue, J. T., Imery, G., Burke, T., Anwar, A., Kelly, E., & Sillers, B. (n.d.). *Independent Advisory Group: Coronavirus powers*. Scottish Police Authority. Accessed on 24 February

2022, from https://www.spa.police.uk/strategy-performance/independent-advisory-group-coronavirus-powers

Scott, P. F. (2020). Responding to COVID-19 in Scots Law. *Edinburgh Law Review, 24*(3), 421–426. Https://doi.org/10.3366/elr.2020.0657.

Scottish Government. (2020). *Criminal trials during COVID-19 outbreak*. Accessed on 24 February 2022, from https://www.gov.scot/news/criminal-trials-during-covid-19-outbreak/

Scottish Parliament Delegated Powers and Law Reform Committee. (2022). *Inquiry into the use of the made affirmative procedure during the coronavirus pandemic*. Scottish Parliamentary Corporate Body. Accessed on 24 February 2022, from https://sp-bpr-en-prod-cdnep.azureedge.net/published/DPLR/2022/2/10/564c1832-ed18-49e5-83e4-3ea890131e07/DPLRS062022R12.pdf

Sheldon, D. (2021). Policing the pandemic: Maintaining compliance and legitimacy during Covid-19. *King's Law Journal, 32*(1), 14–25. https://doi.org/10.1080/09615768.2021.1889809

Shiels, R. (2020). The instant law of coronavirus. *Scottish Law times, 153*, 245.

Shilson-Thomas, A., Rees, S., & Pickles, C. (2021). *A State of Preparedness: How government can build resilience to civil emergencies*. Accessed on 24 February 2022, from https://reform.uk/sites/default/files/2021-03/A%20State%20of%20Preparedness%2C%20Embargoed%20Copy%2C%20Final_0.pdf

Simpson, J. N. J. (2022). *Coronavirus: Police chief forced to back down after threat to search shopping*. The Times. Accessed on 24 February 2022, from https://www.thetimes.co.uk/article/police-must-not-be-heavy-handed-during-lockdown-says-home-secretary-lx7ljwq50

Smith, K., Shaw, G., Deacy, S., Kerr, J., & Tilbury, N. (2011). *Achieving Best Evidence in Criminal Proceedings: Guidance on interviewing victims and witnesses, and guidance on using special measures*. Ministry of Justice. Accessed on 24 February 2022, from https://www.cps.gov.uk/sites/default/files/documents/legal_guidance/best_evidence_in_criminal_proceedings.pdf

Smith, L. E., Potts, H. W., Amlôt, R., Fear, N. T., Michie, S., & Rubin, G. J. (2021). Adherence to the test, trace, and isolate system in the UK: Results from 37 nationally representative surveys. *The BMJ, 372*(608), 1–13. https://doi.org/10.1136/bmj.n608

Sorabji, J., & Vaughan, S. (2021). "This Is Not A Rule": COVID-19 in England & Wales and criminal justice governance via guidance. *European Journal of Risk Regulation, 12*(1), 143–158. https://doi.org/10.1017/err.2020.118

Spencer, J. R. (1994).Orality and the evidence of absent witnesses. *Criminal Law Review*, 628–644

Stone, M. (1990). Instant lie detection? Demeanour and credibility in criminal trials. *Criminal Law Review*, 821–830.

Susskind, R. (2019). *Online courts and the future of justice*. Oxford University Press.

Telegraph Reporters. (2020). *Boris Johnson "scrapped Cabinet pandemic committee six months before coronavirus hit UK"*. The Telegraph. Accessed on 24 February 2022, from https://www.telegraph.co.uk/politics/2020/06/13/boris-johnson-scrapped-cabinet-pandemic-committee-six-months/

Thames Valley Police. (n.d.). *Tell us about a possible breach of coronavirus (Covid-19) measure*. Accessed on 24 February 2022, from https://www.thamesvalley.police.uk/tua/tell-us-about/c19/v8/tell-us-about-a-possible-breach-of-coronavirus-covid-19-measures/

The Conservative and Unionist Party. (2019). *Get Brexit Done, Unleash Britain's Potential*. Accessed on 24 February 2022, from https://assets-global.website-files.com/5da42e2cae7ebd3f8bde353c/5dda924905da587992a064ba_Conservative%202019%20Manifesto.pdf

The Scottish Government. (2021). *Covid Public Inquiry*. Accessed on 24 February 2022, from https://www.gov.scot/news/covid-public-inquiry

The Scottish Government. (n.d.). Information Governance: Use of your data for Contact Tracing. Accessed on 24 February 2022, from https://www.informationgovernance.scot.nhs.uk/use-of-your-data-for-track-trace-isolate-tti

UK Covid-19 Inquiry. (2022). *Baroness Hallett makes recommendations to the Prime Minister on the Inquiry's Terms of Reference*. Accessed on 24 February 2022, from https://bit.ly/39fdS6S

UK Government. (2021). *Working safely during coronavirus (COVID-19): Restaurants, pubs,bars, nightclubs and takeaway services*. Accessed on 24 February 2022, from https://www.gov.uk/guidance/working-safely-during-covid-19/restaurants-pubs-bars-nightclubs-and-takeaway-services

UK Health Security Agency. (2020). *NHS Test and Trace: what to do if you are contacted*. GOV.UK. Accessed on 24 February 2022, from https://www.gov.uk/guidance/nhs-test-and-trace-how-it-works

Vize, R. (2020). Too slow and fundamentally flawed: Why test and trace is a weak and inequitable defence against covid-19. *British Medical Journal, 369*, 1–3. https://doi.org/10.1136/bmj.m2246

Walker, C. (2014). *The anti-terrorism legislation*. (3rd ed.). Oxford University Press.

Walker, C. (2015). *Contingencies*. Routledge.

Walker, C., & Broderick, J. (2006). *The civil contingencies Act 2004: Risk, resilience and the law in the United Kingdom.* Oxford University Press.

Walklate, S., Godfrey, B., & Richardson, J. (2022). Changes and continuities in police responses to domestic abuse in England and Wales during the Covid-19 'lockdown.' *Policing and Society, 32*(2), 221–233. https://doi.org/10.1080/10439463.2021.1896514

Wang, C. J. (2021). Contact tracing app curbed the spread of COVID in England and Wales. *Nature, 594*, 336–337. https://doi.org/10.1038/d41586-021-01354-8

World Health Organization. (2016). *International Health Regulations (2005)* (3rd ed.). World Health Organization.

Wymant, C., Ferretti, L., Tsallis, D., Charalambides, M., Abeler-Dörner, L., Bonsall, D., Hinch, R., Kendall, M., Milsom, L., Ayres, M., Holmes, C., Briers, M., & Fraser, C. (2021). The epidemiological impact of the NHS COVID-19 app. *Nature, 594*, 408–412. https://doi.org/10.1038/s41586-021-03606-z

Zhang, J., Zhang, R., Ding, H., Li, S., Liu, R., Ma, S., Zhai, B., Kashima, S., & Hayashi, Y. (2021). Effects of transport-related COVID-19 policy measures: A case study of six developed countries. *Transport Policy, 110*, 37–57. https://doi.org/10.1016/j.tranpol.2021.05.013

